THE
NORTH BRITISH
RAILWAY

Volume Two

UNIFORM WITH THIS BOOK

Graham S. Hudson, *The Aberford Railway and the History of the Garforth Collieries*
John Thomas, *The Callander & Oban Railway*
Rex Christiansen and R. W. Miller, *The Cambrian Railways: Volume 1: 1852–1888, Volume 2: 1889–1968*
N. S. C. Macmillan, *The Campbeltown & Machrihanish Light Railway*
Patrick J. Flanagan, *The Cavan & Leitrim Railway*
Peter E. Baughan, *The Chester & Holyhead Railway, Volume 1*
Peter E. Baughan, *The Railways of Wharfedale*
Edward M. Patterson, *The Clogher Valley Railway*
Edward M. Patterson, *A History of the Narrow-gauge Railways of North East Ireland*
  Part One: The Ballycastle Railway
  Part Two: The Ballymena Lines
Edward M. Patterson, *A History of the Narrow-gauge Railways of North West Ireland*
  Part One: The County Donegal Railways (second edition)
  Part Two: The Londonderry & Lough Swilly Railway
H. A. Vallance, *The Great North of Scotland Railway*
H. A. Vallance, *The Highland Railway*
H. W. Paar, *A History of the Railways of the Forest of Dean*
  Part One: The Severn & Wye Railway
  Part Two: The Great Western Railway in Dean
K. Hoole (editor), *The Hull & Barnsley Railway, Volume 1*
John Marshall, *The Lancashire & Yorkshire Railway, Volumes 1, 2 and 3*
David L. Smith, *The Little Railways of South West Scotland*
R. A. Williams, *The London & South Western Railway, Volumes 1 and 2*
D. W. Ronald and R. J. Carter, *The Longmoor Military Railway*
G. A. Brown, J. D. C A Prideaux and H. G. Radcliffe, *The Lynton & Barnstaple Railway*
John Thomas, *The North British Railway, Volume 1*
Rex Christiansen and R. W. Miller, *The North Staffordshire Railway*
J. R. L. Currie, *The Northern Counties Railway, Volumes 1 and 2*
Susan Turner, *The Padarn & Penrhyn Railways*
G. Whittle, *The Railways of Consett and North West Durham*
W. J. K. Davies, *The Ravenglass & Eskdale Railway*
A. D. Farr, *The Royal Deeside Line*
Keith Turner, *The Snowdon Mountain Railway*
Robin Atthill and O. S. Nock, *The Somerset & Dorset Railway*
John Thomas, *The West Highland Railway*
H. Fayle and A. T. Newham, *The Waterford & Tramore Railway*
Ralph Cartwright and R. T. Russell, *The Welshpool & Llanfair Light Railway*

NB Atlantic No 868 *Aberdonian* at Aberdeen (*painting by Victor Welch*)

THE NORTH BRITISH RAILWAY

Volume Two

by

JOHN THOMAS

DAVID & CHARLES
NEWTON ABBOT LONDON
NORTH POMFRET (VT) VANCOUVER

ISBN 0 7153 6699 8

© John Thomas 1975

All rights reserved. No part of this publication may be reproduced, stored in a retrieval system, or transmitted, in any form or by any means, electronic, mechanical, photocopying, recording or otherwise, without the prior permission of David & Charles (Holdings) Limited

Set in 10 on 12 Pilgrim and printed in Great Britain
by John Sherratt & Son, St Ann's Press, Park Road, Altrincham
Cheshire WA14 5QQ, for David & Charles (Holdings) Limited
South Devon House Newton Abbott Devon

Published in the United States of America by
David & Charles Inc North Pomfret
Vermont 05053 USA

Published in Canada by Douglas David & Charles Limited
3645 McKechnie Drive West Vancouver BC

Contents

	LIST OF ILLUSTRATIONS	7
	AUTHOR'S INTRODUCTION	11
1	THE BRIDGES ROUTE	17
	Dark days - William Arrol and the Forth Bridge - chaos - The Forth Bridge Railway Company	
2	TWO GREAT RAILWAYMEN	32
	John Conacher - David Deuchars - A dynamic partnership	
3	MIDSUMMER MADNESS	44
	The gathering storm - the 10pm special - the daft days - counting the cost	
4	LOCOMOTIVE MATTERS 1880–1903	63
	Drummond consolidates - NB coaches - exit Drummond - horse power - 'every inch a gentleman'	
5	EAST COAST OCCASIONS	78
	A quasi partnership - whose engines? - The dining car dispute	
6	CONQUEST OF THE WEST	100
	The road to the west - to Carlisle - the West Highland - the beer line	
7	THE CLYDE AND LOCH LOMOND	117
	The Clyde, Ardrishaig & Crinan Railway - the NB boats - Loch Lomond - the lure of the Trossachs	
8	HERE AND THERE	133
	Fife - dropping the pilot - suburban trends - the Edinburgh hotel	
9	LOCOMOTIVE MATTERS 1903–1923	152
	Reorganisation - the Atlantics - retrenchment - locomotive famine - the quest for an 8-coupled engine	

10 THAT NB FLAVOUR 183
    The last days - serendipity shop - the great silence - tailpiece

APPENDIX
    North British chronology 204

BIBLIOGRAPHY 217

ACKNOWLEDGEMENTS 219

INDEX 221

List of Illustrations

NB Atlantic No 868 *Aberdonian* at Aberdeen *(painting by Victor Welch)* — Frontispiece

PHOTOGRAPHS

	page
Main Up platform Waverley station in the 1890s (*M. M. Deuchars collection*)	33
Cover of NBR public timetable, summer 1914 (*Scottish Record Office*)	34
East Coast Express leaving the Forth Bridge (*C. L. Kerr collection*)	51
East Coast express leaving Dundee about 1888 (*Rev Henry Baron Nichol*)	52
Edinburgh express about to leave Perth (*C. L. Kerr collection*)	52
No 55 at Rhu, West Highland Railway (*C. L. Kerr collection*)	52
Invitation to opening of the Forth Bridge, 4 March 1890 (*M. M. Deuchars collection*)	85
Cantilever tower of the Forth Bridge under construction (*Scottish Record Office*)	85
Holmes 4-4-0 No 592 posed against an Edinburgh background (*British Rail*)	86
David Deuchars, superintendent of the line (*M. M. Deuchars collection*)	103
Waverley station with London express (*Scottish Record Office*)	104
Holmes 729 class piloting NE Atlantic on East Coast express (*L & GRP*)	104
No 875 *Midlothian* at Galashiels on an up express (*Mervyn Robertson collection*)	137

St Johnstoun in a setting of Border hills (*R. B. Haddon*)	137
Fort William station (*Scottish Record Office*)	138
Two Glens hard at work in LNER days (*C. L. Kerr*)	138
West Highland Railway device	138
The Port Carlisle Dandy (*Scottish Record Office*)	155
The NBR horse coach which operated between Musselburgh and Levenhall (*Scottish Record Office*)	155
First class compartment carriage	156
West Highland Railway first class saloon	156
12-wheeled composite dining carriage (*Scottish Record Office*)	156
Gunpowder van	189
Hopper wagon (*British Railways*)	189
The Burntisland roundhouse (*Scottish Record Office*)	190
Eastfield after the fire of 28 June 1919 (*Author's collection*)	190
The North British Hotel, Edinburgh (*Scottish Record Office*)	207
Train departure indicator at Waverley station East End in November 1922 (*Scottish Record Office*)	207
NB 4-4-0 as BR No 62060	208
Line-up of overhauled J37s in BR days (*C. L. Kerr*)	208

LINE DRAWINGS IN TEXT

Map of NBR system at 1922	14, 15
Letter congratulating Conacher on appointment	38
Conacher report extract	40
Six-wheel brake composite	66
Six-wheel third	66
Six-wheel full brake	66
Petrol shunting locomotive	71
Glasgow Fair West Highland excursion announcement	111
Glasgow Fair Aberfoyle excursion announcement	128
NB 4-4-2T built by Yorkshire Engine Co (LNER Class C15)	164
NB Class S 0-6-0 (LNER Class J37)	166
Proposed NBR 0-8-0 mineral engine	174
Corridor brake third	192
Corridor third	193
NB 30ton bogie bolster wagon	194

NB 60ton machinery wagon   196
NB 3ton fish wagon   197
NB 8ton mineral wagon   198
Steel bodied 9ton hopper wagon   199

Author's Note

If five years have passed since publication of *The North British Railway Volume 1* I can only plead that it has taken me that time to sift through the treasure trove of NB original sources. I am not a scissors and paste man. I look for my facts among primary sources, and make sparing use of the printed word. In this way I can ensure that my readers, when they open my books, will find authentic information and a great deal that is new to them. It is painstaking, but rewarding work.

The NB minute books from 1842 to 1923 are intact. There are 80 books each of about 600 pages and I have read every page. Available too are the minute books of many of the small, constituent companies like the Blane Valley and the Forth & Clyde Junction. But minute book material, comprehensive though it is, provides only the skeleton of a railway company history. The researcher must find the flesh to pack round the bones.

No fewer than 984 letter books from the general manager's office have survived, each book containing upwards of a thousand letters—more than a *million* in all. By turning the letters over it is possible to read every word the general manager wrote, day after day, month after month, year after year. There are directors' reports to the shareholders, agreement and contract books spanning 80 years, traffic notebooks and locomotive and rolling stock records, accident books, passenger and goods train special notices and service and public timetables. The private papers of John Conacher, a famous NB general manager, fill three large boxes and the archives of some of the great families associated with the NB are available.

Rummaging in a box of NB documents can be exciting work. I recall the thrill of opening a sheet of creased foolscap and realising that I held in my hand the very sheet of paper on which an Inspector, while riding on two successive nights on the NB train in the race to Aberdeen had recorded point-to-point, minute-

and-second timings. It had always been said that records of these runs did not exist. I found it fascinating to be handling the original telegrams which had arrived at NB headquarters in the fever heat of the racing days. The realisation that the faded purple forms with their terse pencilled messages had first been handled by people intimately involved in the event brought to life the atmosphere of the occasion. It was disconcerting to find that the private letters that passed between the East Coast officials concerning the races gave an impression very different from the accepted romanticised view of the event. Here indeed was the truth about the race to Aberdeen.

Evidence of the rivalry between the NB and the hated Caledonian runs like a thread through NB documentation. I read with incredulity in an NB agent's prosaic report how two NB engines had been used to push a Caledonian running powers train off an NB main line while the Caledonian engine at the other end of the train resisted the attempt. There are reports of the Caledonian running long shunts across NB trains at Aberdeen to prevent punctual arrivals and departures and of Caley men at Carlisle changing the labels on Anglo-Scottish wagons so that freight consigned by the Waverley route went up the Caledonian main line.

Another cache of letters reveals that the so-called East Coast alliance was far from a happy one. There is recorded a bizarre incident when the up *Flying Scotsman* arrived at Berwick in charge of an NB engine and was refused admission to NE metals. The NB engine was forced to run round its train and propel it on to a waiting NE engine.

There is no better way to get to know a man (unless you are personally acquainted with him) than by reading his letters, especially when the writer never dreamed that one day they would become public property. The cosy obituaries of W. F. Jackson, NB general manager, in the contemporary railway press contain no hint of the tyrant revealed by his letters. John Conacher's private letters, some of them with his doodles still in the margins, are so touching that you feel you are prying into his personal affairs and have no right to be reading them at all. But what a picture they give of the man and his work.

There are documents that add significantly to NB locomotive history. I am thinking especially of the private correspondence between officials of the NB and GWR concerning the trial of a

GWR engine on the NB, and the subsequent evaluation of the trial. There are reports of NE and GCR engine trials on the NB and a coal consumption trial hitherto unrecorded which are so favourable to the supposedly coal-hungry Atlantics that the chairman would not believe it until the facts had been re-checked and verified. And what is one to make of the enigmatic minute book entries which seem to suggest that the most revered of Scottish locomotive men left the NB under a cloud?

It proved impossible to distil all the fruits of my researches into two compact volumes. The story of the Tay Bridge disaster, originally planned as the first chapter of this book, made a full book. Likewise the material unearthed about the NB Atlantics could not be compressed into a single chapter so a whole book had to be devoted to those exciting engines. Earlier the West Highland Railway had been given a volume to itself. In this volume I have selected my material carefully and woven it into a narrative which I think gives a balanced picture of NB activities during the second half of the company's existence.

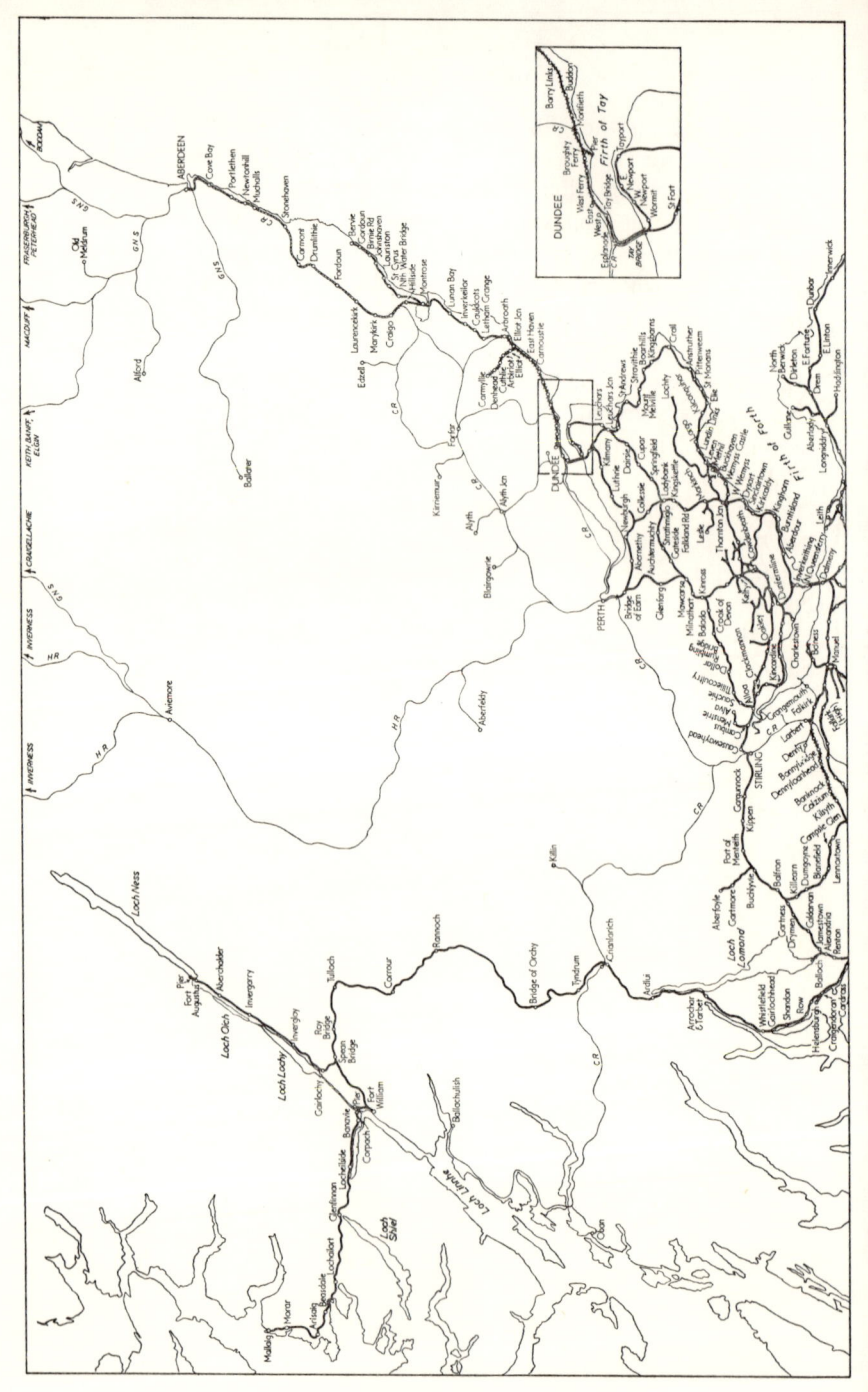

Map of NBR system at 1922

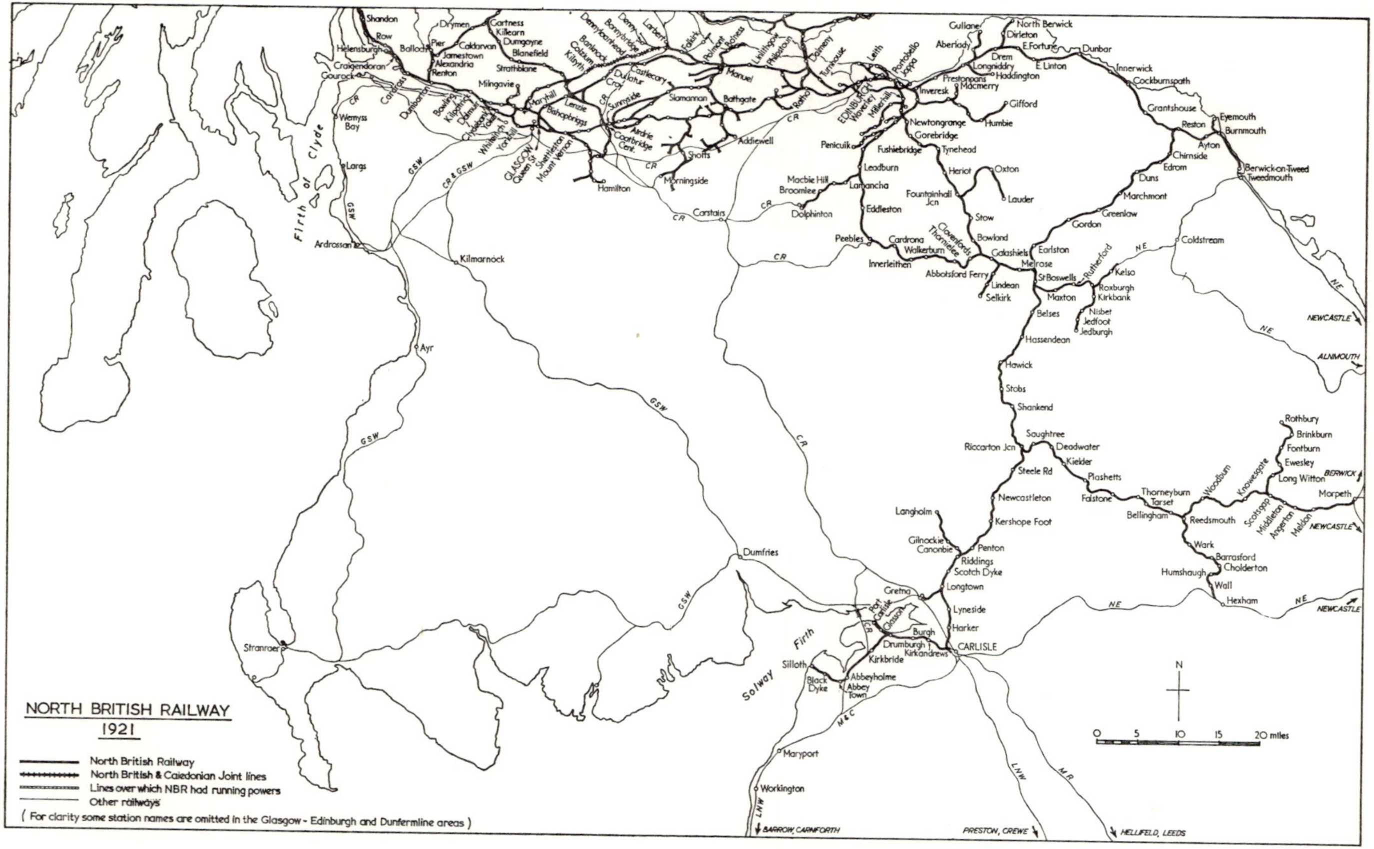

NORTH BRITISH RAILWAY
1921

North British Railway
North British & Caledonian Joint lines
Lines over which NBR had running powers
Other railways
(For clarity some station names are omitted in the Glasgow - Edinburgh and Dunfermline areas)

CHAPTER I

The Bridges Route

DARK DAYS

'I will cross by the 9.30 am train tomorrow if the weather is fine.'

So wrote John Walker, general manager of the North British Railway, to Mr Symonds, a company officer at Burntisland, on 18 December 1884. That simple sentence contained the essence of the malaise that afflicted the NB at that time. Walker's office was in Edinburgh, Burntisland is in Fife and the journey between the two involved a five-mile sea passage of the Firth of Forth. If the general manager of the NB saw fit to use his own company's main line of communication to the north only 'if the weather is fine' how many ordinary passengers forsook the NB for the longer but all-rail route of the Caledonian on the many days when the winds blew strong in these latitudes?

By the last week in December 1879 the NB was within sight of winning the 25-year struggle to bridge the formidable estuaries of the Forth and Tay to create a continuous route from Aberdeen through Dundee to Edinburgh and on to London. The Tay Bridge had been in service for 17 months and its engineer, Sir Thomas Bouch, had designed a spectacular suspension bridge to span the Forth at Queensferry, for which the NB was on the point of letting contracts. The company's future had never looked brighter.

On that terrible night of 28 December 1879 the Tay Bridge had collapsed in a storm with the loss of a train and all its passengers. In an instant the newly-forged route was erased from the map and the NB was left with a broken bridge and an expensive system of approach lines that led to nowhere. Timetables and traffic patterns became meaningless. Seldom had a railway company been dealt so devastating a blow.

The NB accountant's returns at the year's end told a sorry tale. In 1879 the NB had carried 85 per cent of the Edinburgh–Dundee traffic. In 1880 the figure was down to 51 per cent. With the opening of the Tay Bridge the NB had gone out to secure a share of the Glasgow–Dundee traffic, which formerly had been negligible,

B

and in a season had succeeded in winning 29 per cent of this traffic from the Caledonian. In 1880 the figure shrank back to one half of one per cent. Of the through Edinburgh–Aberdeen traffic the NB lost only 9 per cent to the Caledonian. That was due to the lucky chance that the Caledonian was having its own bridge troubles. No fewer than 28 old wooden bridges on the Aberdeen route were being reconstructed and the resulting delays were so great that the NB trains, notwithstanding the two ferry crossings, could beat their Caledonian rivals on the Aberdeen run. That morsel of comfort did nothing to dispel the gloom in the NB boardroom. There was talk of abandoning the Bridges Route and building an NB link from Perth to Dundee along the north bank of the Tay parallel with the existing Caledonian line.

When the tumult died down it was plain to all concerned, not least the government of the day, that only bridges across the Forth and Tay estuaries would solve the transport problems of the east coast of Scotland. When a bill for a new Tay Bridge, designed by W. H. Barlow and to be sited 50 yards east of Bouch's bridge, went before Parliament in 1881 it was passed without demur. The NB shareholders footed the account for the second Tay Bridge, but the building of a great bridge across the Forth was far beyond the company's resources. On 11 June 1881 the three English companies likely to benefit from such a bridge— the North Eastern, the Great Northern and the Midland—met the NB at York and formed the Forth Bridge Railway Company, the purpose of which was to build and operate a new bridge at Queensferry. It was agreed that the NB would contribute 35 per cent of the cost of the bridge, with the Midland contributing 30 per cent and the North Eastern and Great Northern $17\frac{1}{2}$ per cent each. As part of the deal the NB undertook to build approach lines and improve certain of its existing lines in the area. The single line through Fife to Mawcarse was to be doubled and extended through Glenfarg to a junction with the Caledonian at Hilton Junction just south of Perth, thus creating an entirely new first-class route between Edinburgh and Perth. A new line was to run from Inverkeithing along the north shore of the Firth of Forth to join the existing NB main line at Burntisland. From the south end of the bridge spurs were to strike west to join the Edinburgh and Glasgow main line to give a direct connection with Glasgow and east to form a new direct route to Edinburgh. As a result of the York conference the Forth Bridge (Abandonment) Bill was withdrawn and a new bill presenting a design by John Fowler and Benjamin Baker was put forward. It was passed in 1882, and the work of creating the Bridges Route began all over again.

WILLIAM ARROL AND THE FORTH BRIDGE

The contractor for Bouch's Forth Bridge had been William Arrol. One of the tragedies of the story of the Bridges Route is that the NB did not discover Arrol five years before it did. If he had had a hand in the building of the first Tay Bridge it would not have fallen.

William Arrol was one of those uncanny geniuses that the Victorian age threw up to fill a pressing need of the time. He began by patching porridge pots in his native Renfrewshire and finished by building the second Tay Bridge, the Forth Bridge and, for good measure, the Tower Bridge—and all at one time. In passing he had supervised the making (in Glasgow) of Deal pier and Brighton's West Pier and had erected these structures in Kent and Sussex respectively. At the age of 29, as proprietor of his own works, he had built bridges to carry the new suburban railways over the streets of Glasgow and when the Caledonian at last decided to come into the heart of Glasgow he built the bridge that was to carry its metals across the Clyde. Arrol was a born contractor. If a design presented new problems he devised new techniques to meet them. If an existing machine was unequal to a job he invented a new machine. Such was the man who was to build one of the most remarkable steel bridges in the world.

Arrol now had more to think about than a bagfull of iron patches for porridge pots. His task was to fabricate and erect into a gigantic mile-and-a-half-long bridge 54,076 tons of steel, 640,300 cu ft of Aberdeen granite and 62,250 cu ft of rubble masonry.

Nearly three years were to pass before the piers that were to support the massive superstructure rose above the water. Then the plates, shaped at Arrol's South Queensferry works into tubes only a foot narrower than those traversed by London's underground trains, were taken out to the piers and erected. Only then could spectators deduce what the Forth Bridge would look like. The three great diamond-shaped towers that were to support the main spans slowly climbed upwards until in the end their tops stood 341ft above high water. Only Monsieur Eiffel had built a structure higher than that.

Tradesmen of many nationalities came in their thousands to work on the bridge. Theirs was a hazardous life. Before the bridge was ready to receive its first train it had killed 57 men and maimed 510. Illness due to exposure was prevalent. In the eight years the bridge was building the resident doctors issued 26,000 sickness certificates.

The work went on day and night, summer and winter, in all weathers. The labour force worked in two 12-hour shifts. Watchers on the shore saw the men spread like spiders against a tracery of girders. At shift changing times the little black specks moved down the structure towards the wooden piers at water level and, after a suitable interval more black specks swarmed upwards to the working positions. They were a motley crowd.

The new Tay Bridge was much less spectacular than the Forth Bridge and its erection raised fewer problems. It was squat and double-tracked, as sturdy-looking as its forerunner was frail. Arrol spent every Monday and Tuesday at the Forth Bridge and every Wednesday at the Tay Bridge. On Thursday he was back at his Glasgow works thrashing out with his staff means of solving the problems that had arisen during the week. Friday and part of Saturday he spent in London looking at Tower Bridge. Sunday he spent leisurely at his Ayrshire home before embarking yet again on the weekly round.

By the spring of 1889 the three cantilever towers of the Forth Bridge were complete and ready to receive the two main girders. The distance to be spanned was 1,700ft. Normally the girders would have been prefabricated on the shore, floated out on barges and raised into position. Because of the great weight involved this procedure was impracticable, so Arrol devised a new technique. He built the main spans out from the ends of the cantilever arms until the halves met in mid channel. During their construction the half spans were extensions of the cantilever arms. When the halves met they were riveted together to form a continuous span, but each span was cut free of the inner cantilever arm to allow for expansion. The finished span was thus fixed to the outer cantilever but free to move on the inner cantilever.

On a winter morning in 1889 the very last two girders were

due to be joined. The practice was to have the ends not quite touching but to let the air temperature expand the girders until they slid alongside each other when bolts were inserted in holes already drilled in both girders. A mild morning with a steadily rising temperature had been forecast, and the senior staff stood by to witness the historic moment when the holes would slip into alignment and the bolts which would complete the bridge would be slipped into place. But at the critical time an unexpected cool breeze blew in from the sea. Expansion stopped. An Arrol man saved the day by packing wood shavings and oily rags into the troughs of the girders and setting them alight. The holes slowly moved into alignment. The bridge was complete.

The designers of the bridge duly reported to the board of the Forth Bridge Railway Company:

Gentlemen,
On 14 November 1889 the last permanent connection was made with the girders of the Bridge and it then became a complete structure sustaining the full strain arising from its own weight, from wind and from change of temperature. The only additional strain to which it will be subject in future is the rolling or passing load. The results of examination of various parts of the Bridge after connection was perfectly satisfactory. We have no doubt that the Bridge will be quite ready for traffic on 4 March 1890.

Only 10 years had passed since the nation had been stunned by the fall of the first Tay Bridge and British engineering prestige had suffered a severe blow. The Forth Bridge was seen not merely as a link in an important line of communication but as a vindication of the engineering profession. Its inauguration was planned as a national event, a royal occasion. The engineering world had to be shown that the Forth Bridge was a truly great bridge.

March can be a wild month on the east coast of Scotland. The day chosen for the opening of the bridge—4 March 1890—was bitterly cold and spiced with blustering, driving rainshowers. It was not a day for pageantry—especially pageantry carried out on a cold steel bridge deck 150ft above sea level.

The royal train stopped at the new Forth Bridge station (soon to be renamed Dalmeny) at the south end of the bridge where the Prince of Wales received Fowler, Baker and Arrol. A salute from a warship down on the firth crashed out as the train slowly entered on the bridge. Sailors blue with cold, stationed at intervals along the bridge footwalk, presented arms as the royal carriage approached.

On the return journey the train stopped in the middle of the wind-swept centre cantilever tower. As the Prince and his guests alighted, top hats were whisked away in the wind. William Arrol showed the royal guests how to insert the ceremonial last rivet. Two turns, two clicks and the job was done. An eye witness wrote,

> The sightseers presented a pitiable spectacle. Some two score gentlemen—some of them titled but others just plain plebians—elbowed their way on to the meagre platform. Lords and common people stood cheek by jowl all mixed up higgeldy piggeldy in a delightful confusion. Among the crowd were some of Mr Arrol's workmen others of whom were hanging on to parapet or girders like bluejackets manning the yards of a warship.

The train halted again at the exit from the south cantilever tower where many guests had been waiting for upwards of an hour to see the Prince perform the official opening ceremony. 'They had been dangling so long between earth and heaven', said a newspaper report next day, 'that it was small wonder that their faculties were frozen up within their chilled frames'. The Prince's words as he declared the bridge open were carried away in the wind. Few heard his brief speech and all trooped off thankfully to Arrol's drawing office which had been pressed into service as a banqueting hall. At the end of the day the erstwhile porridge pot patcher emerged as Sir William Arrol.

Through traffic did not start on the Forth Bridge until 1 June 1880, the approach lines not being ready. Meanwhile the Tay Bridge had been opened quietly in 1887. The NB now found itself with the fastest route from Edinburgh to Perth and the fastest route from Edinburgh to Aberdeen. NB trains used the Arbroath & Montrose Railway to reach the Caledonian at Kinnaber Junction then exercised its running powers over 38 miles of Caledonian main line to enter Aberdeen. For the first time the NB could compete with the Caledonian for the Glasgow–Dundee–Aberdeen traffic. On a broader front the east coast combine was presented with the fastest route between Aberdeen and London. A new era had opened for the NB.

CHAOS

The summer of 1890 should have been a season of triumph for

the NB. But it turned out to be the most unnerving in the company's history. Waverley station was the cause of the trouble.

The NB station in Edinburgh, squashed as it was into the narrow valley separating the old and new towns, had been struggling to expand for 40 years. In 1890 Waverley station was in effect two back-to-back stations, one facing east and serving the Borders and England, the other facing west and serving the west and north. In between were the administrative buildings and round the sides passed the east-west through lines. The station was incredibly cluttered and congested. The principal waiting room was only 16ft square, the main departure platform was only 4ft wide. One tall man could stand astride it. Passengers trying to reach the trains found the platforms blocked by luggage, carts of cabbages, barrels of beer and other impedimenta. Some platforms were so short that carriages in a normal train overlapped them and could not be boarded. It was common for the trains to be nowhere visible at departure time and station staff when appealed to professed to have no knowledge of their whereabouts or when they were likely to put in an appearance.

The new traffic pouring in from the Forth Bridge precipitated the crisis. The trains approached Edinburgh on an ordinary double line. From Saughton Junction, where the Forth Bridge line joined the Glasgow-Edinburgh line, it was common to see trains standing at every signal. Sometimes an express took an hour or more to cover the three miles from Saughton to Waverley. Some of them coveyed carriages from Inverness, Aberdeen, Perth and Dundee for transfer to East Coast and Midland expresses at Waverley. Day after day the English expresses left late and timetables were disorganised the following day as far away as the English Channel.

The Edinburgh Trades Holiday in July was the straw that broke the camel's back. Fife was a favourite haunt of the Edinburgh masses. Hitherto they had crossed the Forth by the Granton ferry, but now they flocked to the new, much-vaunted Forth Bridge trains. The already congested platforms were stacked with paraphernalia of the Victorian urban holidaymaker—perambulators, baths, bedding, bicycles and tricycles. Patiently the passengers waited for trains that never came. The station pilots shunted to and fro topping and tailing through expresses already running hopelessly late, in the process using platform roads that should have accommodated the holiday trains. Local trains had to take their chance of finding a space. Goods trains were conveniently forgotten for long periods. A Glasgow–Carlisle express goods on one occasion took 24 hours to get through Edinburgh.

At the height of the crisis Winchburgh tunnel (12 miles west of Edinburgh on the Glasgow main line) collapsed, totally blocking the line. Some of the Glasgow traffic used the Bathgate route, but much of it was sent down to Dalmeny on the new spur from Winchburgh Junction and sent to Edinburgh along the new Saughton spur. The reversing of the Glasgow trains in the face of the traffic coming off the Forth Bridge added further to the chaos.

The public sought relief for their frustration in the correspondence columns of the daily press. In a letter headed 'Railway Travelling in the 19th Century. The NBR Again', the writer began 'At intervals during the last ten years I have been a silent sufferer at the hands of the NBR.' Another writer suggested that the motto 'Abandon hope all ye who enter here' be hung over the main entrance of Waverley station. At Galashiels a protest meeting was asked 'to exercise the Christian grace of self denial and abstain from railway travelling.' Yet another critic analysed the NB's troubles in a fine burst of metaphor: 'The heart is congested and the arteries are choked. The new wine of the Forth Bridge traffic goes far to burst the old bottle.' In the *Leith Herald* there appeared a bogus announcement in the style and format of an official NB announcement:

> New timetable for August. Trains at the Waverley Station will, until further notice, start as soon as they can be got away and will arrive as they can immediately be brought in. It is guaranteed that no trains will arrive or depart more than 3 hours behind time. Passengers anxious to reach their destinations at a certain hour had better start the day before. All this wonderful acceleration has been brought about by the opening of the Forth Bridge.

In the end the NB was accorded the accolade of a *Times* leader:

Waverley or 'Tis Sixty Minutes Late

Millions of passengers who have never seen Waverley and who may have only wished to travel locally, say from Gloucester to Bristol or from Aberdeen to Elgin have just cause to know that Waverley station is the key to the railway situation throughout the length and breadth of Great Britain; that a block of half an hour at that point will be felt in the derangement of the service 10 to 15 hours afterwards as far west as Plymouth and as far north as Wick.

There was no quick solution to the problem. What was called for was nothing less than a radical reconstruction of Waverley station and the quadrupling of the main line from Saughton through the heart of Edinburgh to Portobello in the east. That in turn meant the boring of additional tunnels at Haymarket, the Mound and Calton Hill. The whole expensive scheme was authorised by the NB board, but three years passed before work could start. The same citizens of Edinburgh who had protested so loudly about the traffic delays protested just as loudly when the NB sought a strip of Princes Street Gardens essential to them if they were to widen the 'choked arteries.' The reconstruction of the station was carried out between 1892 and 1900. In its new form Waverley provided more platform accommodation than any station in Britain except Waterloo. The Up Main and Down Main through platforms each could take two full-length express trains. A system of loops and crossovers made the rapid handling of trains possible even at the busiest times, and there were two entirely separate through platforms for suburban traffic. The huddle of old buildings in the central area was cleared away and an attractive booking hall provided.

The NB never again experienced the horrors of that summer of 1890. It learned to live with its problems until the improved facilities were ready. The value of the Forth Bridge to the NB, measured at the till, was £22,000 in increased passenger and parcels traffic alone in the first year of operation. In that period 20,695 passenger and 8,488 goods trains crossed the bridge. Their combined weight was 9,888,752 tons.

The bridge was more than a railway structure. It was a totem, a status symbol, a sign of success which the NB exploited to the full. It was emblazoned on the covers of NB timetables and took pride of place in NB promotional literature. It appeared on biscuit tins and chocolate boxes. Within months the exciting contours of the bridge were familiar to millions. The Bridges Route was a fait accompli.

THE FORTH BRIDGE RAILWAY COMPANY

The Forth Bridge Railway Company functioned independently of the NB and it prized its autonomy. No love was lost between the owning and the operating company. The FBR maintained the bridge in working order and derived its revenue from the tolls paid to it by the operating company, the length of the bridge for rating purposes being reckoned as 19 miles. The resident engineer of the bridge had a permanent staff of 44 men covering trades ranging from painting to plumbing.

The painters—28 including the foreman—formed the most numerous group. Their job became legendary as one that never ended; when they finished painting the bridge they went back to the other side and began to paint it again. There were 145 acres to paint. Each painting took three years and added 50 tons to the weight of the bridge. The paint came in steel drums labelled 'Forth Bridge Paint.' It was an aristocrat among paints. The order for the materials for the first painting after the opening read as follows:

Pure oxide of iron paint ground in genuine linseed oil guaranteed over 90 per cent in the dry of oxide of iron F_2O_3 of natural origin	9 tons
Red lead	3 tons 12 cwt
White lead	1 ton 6 cwt
Boiled linseed oil	1,000 gallons
Terebine	50 gallons
Turpentine	70 gallons
Tar oil	20 gallons
Bituminous viaduct solution	200 gallons

The contract stipulated that a paint supplier would be required to make an immediate payment of £50 to the FBR if any sample of the paint contained less than 90 per cent of iron oxide. So stringent were the conditions that only two firms tendered and the contract was shared between them. Although both consignments of paint were made to the same specification, on delivery one proved to be bright red and the other dark brown. An additive was used to bring the red paint to the authorised shade.

The Forth Bridge was almost like an ocean liner. The engineer's office high on a cantilever tower was the navigating bridge from which the duties of the 'crew' were controlled and a watch was kept on the weather. The bridge even had lifeboats permanently manned and ready to go to the aid of the men who fell off the structure from time to time. Thomas Smith dived 60 feet into the water to rescue a fellow worker who had toppled from a girder.

His deed won him the Royal Humane Society Medal and the Carnegie Award for Heroes. The FBR gave him £50, the secretary specifying 'that I keep control of the money and let him have from time to time such instalments as might appear reasonable.'

When the needle of the wind gauge in the engineer's office reached 30mph an alert was sent out to the bridge workers. Men were removed from the more exposed places and put to work on the girders under the deck or inside the tubular columns. Word was sent to the workshop staff at Dalmeny to stop all goods trains and lash the wagon sheets down with new ropes before allowing the train to enter on the bridge. Even then severe gusts got under the sheets and, ropes notwithstanding, sent them sailing like autumn leaves towards the water.

For 16 years the NB refused to recognise the employees of the FBR as railwaymen. The bridge men claimed that since they worked for a *railway* company they were railwaymen and therefore entitled to the cheap travel facilities enjoyed by their NB colleagues. This view the management of the NB hotly contested. It was not until 1906 that the NB grudgingly granted privilege tickets to the Forth Bridge men. The official list of men entitled to cheap tickets is interesting in that it shows the composition of the Forth Bridge staff at that time. Unlimited privilege tickets were granted to the bridge inspector, the foreman painter, two bridge watchmen, one joiner, one fitter and one clerk. Privilege tickets to cover holidays only were granted to 27 painters, four riveters, two boatmen, two works watchmen, one smith, one striker, one plumber, one lighthouse keeper, one carpenter and one fitter.

A Forth Bridge man, John Currie, unwittingly abused his privilege and found himself the centre of a *cause célèbre*. The relevant correspondence vividly illuminates the curious relationship that existed between the FBR and the NB.

An applicant for a privilege ticket was required to present to the booking clerk at his departure station a form giving details of the ticket required and the relationship of the passenger to the applicant if the applicant himself was not the passenger. John Currie presented to the booking clerk at Inverkeithing a privilege ticket order requesting a ticket for his daughter to enable her to travel from Inverkeithing to Gloucester and back. The booking clerk knew Currie, and he was aware that he had a daughter living with him. What he did not know was that the ticket was for his married daughter who, under the rules, was not entitled to a privilege ticket. John Currie had never been shown the rules governing the issue of tickets and he was unaware that his daughter was not eligible for a ticket. A few days after the outward journey had been completed Currie learned the true position. He at once retrieved the unused return half and handed it back to the Inverkeithing booking clerk along with the sum of 14s 4d which was the difference between a privilege and an ordinary single from Inverkeithing to Gloucester.

This trivial transaction was brought to the attention of the general manager of the NBR, at that time William Fulton Jackson, a good railwayman but a firebrand of the first order. He demanded that Currie be punished. Reluctantly John Martin of the FBR barred Currie from having privilege tickets for six months and he notified the NB general manager accordingly. Jackson was furious. 'It must be understood,' he told Martin, 'that privilege ticket facilities will not be granted to him for a period of 12 months in place of six months as suggested by you. You will kindly let me hear from you further.' Martin asked Jackson to modify the penalty in view of the fact that Currie had not committed a deliberate offence and that he had taken steps to put matters right as soon as he had become aware of his infringement. 'Had I been dealing with the matter personally,' replied Jackson 'I probably would have made the period more than 12 months.'

Martin, stung by Jackson's interference in which he considered to be an FBR matter replied, 'It has hitherto been the province of this company to deal with its own staff and I propose to continue that practice'. Jackson retorted, 'If you are to take the course suggested I will advise the NB directors to withdraw the concessions granted to Forth Bridge employees'. Few men had the guts to stand up to Jackson, but Martin was one of them. 'You apparently suggest,' he wrote to Jackson, 'that I am no longer free to deal with this company's staff, but must do as you insist. I object, naturally, and if you prefer it I can put the subject on the agenda for our next board meeting.' Jackson replied that there was no point in putting the matter on the agenda as it had nothing to do with the FBR.

Mr Hunter, the manager of the FBR, was distressed over the case, and a letter he addressed to Martin gives an intimate, touching picture of life on the Forth Bridge as it was then.

I was vexed to hear it is proposed to punish Currie so heavily. I hope you will not do that for he really is not to blame. He is a good workman, straight and honest and has been employed on the bridge for 29 years. There will also be the risk of putting the men in an ill temper and we might very easily get into more trouble with them. As it is they are not easily handled and it would be easy enough for any of them to get better wages close at hand, but I could not fill their places with men of the same experience. It is their good little houses near their work, the low rents and the cheap travelling chiefly between here and Edinburgh that helps to keep them together. Does it not say something for us that this is the only mistake of the kind that has happened in the 9 years the men have been getting these tickets?

Martin made a final appeal to Jackson and back came the cold reply, 'I will be glad to hear from you by return that this understanding is accepted unconditionally so as to avoid the necessity of putting the matter before the NB directors'.

The bridge engineer was proud of his unique charge and conscious of his responsibilities. He hated drivers who abused the bridge by exceeding the 40mph speed limit he had laid down. The first complaints of excessive speed were made within a few months of the opening and continued year in year out for decades. The FBR sent details of offenders to the NB general manager who passed them to the locomotive superintendent who in turn exhibited a notice headed 'Excessive Speed on Forth Bridge' at the relevant engine sheds. There is little evidence that the NB took systematic action against the offenders.

Here is a 'black list' sent by the FBR to the NB following observations on a measured half mile on the down line on two consecutive days:

Train	Engine No	Time in seconds	Speed mph
10.30am	868	37	48·65
2.3 pm	866	42	42·86
4.53pm	868	44	40·91
7.59am	877	44	40·91
9.50am	325	43	41·86
10.29am	868	42	42·86
2.6 pm	866	44	40·91
4·56pm	868	42	42·86

The same engines and therefore the same drivers were persistent offenders. No 868 was the Atlantic *Aberdonian*. It did not appear in the black list again for more than six months, which suggests that the driver was cautioned. The speeds recorded by the FBR very likely are less than the actual speeds attained by the engines. Drivers kept a lookout for the bridge inspector and when they spotted him they began to brake. Some drivers made a habit of running on to the approach viaduct at high speed then checking down as they approached the measured half mile. The bridge inspector knew the culprits. The driver of No 339 was one and he set a trap for him. Unobserved he timed him over the south approach viaduct and got a reading of 44·7mph. On the following two days the driver, still unaware that he was being watched achieved 43·2 and 44·7mph respectively. A particularly outrageous violation brought the following protest from the FBR office. 'On Sunday 21st inst the 7·25 passenger train ex Edinburgh to Perth crossed the bridge from end to end in 1min 30sec, a speed of 62·8 miles an hour—22·8 miles an hour above regulation speed.' That was something the NB could not ignore. The driver got three days' suspension and the promise of dismissal if he repeated the performance.

It became fashionable for privileged persons to walk across the Forth Bridge. Permits were issued to approved applicants by the NB in consultation with the bridge engineer. But the pedestrian traffic raised an unexpected problem which was first ventilated in a letter on 22 July 1900 from John Walker, general manager of the NB, to Matthew Holmes, his locomotive superintendent.

> I have your letter of 21st inst and send herewith the order to Mr Hunter to admit Mr C. M. Smith and two friends to the Forth Bridge. I presume neither of the friends is a lady, because we hesitate to allow ladies to walk across the bridge owing to the great danger there is to them, especially when express trains are passing.

Walker did not explain whether the danger was to their modesty or their person, but the engineer, measuring the girth of Victorian skirts against the narrowness of the footwalk pressed for the total exclusion of ladies from the bridge. The NB thought it invidious to print 'No Ladies' on the permits, but agreed that permits would be issued only on condition that the applicants were gentlemen! 'No ladies' became a Forth Bridge tradition.

Passengers travelling over the bridge invented a tradition that it was lucky to throw a penny from the carriage window during the passage. Money cascaded out of the holiday trains and especially from the Sunday School excursion trains that ran from Edinburgh to the Fife resorts in May and June. Most of the coins never reached the water. They struck the girders and bounced back usually to lodge in the troughs carrying the rails. The lucky pennies provided a bonus for the bridge men. A bag of 51 pennies was recorded in one day.

The Forth Bridge office kept meticulous records of every train movement on the bridge. The weight of every engine and train was noted, as was the type of train and whether or not it was double-headed. Separate records were kept for up and down lines. The books for the bridge's fifth year show that the up line passed 13,037 passenger trains weighing with their engines 2,450,956 tons, and 9,443 goods trains weighing 3,663,884 tons, while 1,339 light engine movements accounted for 106,952 tons. On the down line there were 13,414 passenger train movements, with trains weighing 2,521,832 tons, 9,334 goods trains with a weight of 3,621,592 tons and 1,339 light engines giving a weight of 100,425 tons. An analysis of the bridge figures for the tenth year showed that the average weight of a passenger train had risen from 188 to 200 tons, the average weight of goods trains had risen from 388 to 400 tons and the average engine weight had remained constant at 75 tons. In 1907 14,717 trains crossed the bridge in the up direction (1,082 of them double-headed) while the down line carried 14,958 passenger trains (807 double-headed). The gross tonnage carried that year was 14,674,750. The gross tonnage between 1900 and 1907 was 226,470,821. That figure tells us all we need to know about the importance of the Forth Bridge to the NB and its East Coast partners.

CHAPTER 2

Two Great Railwaymen

JOHN CONACHER

I *know* you are competent to a degree that may fairly be called superlative, honest and upright and hardworking.
                       Sir Henry Oakley general manager of the GNR in a letter to John Conacher.

It was said of John Walker that he spent nine months of the year fighting the Caledonian and three months promoting NB bills. On 23 April 1891 he was doing both. The North British (Lanarkshire) Bill was in Parliament and was having a stormy passage at the hands of the Caledonian lobby. At one stage Walker angrily accused the opposition of nobbling witnesses. On the following day Walker was back in the House pushing the Alloa Docks Bill, again against Caledonian opposition. He left Westminster late that afternoon (it was Friday) with the intention of spending a restful weekend at Ryde on the Isle of Wight. When he stepped from his cab at Waterloo he faltered and said, 'Nearly stumbled there'. These were the last words he spoke. He was carried unconscious into the station and died shortly afterwards of a stroke in the first class waiting room. He was 60.

Walker had been general manager of the NB since 1874 and had served under three chairmen—Kippendavie, Sir James Falshaw and Lord Tweeddale. He was the right man in the right place at the right time. His legal training and flair for combat in court and committee had stood the NB in good stead at a time when it was constantly engaged in a battle to extend its rule and promote its interests. By 1891 the main battles were over and the company's task was to consolidate its gains. It is doubtful if Walker, had he lived, would have been as successful a general manager in the 1890s as he had been in the 1870s and 1880s. What the NB needed in 1891 was not a legal mind but a first class, down-to-earth railwayman who would join with his English counterparts in developing the East Coast route as well as getting the best out of internal services. The NB was fortunate in getting two such men in John

THE NORTH BRITISH RAILWAY

Page 33:
East Coast express at Edinburgh Waverley station Main Up platform in the 1890s

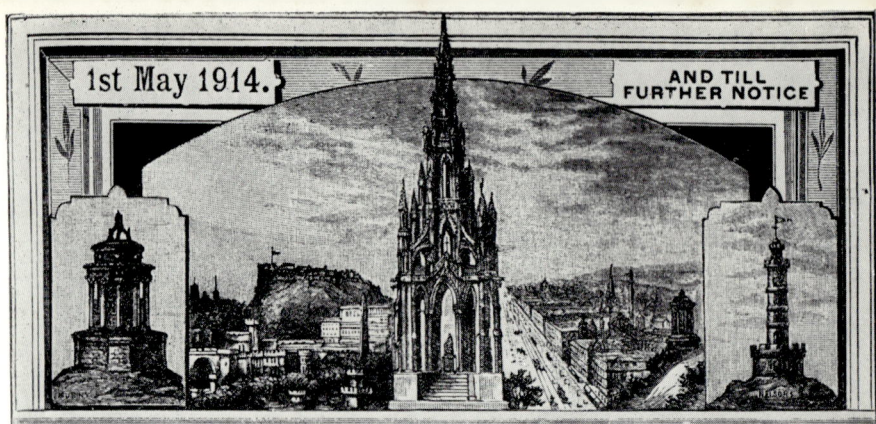

Page 34:
Cover of NBR public timetable, summer 1914

Conacher and David Deuchars. Their names loom large in this narrative and now is the time to take a close look at the men who were to guide the destiny of the company through the next turbulent decade and beyond.

Shortly after Walker's death Queen Victoria travelled from Windsor to Ballater, and on that occasion George Wieland and G. P. Neele, superintendent of the LNWR, met in the officers' saloon of the royal train. They were old friends and they discussed the topic that was currently engaging British railway circles; who would get the North British? The name of Charles Mason, assistant manager at Euston, was mentioned; his brother, S. L. Mason, was a former general manager of the North British. Another name that cropped up was that of John Conacher, secretary and general manager of the Cambrian Railways, a gentleman who had a remarkably good reputation among the elite of British Railway management.

Meanwhile Sir Henry Oakley was writing to Conacher:

> The North British are looking for a successor to Walker. They want a man who *will work* the railway and not one to engineer its policy. I have mentioned you to Wieland, and he has asked me to tell you to write to him if you are still open.

John Conacher had joined the Scottish Central Railway at Perth in 1861 as a boy of 16. In 1865, when the SCR was absorbed by the Caledonian, he was moved to Glasgow. His career with the Caledonian lasted six weeks; in September 1865 he went to Wales to seek his fortune on the Cambrian. In 1867 at the age of 22 he became the company accountant. In 1882 he was appointed secretary and in 1885 secretary and general manager. By 1891 Conacher's name was synonymous with the Cambrian. He loved the line and he was held in affection and respect by management and staff, travellers and traders. Above all he was a fine railwayman.

Much as he loved the Cambrian the North British was a prize worth having and Conacher wrote to Wieland expressing interest. The NB secretary instructed Conacher to make a formal application for the vacancy. While he was willing to engage in private negotiations he was not willing to be named as one of a panel of contenders for the job. To put himself in the public market would, he felt, be discourteous to the Cambrian board. 'My relations with the Cambrian directors are so harmonious,' he explained, in a letter to his friend, Henry Oakley. Oakley replied:

> I have your note. Don't apply. I think it would be better for the North British to make the first move. I have written to Wieland and suggested that when they are ready to make a serious advance he should invite you to see him or his directors. I don't think there are to so many *eligible* candidates that you need fear being omitted, and as you should do well your position will be strengthened by the knowledge that you are not a candidate though willing to consider any proposal. The North British will, I suppose, give £2,500 to £3,000 for the right man. I hope you will join them. The work will be hard and the position not a bed of roses, but I rely on your ability to bear all and to succeed.

Conacher received Oakley's letter on 26 May and for six weeks neither side made a move. Then on 14 July when Conacher was in London on Parliamentary business he was, in his own words, 'asked to allow himself to be introduced to Lord Tweeddale'. A 'little conversation' took place in a lobby of the House during which the North British was not mentioned. Tweeddale was sizing up the prospective candidate. Two days later the NB chairman was in Manchester discussing various names with Pollitt of the Manchester, Sheffield & Lincolnshire Railway, and he strongly recommended Conacher.

On 31 July Conacher was called to London to meet Tweeddale. At the end of a friendly interview the Cambrian general manager was invited to obtain testimonials from certain leading figures in the railway world, among them Oakley, Sir E. Watkin, Pollitt, Lambert of the GWR and Tennant of the NE.

That night when Conacher got back to Oswestry he found waiting for him a letter offering the Taff Vale. He sent an appropriate reply and received the response, 'If you are for the North British you will not look at the Taff Vale'. (Later he was to learn that the LB & SC board had decided to offer him the general managership of its company but had desisted knowing that the candidate would not be lured to Brighton when Edinburgh was in prospect.) That same evening Conacher, with a heavy heart, informed the Cambrian board of the turn of events. The reply from the chairman was dated 2 August.

> I cannot tell you how sorry I am to think that the relations which have lasted so long and been so cordial should be interrupted, I

don't say closed. But I cannot wonder at your being ready to accept such promotion as the general manager of the North British and indeed the fact that it was open had more than once made me wonder whether it might have been offered to you. I have written to Lord Tweeddale a letter giving a summary of your service to the Cambrian. I hope it will be what is wanted.

It says much for the esteem in which Conacher was held that several of the distinguished railwaymen from whom he solicited testimonials had already, uninvited, suggested his appointment to NB officials. Tennant of the NE informed Conacher, 'I have said to him (Wieland) all that I would write and you may rest satisfied that I expressed no opinion unfavourable to you'. Lambert of the GWR also had been in touch with Wieland and had emphasised Conacher's 'fitness for the position'.

On 6 August Tweeddale informed Conacher that the job was as good as his and asked him to come to Edinburgh to attend the meeting at which the committee would make its official decision. In the train going north Conacher was distressed to read in the newspapers that there was dissension on the board over the appointment of an outsider. On his arrival at the NB headquarters Conacher told Tweeddale and the vice chairman of the company, Charles Tennant, 'Unless there is perfect unanimity on the subject I will at once return and regard the negotiations as closed'. He was prevailed upon to stay until the end of the meeting, when he was informed that he had been appointed by the unanimous vote of the committee. But not until he had asked each member individually for an assurance that the appointment had his entire approval did Conacher accept the post. Tweeddale warned him, 'The work you are about to undertake is far more arduous than any you have hitherto experienced and to succeed will require on your part the most unrelenting attention'.

The impending departure of Conacher from Oswestry was greeted with regret, indeed almost dismay, for the family was very much a part of the place. Letters poured into the general manager's office and to his home from traders, from railwaymen, from old schoolfellows, from a one-time colleague on the Scottish Central and from organisations of all kinds. The letters give a vivid picture of the man who was coming to the NB. From the secretary of the Scottish Permissive Bill & Temperance Association came this appreciation:

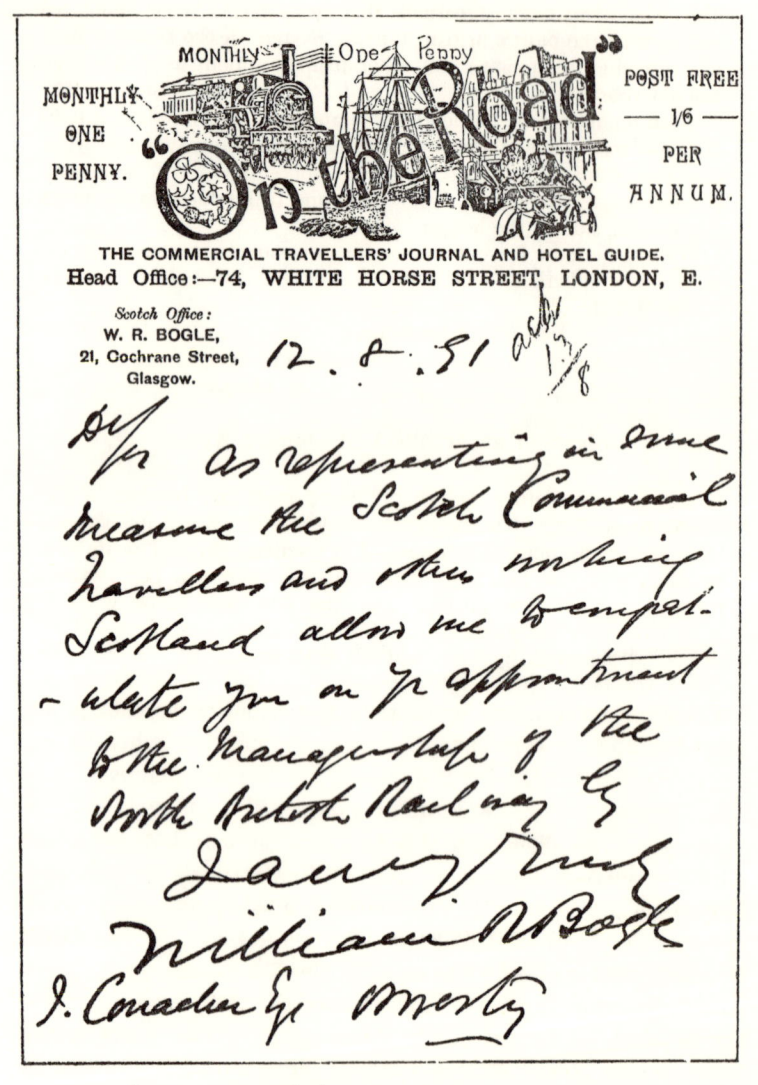

> **"On the Road"**
> MONTHLY — One Penny — POST FREE
> MONTHLY ONE PENNY.   1/6 PER ANNUM
>
> THE COMMERCIAL TRAVELLERS' JOURNAL AND HOTEL GUIDE.
> Head Office:—74, WHITE HORSE STREET, LONDON, E.
>
> *Scotch Office:*
> W. R. BOGLE,
> 21, Cochrane Street,
> Glasgow.
>
> 12. 8. 91
>
> Dr Sir
>
> As representing in some measure the Scotch Commercial Travellers and others working Scotland allow me to congratulate you on yr appointment to the Managership of the North British Railway Cy
>
> Yours truly
> William R Bogle
>
> J. Conacher Esq

Letter congratulating Conacher on appointment

The executive having learned that you have been appointed manager of the North British Railway System desire to offer their hearty congratulations to you on your appointment to such a high and onerous office.

Your reputation as a friend of Temperance and Sunday Schools and also the friend of those on the Cambrian railway under your care lead them to anticipate that your appointment will be greatly conducive to Temperance, Early Piety and to kindness to all under you on this side of the border.

With their most fervent wishes for your steadfast, signal success in the new sphere to which you have been called, I beg to subscribe myself,

      Dear Sir,
      Yours very truly,
      R. Mackay

J. Murray Robertson an architect of Dundee wrote:

It was only the other day that I heard from my brother in the Union Bank, Perth that the new manager of the North British was my old school companion in Mr Moir's school, Perth. I write this to offer you my heartiest congratulations and my best wishes for you in your new position and that you may know what it is to have ever the guidance of Him who alone can direct. In all thy ways acknowledge Him and He shall direct thy steps.

Conacher returned to Scotland as a conquering hero of whom great things were expected.

DAVID DEUCHARS

In 1861 when the youthful John Conacher was finding his feet with the Scottish Central at Perth, 22 miles away in Dundee a boy one year his junior was appointed to a lowly post in the goods manager's office of the Dundee & Arbroath Railway. He was David Deuchars, and his home was in Arbroath. Like Conacher he gravitated to Glasgow during the upheaval of the 1865 amalgamations, but he went no further south. After spending two years in the North British goods office in Glasgow he returned to Dundee as assistant to the district goods manager there. In 1875 he became district goods manager himself with responsibility for all territory north of the Forth. Even before Walker died in 1890 it was being said that David Deuchars was his likely successor. It was of course Conacher who got the job, but Deuchars moved to Edinburgh to be his assistant.

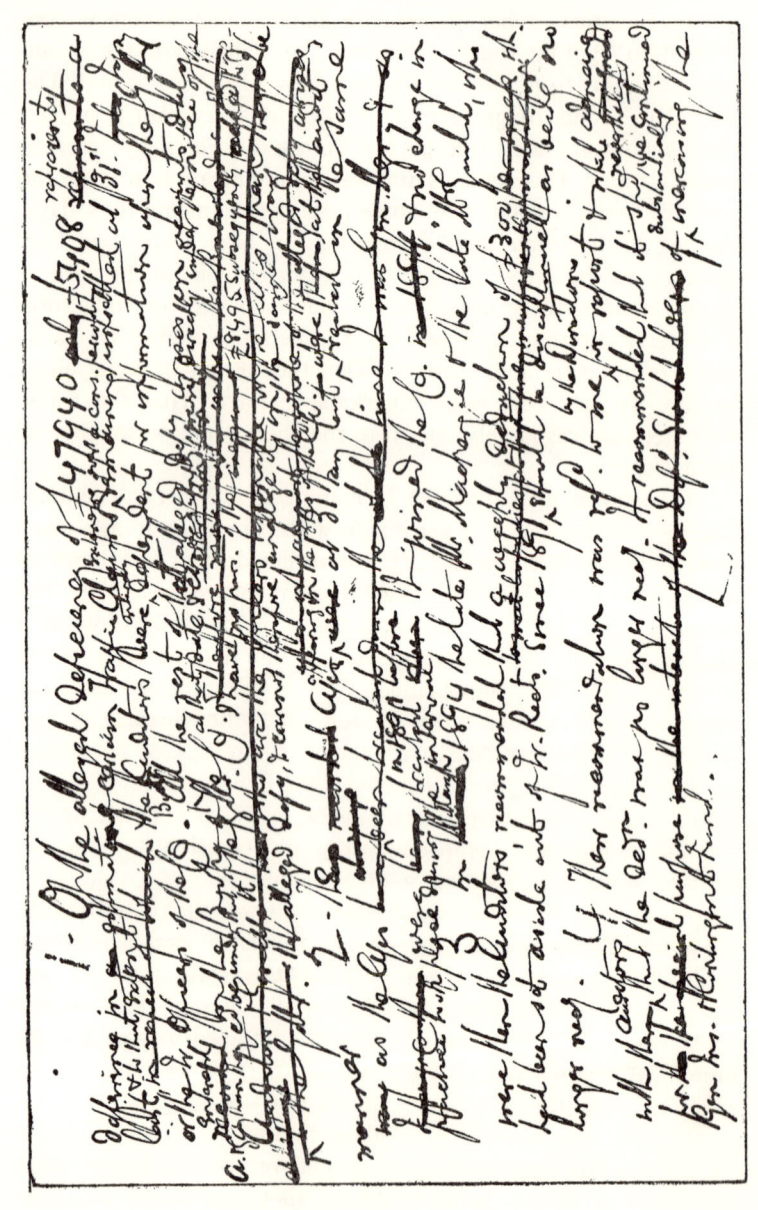

Conacher report extract

From the start of his career with the NB Deuchars was conditioned to fighting the Caledonian. The Caledonian could run through freight from Dundee direct to any place in England. The NB had to get its freight across the Tay by ferry, run it by rail through Fife and then transport it across the Forth by ferry to reach Granton. This tenuous line of communication was at the mercy of wind, fog and tide. Sometimes consignments took days, even weeks to reach their destination. In later years Deuchars spoke of looking across the Tay and seeing wagons in the yard at Tayport waiting to be ferried across, but such was the congestion at the ferry slip that the wagons had to be taken by rail via Ladybank, Perth, Forfar and Arbroath. That the NB got traffic at all in the face of such odds was remarkable enough. That the traffic was extensive was largely due to to the energy and personality of David Deuchars.

Deuchars was like Conacher in many ways. He was a churchman. He had the knack of getting on with people. In an age when senior railway officers ranked with ministers, doctors and dominies in the community Deuchars filled his social role to perfection. The traders trusted him. All were impressed by his dedication to a difficult job. One acquaintance said of him that he was 'North British on the brain'. The opening of the first Tay Bridge eased his burden and extended his scope for furthering the NB cause. When the bridge fell he was faced with the agonising task of re-organising the ferries and trying to cope with the newly-generated traffic. Before he left Dundee Deuchars had the satisfaction of seeing the new Tay Bridge and the Forth Bridge in operation and the NB fortunes in his area booming as never before.

By 1891 Deuchars was something of a civic hero in Dundee. When he left the citizens gave him a farewell dinner over which the Lord Provost presided. Many of the townsfolk went to look in a shop window in which was displayed a marble clock—a gift from his church. All grades of NB staff combined to give him an illuminated address and his good lady a gift of silver plate.

A DYNAMIC PARTNERSHIP

Conacher was appointed general manager on 11 August 1891 at a salary of £2,500. In December of that year David Deuchars joined him as his outdoor assistant and John Cathles, formerly chief clerk, became his indoor assistant, both with salaries of £550.

On the death of James McLaren, general superintendent of the company, in November 1893, Deuchars assumed the title of superintendent of the line and had his salary raised to £1,000. The formidable team of administrative and practical men at headquarters set out to transform the NB. Deuchars could put his finger on the company's weaknesses and Conacher knew how to overcome them.

That Conacher and Deuchars were successful was evident from the unwonted compliments that appeared in the press. From being everybody's aunt sally the NB became a respected institution. That unrelenting critic of the railway the *Dundee Advertiser* spoke of the 'salutary improvement' in services and the 'spontaneous alacrity of the staff. 'The esprit de corps of the whole staff is transparent and is the agreeable substitute for half-hearted service dissention and friction', the paper went on. 'He [Conacher] has inspired confidence in his subordinates. Guards frequently wave their green flags triumphantly and cheerfully shout as they steam out of a station.'

Major Marindin, inspecting officer of the Board of Trade, was more accustomed to throwing brickbats than proffering bouquets as far as the NB was concerned. But the nineties were not far advanced before he was telling Deuchars, 'I know nothing of railway finance and policy but I flatter myself that I do know something about the condition of a line and the service of trains; and I can only say this, that the improvement on your line has been extraordinary, and is generally admitted'.

Deuchars' success at first went unrewarded by the NB board, and it appears that the superintendent of the line, dissatisfied with the absence of financial recognition threatened to offer his talents to another (unnamed) company. Lord Tweeddale himself took the matter in hand and the following minute was the result.

> The board confirmed a provisional arrangement which the chairman reported he had made since the last meeting with Mr Deuchars' superintendent of the line in order that his services might be retained by the company, viz. that his salary shall be increased from £1,000 to £1,250 as from February 1896 and to £1,500 as from 1 February 1898.

The proposed increase in Deuchars' salary was strongly opposed by Randolph Wemyss, one of the directors. He explained to the chairman, 'The reason I object to Mr Deuchars receiving an eventual salary of £1,500 per annum is because the post of superintendent of the line in this system, I consider, as chairman of the traffic committee, should not exceed anyway and under any circumstances £1,250 per annum'. Wemyss asked that his letter be recorded in the minutes. The director disliked Conacher and Deuchars and had already formed a cabal with two other members of the NB hierarchy which was to destroy not only Conacher but Lord Tweeddale. But that is a tale for another chapter.

It was not only internal affairs that engaged the attention of Conacher and Deuchars. When the partnership began the East Coast route was just coming into its own and the two men immediately found themselves embroiled with their North Eastern and Great Northern counterparts in the battle for supremacy over the West Coast companies.

CHAPTER 3

Midsummer Madness

THE GATHERING STORM

The summer of 1890 was the first in its history in which the NB was able to carry passengers between Edinburgh, Perth, Dundee and Aberdeen by a direct route without change of carriage. As the tourist traffic built up the East Coast general managers kept a close watch on the effect of their new challenge on the West Coast's through traffic from London to the north. Every morning the NB agent at Aberdeen telegraphed details of the arrival times and loadings of the night trains to Walker who passed them on to Gibb of the NE and Oakley of the GN.

The NB did not expect wonders in view of the Waverley bottleneck. Acknowledging receipt of traffic statistics from Aberdeen on one occasion Walker replied, 'I am pleased to learn that our running to Aberdeen this morning was quite up to the mark the train having arrived here [Edinburgh] from the south 46 minutes late and reached Aberdeen the same number of minutes late'. For the time being Walker was content to see the company holding its own. But there were mornings when NB performance justified the dispatch of more enthusiastic telegrams to the south. For instance on 6 August Walker wired Oakley:

> East Coast arrived this morning at Aberdeen 37 minutes late, 15 minutes reduced by us with 62 passengers. West Coast arrived at 10.20 with 40 passengers. This shows that exceptional efforts must be made to maintain our superiority.

Walker was not slow to chide Oakley if he thought his southern partner had let him down. On one occasion he wired, 'We gained 9 minutes this morning between this and Aberdeen. Yours was 6 minutes late on arriving here'. A few days later he was complaining to Oakley, 'I heard when passing through Perth this morning that passengers had been refused accommodation at King's Cross last night and had gone over to Euston'.

Part of Walker's strategy in improving the service north of

Edinburgh was to lure the mails to the Forth Bridge route. Once the peak of the tourist season was past he wrote the following strictly private, some might think improper, letter to F. E. Baines of the GPO.

> I do not wish to influence you, because I know that it is impossible but, seriously, would it not be a great advantage to you to forward the mails for Aberdeen by the Forth Bridge route? I observe from today's report that the East Coast express arrived at Aberdeen at 8.14 one minute before time; that the postal train arrived at 9.27 and the West Coast train at 9.53. Now that the pressure is over I think we can run from London to Aberdeen in 12 hours, but you ought to assist us and if you do handsomely we will afford a good service which must benefit the Post Office.

The North British never had been a welcome guest at Aberdeen. From time to time the Caledonian employed obstructionist tactics to impede NB movements in and around the station. A favourite Caledonian trick was to plan a shunt so that it delayed an NB arrival or departure. In the summer of 1890 the Caledonian deliberately and blatantly intensified the war of nerves against the NB. On 29 July Walker reported that a Caledonian shunt had delayed the placing of the stock for the East Coast 3.30 pm express from Aberdeen to London by 40 minutes. A week later he was protesting to the Caledonian general manager, 'Our traffic is being seriously prejudiced by the interruption and obstruction at Aberdeen. I must ask you to provide a remedy forthwith'. When Walker asked for a copy of the CR manual of rules governing the movement of traffic at Aberden his request was refused.

NB goods trains arriving from the south often had to work traffic destined for the GNS through the station to Denburn Junction, and this meant running the gauntlet of Caledonian signals. In a report presented by Walker to his Caledonian counterpart during the 1890 confrontations, the NB general manager cited the example of the 6.45 am goods train from Dundee which arrived at Aberdeen at 12.30 and at 12.35 had whistled for the Denburn signal. The train stood ignored for an hour when a Caledonian pilot also bound for Denburn came up, whistled for the road and was given the signal immediately. The NB train was allowed through at 2.43. Walker claimed that because of the obstruction 'delay visited our afternoon trains'. A week later an NB engine whistled for the Denburn signal at 1.40 pm. The driver waited until 3.10 when he gave up. He came forward again at 5.40 and was given the signal at 7.8. During this time a Caledonian pilot made several trips to Denburn and a GNS engine was allowed through. The episode cost the NB demurrage on the GNS wagons it was trying to deliver.

The season ended well for the NB. By September the East Coast trains had won a share of the mails and the bulk of the passenger traffic. Conacher, who was now in command, on his own initiative speeded up the 4.50 am departure from Edinburgh to give the train an 8 am arrival at Aberdeen, and a 12-hour London to Aberdeen schedule. 'Kindly ensure the speedy arrival of the 8 pm from King's Cross,' the new NB general manager wired Oakley.

The East Coast down day express was due in Aberdeen at 10.20 pm followed at 10.55 pm by the West Coast express. This arrangement seemed to work well enough and for three years the running of the trains provoked no scenes between the rivals. On 1 January 1893 the West Coast re-timed its day express to leave Euston half an hour earlier than before, with a corresponding earlier arrival at Aberdeen. This meant that the West Coast train was now reaching its destination 5min after the East Coast train. The margin was small but it induced the NB to ensure good time keeping with a view to getting to Kinnaber first.

It was not until mid-February that the NB management realised that the East Coast train, despite commendable timekeeping, was being subject to frequent delays at Kinnaber. On 16 February the train was 4min ahead of the Caley, but was held at Kinnaber for the West Coast train to go through, with the result that it was 13min late at Aberdeen. On the following day, with 7min in hand at Kinnaber the train was again held at the junction and reached Aberdeen 15min late. An examination of the Caledonian working timetable revealed that while all the down expresses were given 2min over the Caledonian section immediately south of Kinnaber the day express from London was allowed 6min for the 1 mile 18 chains. This enabled the Caledonian signalman at Dubton Junction to offer the train to Kinnaber 6min before it was due there whether or not it had entered the section to the south of Dubton.

The NB got over this piece of Caledonian skulduggery by the simple expedient of reversing the times of their Perth and Aberdeen departures from Waverley. The 5.40 departure for Perth was allotted to the 6.55 for Aberdeen, and the Perth was given the former Aberdeen timing. The East Coast express was thus assured of a 20min margin over the West Coast train at Kinnaber.

Four months later the Caledonian struck again. It was the custom for railway companies to exchange, for verification purposes, proof copies of their forthcoming timetables where connections were shown to the foreign company concerned. In accordance with routine the NB in May 1893 supplied the Caley with a proof copy of its June Edinburgh–Perth service showing a connection from the 5.45 am NB arrival at Perth into the 6 am Caledonian departure for Forfar, Brechin and other points north. The proof was returned to the NB with the connection deleted. When the NB superintendent asked for an explanation he was told that the Caledonian train had been retimed to leave Perth at 5.45 am which was precisely the arrival time of the NB train.

That afternoon the NB superintendent, after consulting the Caledonian working timetable to assure himself that there was no conflicting movement on the main line south of Perth, retimed his train to arrive at Perth at 5.40 am. The Caledonian promptly retimed one of its down trains to arrive at Perth at 5.40 am. Both trains were due to arrive at Hilton Junction at 5.35. 'I am timing your train to pass Hilton Junction at 5.38 and arrive at Perth at 5.43,' the Caledonian wired the NB superintendent. The NB refused to accept the Caledonian timings and the timetables of both companies that month showed trains arriving at Perth at 5.40.

The situation at Hilton Junction had all the ingredients of a classic Caledonian–NB confrontation. But if there was a daily race by contesting trains to gain possession of the Hilton–Perth section there is no extant record of the event.

THE 10 PM SPECIAL

In June 1895 Sir Henry Oakley decided that the interests of the East Coast route could best be served by the introduction of an entirely new prestige Anglo-Scottish train which would be run during July, August and September to the following timings:

King's Cross dep.	10.0 pm
Peterborough	11.33
Grantham	12.14 am
York	1.19

Newcastle	2.7
Edinburgh	3.5
Perth	8.16
Glasgow	9.0
Dundee	8.50
Montrose	9.52
Aberdeen	11.0

The new train was Oakley's idea. The NB was not consulted, and Conacher was far from pleased when, six days before the new service was due to start, he was presented with the timetable. He protested at once to Oakley on the grounds that there was insufficient through traffic to justify the new train and that it was timed to arrive at Waverley at a time of peak congestion when the staff was already hard pressed handling seven main line arrivals or departures. Conacher urged that instead of instituting a new train the East Coast companies should concentrate on improving the running of the 8 pm from King's Cross so as to compete effectively with the West Coast's 8 pm. Oakley insisted that the NB must cope with the 10 pm. In a letter dated 29 June he reminded Conacher where his duty lay.

> I have your telegram of yesterday's date. I cannot, of course, express any opinion on the necessities of your working at Edinboro, but I think you must bear in mind that nothing short of *absolute impossibility* ought to prevent the utmost use being made of this train with a view to rendering it attractive to the East Coast route. Happily for you the train will reach Edinburgh admirably suited for trains that are already running, therefore you will gain all the advantages to be derived from it without additional expense. This should I think influence you to insist upon the utmost being done to make this train a popular one.
>
> Please recognise also that it is not a question of convenience but of upholding the East Coast against the West Coast.

The first night's working of the new train confirmed Conacher's worst fears. The 10 pm arrived in Waverley with only five passengers, all of them for Edinburgh. The NB did not even trouble to run the train forward to Aberdeen. But that same morning an event took place the significance of which was not appreciated at the time. The East Coast companies had, after all, decided to accelerate the 8 pm from King's Cross to reach Aberdeen at 7.20 am compared with the West Coast 8 pm's arrival time of 7.40. On 2 July the NB agent in Aberdeen wired Deuchars to the effect that the East Coast train with 75 passengers was in Aberdeen 36min before the West Coast train which carried only 25 passengers.

However, Conacher's main concern was with the 10 pm with which he considered the NB had been unfairly saddled. On the evening of 3 July he was at King's Cross walking down the platform looking into the carriages of 'the Special'. The vehicle next to the engine was a 3rd class corridor for Edinburgh; it contained one passenger. The second vehicle, a 3rd class corridor for Glasgow, likewise housed a solitary passenger. A coach for Fort William with five passengers was followed by an Aberdeen sleeper with three 1st class passengers and an Aberdeen 3rd corridor with one passenger. The two rear vehicles, for Perth, were empty. On the following morning Conacher wrote to Oakley:

> I went to King's Cross last night to see the new 10 pm train start. It contained 11 passengers for whose accommodation 7 carriages were provided. I hope now that steps have been taken to advertise the train specially that we may look for better results but it struck me that meantime while business grows the working might be greatly economised.
>
> As the mileage is unbalanced all these carriages will have to be worked back empty and no inconvenience would have been caused to the passengers if the Edinburgh and Perth carriages had been left behind, and the same might be said with regard to the Glasgow carriage. I noticed all the carriages went out without the gas being turned down as it might have been in the two Perth carriages and in by far the greater number of the compartments of the other carriages. Will you kindly take these suggestions into consideration pending our meeting tomorrow.

THE DAFT DAYS

Plans to publicise the 10 pm went on apace. Special posters were printed, and slips were inserted in the July timetables which had been issued without information about the new train. Then in mid-month there occurred an event which forced the East Coast to push the 10 pm into the background of its thinking. On 15 July the West Coast announced a massive acceleration of its 8 pm; henceforward the train would arrive at Aberdeen at 7 am.

There was a flurry in East Coast dovecotes. Obviously, the West Coast challenge had to be met by an acceleration of the East Coast 8 pm. It was planned to run the train to reach Aberdeen at

6.45 am starting on the following Monday, 22 July, and Conacher was asked what the NB could do to help. The NB was prepared to join in a joust with the Caley, but only if it did not lose money in the process. Conacher made his company's position clear in a telegram he sent to Oakley on 17 July: 'We will carry out our part of the arrangement commencing on Monday subject to our being guaranteed against loss north of Berwick. We could not agree to bear any share of the loss having already a very expensive service to maintain.' The upshot was that Oakley and Gibb had to guarantee the NB against loss in the operation of the racing trains.

The NB operating staff had its work cut out to maintain the schedule called for by the racing train over its heavily graded and curvaceous route. Getting the train through the eternal congestion of Waverley station was a nightly headache, especially since the exact arrival time was not known until the train was approaching Edinburgh. Conacher toyed with the idea of running the 8 pm over the Suburban line on a route that would have taken it direct from the main south line to the main north line without touching Waverley. Engines could have been changed conveniently at Haymarket. The difficulty in implementing this plan was that the 8 pm carried Edinburgh mails, and the PMG would not have been amused if these had been dumped on some suburban platform in the middle of the night. Reporting on happenings on the NB on 24 July Conacher informed Oakley: 'West Coast line advertises arrival of their eight o'clock at Aberdeen 6.35. We can better this and I will wire you later in the day both regarding 8 pm and 10 pm. If we run the 8 pm over Suburban line here can you prevent mails for Edinburgh being put in 8 pm train?'

Oakley got the GPO to agree to the mails being transferred to the slower 8.10 pm from King's Cross, but there is no evidence that the 8 pm in fact used the Edinburgh Suburban line.

With the East Coast and West Coast determined to get the better of each other the situation got out of hand. On 25 July Oakley made a commendable effort to call off the dogs of war when he sought the NB board's view on the desirability of getting round the table with the West Coast to discuss a sensible compromise. Tweeddale's answer was that he would sit at a table with the West Coast only after they had been beaten into the ground by the East Coast. So it was war. By then the newspapers

Page 51:

Drummond engines at work (1): (above) *East Coast express leaving the Forth Bridge with 476 class 4–4–0 No 488;* (below) *East Coast express leaving Dundee about 1888; third and fourth coaches are Midland & North British Joint Stock on Anglo-Scottish service via the Waverley route*

Page 52:
Drummond engines at work (2): (above) Edinburgh express about to leave Perth; (below) No 55 0–6–0 on a Garelochhead train at Rhu, West Highland Railway

were aware of what was afoot. A railway race to the north was a gift horse that could not be ignored in the traditional silly season, and the press geared itself to make the most of it.

The five days in which the racing grew to a crescendo have become legendary. There was the dramatic night of 20–21 August when after a night of racing the competing trains found themselves at daybreak within sight of each other and only two miles from Kinnaber. The Caledonian train whisked over the junction a bare minute ahead of its rival. On the following night the East Coast was through Kinnaber a decisive $14\frac{1}{2}$min before the Caledonian and covered the $523\frac{1}{2}$ miles between London and Aberdeen in 520min. The railway writers half crazed with excitement described the event in extravagant prose.

But General Inspector W. McLelland of the NBR, who rode on the trains on both nights, was concerned neither with satisfying the public demand for thrills nor with creating legends. His job was to produce a sober, factual report for his general manager and the following is, in part, what he wrote.

> The speed as you will see from the statement of today's running was very high and the restrictions through junctions and over the Tay Bridge and picking up and leaving tablets, were pretty well put aside, and my opinion is we cannot improve upon it. One minute 50 seconds over the Forth Bridge and 1 minute 40 seconds over the Tay Bridge was very sharp work, and I heard a gentlemen complain of the excessive speed at which the train was run to our Aberdeen agent.

That was the most significant statement to come of the racing as far as the NB was concerned. If speed restrictions were imposed for the protection of passengers then by wantonly disregarding the restrictions the NB was exposing its passengers to a known danger. Fear of disaster was the chief motive for Conacher deciding on the arrival of the train at Aberdeen on the final night that enough was enough and the nonsense must end. First thing that morning the NB general manager drafted a telegram to Oakley calling for a cessation of the racing and gave orders that it had to be handed in at the post office when it opened at 9 am.

It was August and the general managers of the NE and GN were on holiday, Gibb at Dornoch, Oakley in Dublin, while Conacher himself was in Aberdeen. The vital telegram had to be re-transmitted from the head offices of the English companies to the holiday addresses of the executive officers. It was not until 12.13 pm that Oakley's reply reached Conacher. It said, 'I think we ought to continue to show our friends the hopelessness of their effort. Stopping now would be commented on. Please reply'. Seven minutes later Gibb's reply was in Conacher's hands. 'Having made record this morning my opinion in favour of confining racing to this week. Best policy to be able to prove that except this week we have worked our trains not as racers but under ordinary traffic conditions.' Conacher alone seemed determined to hold to a sane course.

Meanwhile a meeting of the GN board had taken place in London and while it was sitting a further telegram arrived from Conacher urging an end to the racing but agreeing, with obvious reluctance, to continue the struggle if the GN thought it necessary. At 1.50 pm Conacher received from the GN board the message, 'Feeling of directors here that we should cease having shown what we can do'. Conacher's relief shows in his telegraphed reply. 'Am glad your directors agree to view expressed in my first telegram. I think it the safest course and the most dignified.' *Safety* was the key word.

At 3.20 that afternoon Gibb capitulated. In a wire to Conacher he said, 'I agree your view and have so wired Oakley. Think we should publish tonight official notice of intention to return to advertised time'. However, at York there was confusion. Amid the welter of conflicting messages and telegrams the NE officers did not know whether the race was on or off and at 4.18 pm Burtt asked Conacher for clarification. It was not until 5 pm that the East Coast companies decided that the 8 pm would run to its advertised times that night.

But the 8 pm from Euston did not revert to its advertised times. The West Coast train, racing without a competitor, covered the 540 miles to Aberdeen in 512 min thus wiping out the East Coast triumph of the previous night. The news of the West Coast run had a startling effect on the NB general manager. The cautious Conacher at once embarked on a hot-headed campaign to restart the races. On the morning of 23 August he asked Holmes if the previous best performance could be improved on. Holmes replied, 'Might possibly arrange three ordinary carriages but risky seeing such high speed has to be maintained'. In spite of his locomotive superintendent's warning of danger, and the lesson of McLelland's reports, Conacher continued with his scheme for staging a 'special effort' run. The English officers whom the day before had been urged to stop the races now received telegrams asking them to renew the struggle. It was an amazing *volte face*. Gibb was sympathetic. He wired Conacher at 10.40 on the morning of 23 August, 'Think we must run special again tonight'. But at 2.50 pm came a cold douche from Oakley. 'I think it would be childish to begin to run again at present. Let us wait and see the effect on the public mind. From all I hear action is approved.' Andrew the NB goods manager was standing in for Conacher at Edinburgh, the general manager still being on holiday, and he had been briefed to stand by for a resumption of the race that night. But late in the afternoon he received a telegram from Conacher: 'I think we should wait a few days before running another special and see details of last night's runnings first.'

It was important that Conacher should see the official figures of the record Caledonian performance. Normally the rival company did not release details at once, but on this occasion Conacher had a stroke of luck. Inspector McLelland went to Fort William on 23 August to attend an inquiry into a derailment on the West Highland Railway and it transpired that the Board of Trade inspecting officer had a copy of the official Caledonian figures in his possession. He allowed McLelland to copy the information which was forwarded at once to Edinburgh.

While admitting 'the childishness of the whole business' Conacher tried to persuade Oakley to resume racing, and he told the English manager how, in his opinion, the East Coast could retrieve the laurels. His idea was to pick a quiet night when, unannounced, they would make an all-out effort. But the GN had turned its back on racing. The circus was over.

COUNTING THE COST

If the purpose of the racing was to attract passengers to the 'winning' train the episode was a fiasco. The existing traffic pattern was not influenced one whit by the racing. In early July the East Coast was carrying the bulk of the London–Aberdeen traffic. It continued to attract the biggest share during the races, and when normal services were resumed in September the 8 pm from King's Cross carried almost double the number of through passengers booked on the 8 pm from Euston—608 against 333.

By the time the racing reached its climax the East Coast train was carrying passengers for Dundee and Aberdeen only. The mails, parcels and newspapers had been shed to lighten the train and save time at Waverley, and the revenue from this traffic had been lost to the 8 pm. Passengers for Aberdeen and other northern destinations from stations in the south no longer served by the racer were carried on the 8.30 and 10 pm trains from King's Cross. On the West Coast there was no suitable alternative to the 8 pm and a relief train, quite unjustified by the volume of traffic offered, was put on to follow the racer all the way to Aberdeen, where it was due at 7.40 am. On its first night it arrived with two passengers, on the third night none at all and on two occasions it arrived with only one passenger. On 22 July the West Coast racer conveyed seven passengers, the relief one; two trains for eight passengers—a lot of effort for little revenue.

On the three peak days of the racing (19–21 August departures from London) the East Coast train carried 101 through passengers, the West Coast 35. On the night of 22 August the East Coast train running normally brought 34 passengers to Aberdeen. The West Coast train on its night of nights had already arrived in glory 48min before schedule, but with only 10 passengers. The relief arrived 3hr 16min later also with 10 passengers.

Taking the period of the racing as extending from 16 July to 23 August (arrivals at Aberdeen) the East Coast recorded two on time arrivals, 13 early arrivals and 19 late arrivals. The corresponding figures for the West Coast train were no on time arrivals, 30 early arrivals and four late arrivals. The East Coast totalled 86min early, 262min late and carried 2,156 passengers. The West Coast train achieved 393min in early arrivals, 7 in late arrivals and carried 751 through passengers. From 27 July to 17 August when the West Coast recorded 19 successive early arrivals and the East Coast train was consistently late, the East Coast train held its nearly 3 to 1 loading lead over its rival.

When the fury had subsided the recriminations began, with the various general managers blaming each other for having started the tomfoolery. The West Coast saw the East Coast's introduction of the 10 pm from King's Cross as the start of the competition, while the East Coast dated the West Coast aggression from the Caledonian's obstructive tactics at Kinnaber in 1893.

The East Coast companies regarded it as a divine right that their train should arrive in Aberdeen first. Sir Joseph Pease, chairman of the NE, thought the East Coast had every right to benefit in perpetuity from its shorter route and he 'did not see any reason why they should give up a position which they had earned at the expenditure of a good deal of intelligence and capital'. Jackson, chairman of the GN, likewise announced that 'they were entitled to claim that the old relative time be preserved'. To Conacher fell the task of negotiating details of a settlement with the Caledonian. His aim was to achieve first arrival at Aberdeen with a margin of 15min over the West Coast train at Kinnaber.

Thompson of the Caledonian was incensed at Conacher's suggestion that the Caledonian was responsible for the race situation. On 28 August he wired the NB general manager:

> Your telegram of today. I completely deny that any action of my company justifies your allegation that the recent fast running was brought about by West Coast companies. The first alteration made was that our train arriving at Aberdeen at 7·50 was altered to 7·40 in order to secure connections and this alteration left your train with a margin of 5 minutes in advance. It was then that the East Coast companies took the step of accelerating their train by another 15 minutes and this forced the West Coast companies to take steps to protect their interests. I do not agree with you that a 15 minute margin is required and if your train is run to time there is no need for any question at all as to margin. It is an entirely new departure to seek to set up the necessity for such a margin. I have gone to a great length to meet you in allowing your train the 5 minutes margin in front of the West Coast train and I regret that it has not been appreciated.

On the day this telegram was received Oakley wrote privately to Conacher congratulating him on the stand he had taken against the Caledonian and urging him to stick his ground.

> I am *not* disposed to recommend any arrangement with either North Western or Caledonian. They began and they should finish first. The West Coast already feel the pressure. Last night they were behind us as they must be if they are to run reasonable trains. When they show a disposition to threat I should listen and fix the time of arrival with due regard to our more favourable distance. But I would rather not agree at all. Their action has relieved us from any obligation. I should like to let them see more fully the consequences of their hasty action. Only a stern resolve to show them always that we are neither to be cajoled or outrun will keep them quiet.

Oakley's belligerent message encouraged Conacher to take a provocative line with Thompson: 'Your telegram of 28th. Your denial of the origin of fast running totally irreconcilable with the facts. A 5 minute margin is impracticable, even when both company's trains approach Kinnaber on time, and will as certainly fail now as when you attempted it in the beginning of 1893.' To this Thompson answered: 'I have only to add that you must not assume that West Coast has any other intention than to maintain equality in the working with East Coast.' Conacher replied by telegram within the hour: 'There can be no equality so long as our access to Aberdeen is over 38 miles of your line. A margin of 15 minutes etc. insufficient. Refer case of February 1893. Thompson replied on 2 September:

> Your telegram. We shall certainly insist upon equality in regard to time, and I do not see that I can add anything to what I have already stated. Surely you do not mean to claim a 15 minute margin for working over our main line because your route happens to be a few miles shorter from London. I do not see that anything turns upon the working on the date you refer to in 1893.

One worthwhile achievement emerged from the races. Throughout the episode the traffic needs of the great city of Glasgow had been ignored by both contestants. While the general managers were huffing and puffing on paper the always practical David Deuchars was producing figures to show that the Glasgow–London traffic by the East Coast route, although neglected by the companies, was increasing steadily. It was Deuchars' view that the greatest traffic potential lay not in the largely seasonal traffic to the north but in the solid trade generated by Scotland's industrial capital. The NB superintendent pressed his view on his English colleagues and they accepted it willingly. Gibb in an appreciative letter to Conacher wrote, 'Hitherto we have rather neglected Glasgow traffic, but under the new conditions we must make efforts to get more of it'. Oakley shared his opinion.

When the East Coast winter timetables appeared two trains from London to Glasgow were shown as doing the journey 20 and 25 minutes faster than the corresponding West Coast expresses, this in spite of a distance handicap of no less than 38¼ miles. One East Coast up train completed the inter-city trip in 15min less than the rival West Coast train. Two months earlier that timetable would have triggered off a frantic 'race to Glasgow'. That the West Coast officers took no notice of it was a measure of their disenchantment with the operational and economic folly of racing. Henceforward the competitors conducted their affairs within the framework of closely-observed treaties. When in 1900 the NE wanted to speed up East Coast trains the LNW and the Caledonian joined the GN and NB to thwart the development of a race situation.

Inspector McLelland rode on the NB trains on the mornings of 20 and 21 August and made detailed logs of the journeys. The following extracts are from McLelland's originals in the Scottish Record Office. The inspector was called away to attend the accident inquiry into the derailment on the West Highland Railway and was not available for the record East Coast run on 22 August.

M.	C.		20 Aug. H. M. S.	21 Aug. H. M. S.
		Edinburgh Wav. arr	2.46	2.42.30
		Edinburgh Wav. dep	2.57	2.44
3	41	Corstophine	3.3	2.50
8	55	Dalmeny	3.8	2.55
11	27	North Queensferry	3.10	2.56.50
13	13	Inverkeithing	3.13.30	2.58.30
17	30	Aberdour	3.19	3.3.30
20	11	Burntisland	3.23.30	3.6
22	59	Kinghorn	3.25.20	3.9
25	71	Kirkcaldy	3.27	3.12
27	15	Sinclairtown	3.28	3.13
27	79	Dysart	3.29.30	3.14.40
30	61	Thornton	3.33	3.17
33	20	Markinch	3.34.30	3.19.30
36	12	Falkland Road	3.37.40	3.32.40
38	16	Kinskettle	3.39.30	3.24
39	9	Ladybank	3.40.20	3.25
42	23	Springfield	3.43.40	3.28
44	46	Cupar	3.46	3.30
47	46	Dairsie	3.49	3.33
50	68	Leuchars Jct.	3.52	3.36
54	48	St Fort	3.55.40	3.40
56	42	Tay Bridge S	3.57.40	3.42
58	37	Esplanade	4.0	3.43.40
59	18	Dundee Tay Bridge arr	4.1	3.44

M.	C.		20 Aug. H.M.S.	21 Aug. H.M.S.
		Dundee dep	4.9	3.46
3	40	West Ferry	4.14.30	3.53
3	79	Broughty Ferry	4.15	3.53.40
6	28	Monifieth	4.17.30	3.55.20
		Buddon	4.19	3.56.30
9	21	Barry	4.21	3.58
10	20	Carnoustie	4.22	4.0
12	53	East Haven	4.24	4.1.30
15	49	Elliot Jct.	4.27	4.4
17	3	Arbroath	4.29	4.6
20	1	Letham Grange	4.34	4.9.20
21	71	Cauldcoats	4.36	4.12
23	16	Inverkeillor	4.37	4.13
25	65	Lunan Bay	4.40	4.16
30	53	Montrose	4.46	4.22
32	58	Kinnaber Jct.	4.49	4.26
33	23	Craigo	4.51.30	4.30
35	34	Marykirk	4.33.30	4.34
38	50	Laurencekirk	4.57.30	4.38
41	76	Fordoun	5.0.40	4.41.30
45	70	Drumlithie	5.5	4.45
53	4	Stonehaven	5.12	4.52.30
57	52	Muchalls	5.17	4.57
58	55	Newtonhill	5.18.30	4.58
60	72	Portlethen	5.20.30	5.1
64	20	Cove	5.24	5.4
		Aberdeen Ticket Platform arr	5.28.30	5.9
		dep	5.30.40	5.10.30
69	6	Aberdeen	5.32	5.11

This table shows the running and loading of the East Coast and West Coast trains from 2 July to 31 August 1895.

	East Coast			West Coast		
Date	Time of arrival	Mins late (early)	No of through passengers	Time of arrival	Mins late (early)	No of through passengers
	Due 7.20			Due 7.40		
July 2	7.24	4	75	8.0	20	25
3	7.25	5	18	8.5	25	20
4	7.34	14	22	7.54	14	12
5	7.26	6	13	8.1	21	14
6	7.22	2	23	8.8	28	14
8	7.24	4	3	7.39	1	3

MIDSUMMER MADNESS

	East Coast			West Coast		
Date	Time of arrival	Mins late (*early*)	No of through passengers	Time of arrival	Mins late (*early*)	No of through passengers
	Due 7.20			Due 7.40		
9	7.51	31	49	7.40		14
10	7.30	10	38	7.52	12	8
11	7.18	2	21	7.45	5	13
12	7.39	9	36	8.8	28	23
13	7.44	24	50	8.6	26	11
15	7.59	39	12	8.16	36	3
				Due 7.0		
16	8.12	52	52	6.46	14	9
17	7.29	9	24	6.21	39	12
18	7.35	15	37	6.54	6	17
19	8.10	50	43	6.50	10	9
20	7.55	35	53	6.49	11	15
22	7.28	8	25	6.38	22	7
	Due 6.45			Due 6.35		
23	6.44	1	43	6.38	3	16
24	6.40	5	61	6.30	5	19
25	6.38	7	33	6.25	10	19
26	6.48	3	53	6.36	1	26
27	6.42	3	120	6.31	4	72
29	6.40	5	24	6.14	21	10
	Due 6.25			Due 6.20		
30	5.22	3	66	6.5	15	27
31	6.40	15	88	5.59	21	25
Aug. 1	6.50	25	161	6.16	4	58
2	6.55	30	160	6.17	3	32
3	6.33	8	123	6.16	4	54
5	7.5	40	20	6.10	10	8
6	6.25		56	6.9	11	12
7	6.42	17	96	6.19	1	34
8	6.27	2	92	6.10	10	17
9	6.49	24	85	6.17	3	40
10	6.45	20	107	6.9	11	52
12	6.30	5	39	6.10	10	10
13	6.20	5	43	6.10	10	10
14	6.27	2	35	6.15	5	16
15	6.21	4	52	6.13	7	22
16	6.25		32	6.18	2	18
17	6.27	2	62	6.10	10	29
19	6.17	8	36	6.23	3	11
	Due 5.40			Due 5.35		
20	5.32	8	44	5.16	19	13

	East Coast			West Coast		
Date	Time of arrival	Mins late (early)	No of through passengers	Time of arrival	Mins late (early)	No of through passengers
	Due 5.13			Due 5.20		
21	5.11	2	35	4.58	22	12
22	4.40	33	22	4.55	25	10
	Due 6.25					
23	6.23	2	34	4.32	48	10
				Due 6.25		
24	6.34	9	63	6.24	1	29
26	6.32	7	24	6.22	3	13
				Due 6.30		
27	6.39	14	42	6.29	1	27
28	6.23	3	30	6.32	2	5
29	6.23	2	29	6.35	5	8
30	6.21	4	25	7.9	39	10
31	6.31	4	62	6.37	7	18

CHAPTER 4

Locomotive Matters 1880–1903

DRUMMOND CONSOLIDATES

By 1880 the splendid engines of Dugald Drummond dominated the NB scene. Whether express bogie, branch line tank or six-coupled goods the Drummond product performed superbly. And some of the Old Wheatleys had been given a new lease of life. No contemporary railway owed more to its locomotive superintendent than the NB owed to Dugald Drummond.

The fall of the Tay Bridge had an effect on locomotive policy. Had the bridge survived it is likely that the directors would have called for a new express engine for the prestige Burntisland–Aberdeen trains, in which case the 4-4-0 which subsequently made Drummond's name on the Caledonian might well have appeared on the NB. Only one new Drummond design appeared from Cowlairs after 1879—the small 4-4-0 tank. These little engines—they were only 30ft long—were Drummond's answer to the board's request for a class that would work the company's large number of branch lines economically. The engines were extremely neat and toy-like. The cylinders were 16in by 24in, the coupled wheels were 5ft in diameter and the solid bogie wheels 2ft 6in. The 24 engines of the class carried regional names and for 50 years or more carried out their duties in places as far apart as Morpeth and St Combs.

On 30 March 1882 Drummond was asked to produce two engines for Leith and Stobcross docks 'to be built as early as possible at Cowlairs works unless it should be found that two can be purchased for delivery in two months'. On 20 April it was announced that Neilson & Co had undertaken to deliver two such engines at £1,275 each within two months.

Although only one new design appeared from Cowlairs in the last two years of Drummond's reign there was plenty for the locomotive superintendent to do. The works were extended and partly re-equipped. It was the hope of the directors that Cowlairs would be made capable of coping with all new building and repairs both of locomotives and rolling stock. Between 1880 and 1882 a further 50 of Drummond's 17in 0-6-0s were built at the works and a steady programme of carriage and wagon renewal was carried out.

Progress was made in the fitting of passenger stock with the Westinghouse brake, but the task of Cowlairs was made no easier by the unreliablity of the brake in service. In the first six months of 1882 there were no fewer than 72 brake failures. A report on the situation also listed the mileage of passenger trains still running without continuous brakes during the same period.

NBR	875,505
Blane Valley	2,480
Kelvin Valley	10,710
Newport Railway	5,590
Wemyss & Buckhaven	4,960
Dundee & Arbroath	45,819

THE NB CARRIAGE

Drummond bequeathed a locomotive dynasty to the NB. It is forgotten—perhaps with good reason—that he also bequeathed a carriage dynasty. Photographs of NB passenger trains of the period, and later, tend to give the impression that the carriages were of an earlier generation than the engines pulling them. NB coaches got a consistently bad press; travellers were much given to venting their spite against them in the public prints.

The standard Drummond 3rd class four-wheeler was an austere vehicle. The designer contrived to pack 50 passengers into five compartments in a body length of 28ft 6in; ten people were compressed into a space measuring 7ft 6in by 5ft 6½in. In the corresponding 1st class carriage the passenger density was reduced to 24 persons in four compartments. The wheelbase in each case was 16ft. The 3rd class carriage weighed 10ton 4cwt and the 1st class 11ton 6½cwt. Drummond's six-wheeler was 7ft 0½in longer than the four-wheeler and had a wheelbase of 23ft. The 3rd class traveller was allowed 2⅛in more knee room than his fellow-passenger in the four-wheeler. There were six compartments with a total capacity of 60 passengers. The 3rd class vehicle weighed 13ton 8cwt, and the 1st class 14½ tons.

A feature of the Drummond coach was that the body was some 8in longer and wider than the underframe. The ends and sides were curved inwards from a point about window level to join the underframe, thus giving the vehicle its characteristic contours—the NB look. The roof, flat for most of its width, curved suddenly to meet the cornice. It was not an elegant vehicle.

Carriage heating was by warming pan. Victorian and Edwardian travellers appreciated the importance of jockeying for a seat as close as possible to the communal compartment footwarmer. The footwarmer headquarters was at St Margarets. There the devices were serviced and sent out to the main stations where heating boilers were positioned and men were detailed to prepare and distribute the pans throughout selected trains. The pans were sealed and attached to the end of long poles. They were heated by being immersed in boiling water and then thrust into compartments by porters or other servants detailed for the job.

On short journeys and local trains only 1st class pasengers got footwarmers; 3rd class passengers had the discomfort of an unheated compartment. On long journeys the pans were exchanged or re-heated at certain intermediate stations. West Highland journeys caused special anxiety to the company, especially after the first grim winter. It was no great comfort to the passenger to set off on a five-hour journey over high frozen moors swept by icy winds with only a hot water bottle for company.

A journey on a dark winter night in a claustrophobic NB compartment lit by a fitful oil lamp must have been a test of endurance. One such journey was described dramatically in a passenger's letter to the general manager. A family travelling in the compartment of an express train at night noticed that oil from a faulty reservoir was steadily leaking into the bowl of the roof lamp. Convinced that he was sitting under a potential bomb, one of the passengers pulled the communication cord. Nothing happened. In explanation of the affair the general manager wrote, 'The train was fitted with cord communication throughout, but it appears that the passengers pulled the cord on the wrong side. If he had pulled the cord on the right hand side of the train in the direction in which it was travelling they would have succeeded in stopping it'.

'The historian of the future will find food for thought when he records the fact that the people of the 19th century travelled about in dog kennels.' So ran one of the periodical letters of complaint about NB carriages. Now and again such taunts spurred the NB

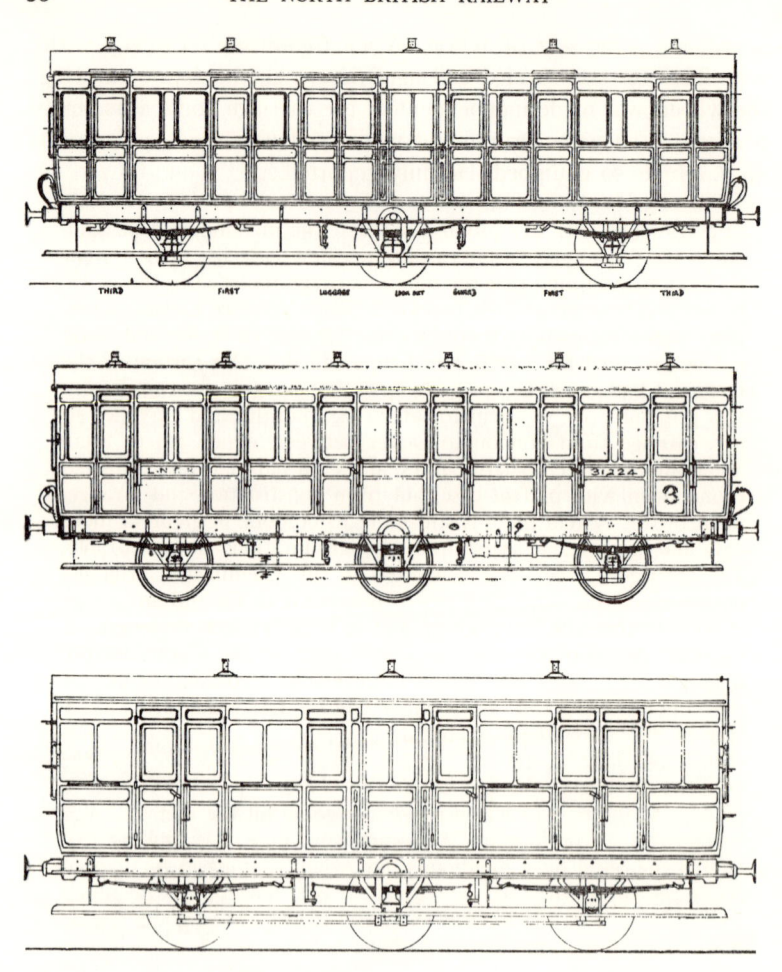

(Above) Six-wheel brake composite

(Centre) Six-wheel third

(Below and left) Six-wheel full brake

board into some sort of action. When Cleminson's Patent Elastic wheelbase for six-wheeled carriages (in which the frame carrying the wheels was made independent of the carriage body) was being praised in the press Drummond was urged to inspect and report on a vehicle so equipped. He duly reported:

> In accordance with my promise made at the meeting held in Edinburgh on Wednesday last regarding the new carriage stock I went to London and found that the saloon carriage reported in the newspapers and belonging to the London & South Western Railway Company was being used by the Prince and Princess of Wales and could not be procured for a trial run. I then called on Mr Kirtley of the London Chatham & Dover Railway who has carriages running on this principle, one of them for about six months, and travelled in this carriage from London to Dover between which places there are a number of very sharp curves, and I am happy to say it moved round them with perfect ease, but from construction and arrangement of this system there is still more to be done in giving a more easy and comfortable seat as the vertical vibrations are unbearable. The carriage 27 feet long converted to suit Cleminson's principle does not give the same facilities of proving it to the full advantage it would otherwise have given had it been 40 feet in length. It takes the curves quite as easy as a bogie carriage and is considerably lighter in its construction but in the event of a collision or any of the connections giving way which control the wheels to radiate true to the curves there is nothing to guide the wheels or prevent them from leaving the rails and doubling up below the carriage whereas the bogie principle has always the two pairs of wheels to guide it to the true path and prevent it going off the metals. I also travelled in an ordinary LC & D carriage which was immediately behind the one I have mentioned, but when running at high speed round the curves the carriage with the elastic wheel base was much freer from side oscillation but vertically it was not so good, and as it is a very important matter to have an easy seat for passengers something will have to be done to attain this object.

Drummond refused to recommend that the Cleminson principle be applied to carriages building at Cowlairs, although he suggested that one might be fitted experimentally and tested against a conventional carriage.

EXIT DRUMMOND

In recording the departure of an administrative figure from the NB scene in the early 1880s a board minute mentioned the 'personal supervision he always offered to the locomotive department with the affairs of which he specially concerned himself to the company's great advantage'. That would have made a fitting tribute to Drummond; in fact it referred to William Muir, a director of the company. When Drummond left the NB with seven years of exceptional achievement behind him his going was recorded coldly in a nine-word sentence. 'The resignation of Mr Drummond locomotive superintendent is reported.' The customary appreciation of services rendered was omitted, and if Drummond received the customary gratuity no mention of it was made in the relevant NB papers.

Muir was chairman of the locomotive committee. He was an old man and he did not always see eye to eye with the ebullient young Drummond. It had been at Muir's instigation that Cowlairs works had been extended and improved and he was of the opinion, after the money was spent, that productivity there was unsatisfactory. There was a clash of personalities in 1881 when Drummond wanted twenty 17in goods locomotives built by Neilson & Co and Muir told him plainly that the engines must be built at Cowlairs. When Drummond remonstrated that Cowlairs was incapable of building them Muir led the locomotive committee on a tour of inspection of the works and forthwith announced the plant 'capable of producing all engines, carriages, etc required, Mr Drummond being instructed to complete the orders on hand with the utmost dispatch'. The board eventually compromised, 10 new engines being built at Cowlairs.

Also in 1881 there was trouble over the failure of tender tyres. There were 29 such failures over a short period, and when five failures occurred in as many days there was consternation in Essen. Krupp was the main supplier of steel tyres not only to the NB but to many of the great railways of the world. Anything that reflected on the great name of Krupp demanded investigation. On 28 January 1881 a 'practical representation from Germany' inspected Cowlairs works in the company of Drummond and the directors. The Krupp investigators concluded that the tyre fractures were due to faulty setting of the brake blocks, and Drummond was informed that the brake blocks were to be altered 'so as not to apply to flanges of tyres'.

One pinprick showed the way the wind was blowing. Drummond applied for a shopping pass for his wife, valid between Lenzie and Glasgow. Railwaymen and Cowlairs shopmen were supplied with similar passes between Cowlairs and Queen Street for their wives or housekeepers. Mrs Drummond was refused a pass.

Drummond irretrievably damaged his standing with the board by his conduct during the Board of Trade inquiry into the Tay Bridge disaster. The company had based its case on the theory that part of the train had become derailed on the bridge and demolished a vital strut thereby producing a chain reaction that had brought down the bridge. Drummond contemptuously rejected this theory. No doubt he was right. But his haughty attitude in court and his relentless browbeating of the luckless Bouch—a boardroom favourite—were not forgotten by the directors.

The locomotive superintendent was responsible for disposing of old timber—usually slab wood and wagon boards—from the carriage and wagon department, and this trade produced revenue of up to £600 per month. Early in June 1882 Drummond was asked to explain an apparent discrepancy in the timber accounts and he duly submitted a report. On 22 June Drummond resigned, ostensibly to take up an appointment with the Caledonian. But George Brittain, the locomotive superintendent of that company, did not resign until July and Drummond was not appointed in his place until 6 August. On the day that Drummond's resignation was reported to the NB locomotive committee, Matthew Holmes was appointed as his 'suitable and economic successor'. Contrary to NB practice the post was not advertised. Evidently Mr Drummond's departure was not unexpected.

On 24 August the new locomotive superintendent and Robertson, the stores superintendent, 'were instructed to inquire into and report upon a statement which has been furnished by Mr Drummond showing a loss upon timber'. On 14 September 'consideration of the reports by the locomotive superintendent and stores superintendent with regard to loss upon timber and the sale of old material lying at Cowlairs was delayed until the next meeting.

On 4 October the locomotive and stores committee met specially at Cowlairs to conduct an on the spot investigation and frame the final report on the disputed accounts. The relevant minute book page is headed, 'Minute of Special Meeting of Locomotive and Stores Committee held at Cowlairs on 4 October 1882' and those present were listed as Sir James Falshaw (chairman of the company), and Messrs Beaumont, Garnett and Grierson—all directors.

The page area below the heading where the report of the meeting normally would appear is blank except for a pencilled note, 'No minute written by chairman'. This is the only example of an un-minuted meeting, board or committee, in the whole history of the company. The general manager's wet tissue copy letter book covering October 1882 is missing. Whether by accident or design the NB hierarchy effectively deprived posterity of learning the findings of that vital meeting.

On 5 October the 'secret' report was presented to the directors, who ordered that a deficit of £4,305 8s in the locomotive department accounts be made up by the transfer of £1,500 per half year from the general reserve.

Drummond was fortunate in being served by a first rate chief draughtsman—Robert Chalmers. The careers of the two men were curiously interlinked. Chalmers, then in his early twenties, was already at Cowlairs when Drummond went there the first time. When Drummond moved to Brighton as Stroudley's assistant he was joined by Chalmers who remained with him for five years. In February 1875 Drummond returned to Cowlairs as locomotive superintendent to be followed a month later by Robert Chalmers as chief draughtsman. Drummond stayed at Cowlairs for a mere seven years, but Chalmers ruled the drawing office for 30 years—from the Drummond 2-2-2 to the Atlantic. What a tale he could have told had he recorded his experiences on paper. But leading draughtsmen, whatever railway they served, were self-effacing men whose lot was to stand unobserved in the background leaving the titular head of the department to take the kudos for ideas which not infrequently had their origin in the drawing office.

HORSE POWER

The NB boasted not only a locomotive superintendent but a horse superintendent. The most distinguished custodian of the company's flesh and blood motive power, John Lingard, was as much a character as any of his steam and steel counterparts. The NB horses bore numbers and were grouped in classes according to the work they were intended to perform. Thus in a departmental report issued on 13 March 1882 Lingard noted, 'Two new ponies for working phaeton and dog cart and two horses for light lorries have been added to stock and are numbered 61, 62, 63 and 64. Two are still on hand alleged to be on trial'.

There were five 'sheds': Glasgow with 104 horses, Perth with eight, Arbroath seven, Forfar (on Caledonian territory) seven, and Greenfield one. Motive power was re-allocated from time to time to suit traffic requirements. In a report on the Glasgow stable there is a reference to 'brown horse No 189 formerly of Perth, now transferred to this station', while a report from Arbroath states 'Horses are in very fair working condition. No 36 is replaced by No 40 ex-Glasgow, the former said to be dead'. Selected animals were army reservists, the NB being paid £15 per annum in respect of horses ear-marked for call-up in the event of a national emergency. There was a journal devoted to the performance of railway horses. A controversy raged through several issues on whether hairy-legged horses were better pullers than smooth-legged horses.

A celebrated NB horse was the one that shunted Kelso yard. The curves at this location were such that no locomotive could negotiate them. The Kelso horse defied the steam horse for many years only to yield to the petrol engine in January 1921. The annual cost of horse shunting was £1,180 compared with £904 using a petrol shunter, although the company had to spend £121 in easing the curves.

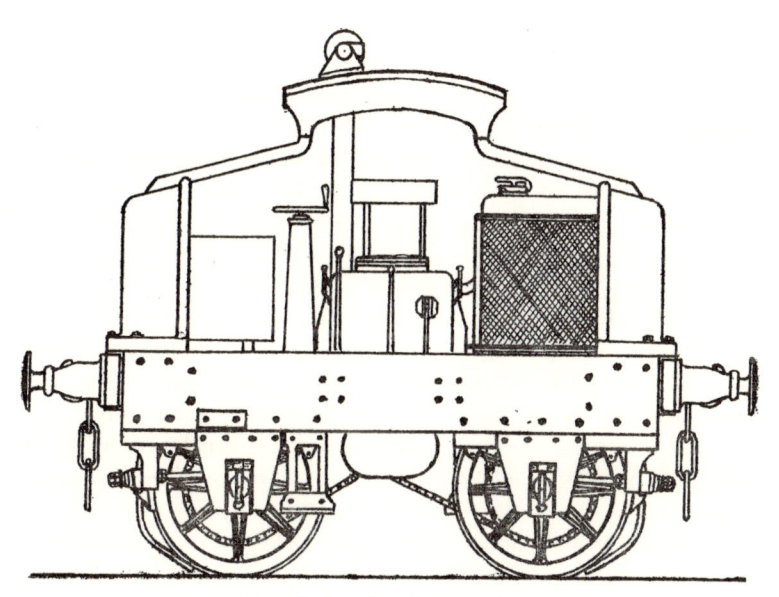

Petrol shunting locomotive

NB horses that did a real railway job were those which worked the Drumburgh–Port Carlisle branch in Cumberland. The first coach used in this service came from Bartons of Carlisle for the opening of the line on 28 August 1856. This vehicle was replaced in 1859 by the St Margarets-built 'Dandy No 1' which had already seen service on the North Leith line and briefly on the North Berwick branch. It was a four-wheeler constructed on stage coach lines with inside accommodation for 12 1st and 2nd class passengers and open benches round the body for 15 3rd class passengers. Traffic justified the introduction in 1863 of the 'New Dandy'. It was 27ft long and 10ft 9in wide and was divided into one 1st class compartment and two 3rd class. 'Dandy No 2', acquired in 1900, was similar in appearance to a tramcar and could accommodate 28 passengers under cover and 20 in open seats.

Freight was steam-hauled until 2 January 1899 when the branch was closed to goods trains. It was however reopened for goods on 1 May of the same year using horse traction. The horse-drawn passenger service was withdrawn in 4 April 1914.

The horse cabs which serviced the main stations on the NB although not owned by the company were liable to inspection by the general manager or his representative. Cabbies were required to provide horses and cabs of a 'superior description' and in the words of the contract 'must not leave their horse's head until engaged'. They were required also at their own expense to paint on both sides and the back of the vehicle the legend 'NBR Station'.

'EVERY INCH A GENTLEMAN'

Like Drummond and Robert Chalmers, Matthew Holmes had known Cowlairs in Edinburgh & Glasgow days. He had been 29 years in railway service when he was appointed locomotive superintendent, the previous 10 as general running foreman over the whole system. In contrast to his rumbustious predecessor Holmes was a mild-mannered man much liked by all who came in contact with him. He stayed longer at Cowlairs than any other holder of the office and he produced the company's most prolific class.

More than a year passed before the first Holmes design appeared. Seven of his 17in 0-6-0 goods were turned out in the latter half of 1883. They were similar to Drummond's 17in engines although the hand of Holmes could be discerned in them. A new design of tender dispensed with Drummond's outside bearings, slotted frames and underhung springs, and the toolbox had disappeared from the traditional Drummond position at the rear of the tender. The Ramsbottom safety valves of the former regime had given way to independent lock-up valves arranged in pairs in beaded-brass columns fitted on the dome. Ramsbottom valves had been removed hastily from all NB engines following a disastrous boiler explosion which demolished No 465 at Dunbar a few months after Holmes took office. It was never proved that the valves were at fault but Cowlairs' mistrust of them was such that engines were called in and lock-ups fitted as soon as they became available.

In 1884 11 more engines of the class came into service. One, No 150, instead of having the usual Drummond square cab had a rounded, Stirling-type cab. Four engines of the batch (582-5) were fited with the Westinghouse brake for passenger working. In 1885 a further 11 engines appeared and of these six had round cabs and eight the Westinghouse brake. The round cab appeared to offer less protection than the square cab, but the drivers swore that it was less draughty than the Drummond cab. The cab became standard, the final six engines of the batch (which totalled 36) were fitted with it and with the Westinghouse brake.

The first express passenger engine to be added to NB stock for 10 years appeared from Cowlairs in 1886. It was the Holmes 592 Class 4-4-0. The Drummond lineage was still obvious, but so also were the Holmes innovations. The engine had the now standard round cab and Holmes tender. Whereas in the Drummond engines the frames above footplate level were cut off flush with the smokebox, in the Holmes engine they were carried forward to join the buffer beam in a graceful curve. The chimney had a more decided taper. The new engine appeared in Drummond colours, but it carried no name. The regional names favoured by Drummond were said to have been causing confusion among passengers who mistook them for destination boards. However, the Holmes engines were provided with moveable destination boards which were curved to the contour of the smoke box and exhibited the destination in white block letters against a brick red background.

The Drummond 18in by 26in cylinders were retained, but Holmes gave No 592 7ft driving wheels in place of the 6ft 6in wheels of the Drummond passenger engine. Boiler pressure was

150psi. Holmes did not like the Drummond sloping grate so he introduced a flat grate.

Six of the new engines were built in 1886 and a further six in 1888. The first of the class appeared just in time to feature at the Edinburgh International Exhibition of Science, Industry and Art. This was the first major exhibition to be held in Scotland and the first at which locomotives had been exhibited. The NB engine took its place in the industrial pavilion along with Drummond's No 124, the soon to be famous No 123, and the Highland Railway 4-4-0 *Bruce*. The site of the exhibition at the Meadows was somewhat remote from a railhead, and at the close of the show No 592 hauled the two Caledonian engines and two carriages through the streets of Edinburgh to the Caledonian depot at Lothian Road. This feat was accomplished by James Bell, chief engineer of the North British, and a team of 30 men who kept lifting and relaying a length of sleepered track on the roadway as the procession progressed. The journey took two days. No 529 and its sisters were employed on the Glasgow, Edinburgh and Dundee fast services.

While the 592 Class was under construction Holmes also had in hand six 0-4-4 passenger tanks. They resembled Drummond's 88 Class after Drummond had rebuilt them in 1881. They had the same size of cylinder (17in by 24in) but the driving wheels of the Holmes engine were 6ft 6in compared with the 5ft 9in of the Drummond engine. These were the only passenger tanks built by Holmes and the last to be built for the NB for 23 years. Six were added to the class in 1888 and all were employed on local services, especially in the Glasgow area.

Between 1887 and 1891 Holmes produced 36 0-4-0 saddle tanks for light shunting duties in dock, colliery and factory sidings. The design closely followed that of the two off-the-cuff dock tanks that Neilson had supplied at short notice in 1882. The engines were only 24ft 4in long over buffers and the centre line of the boiler a mere 5ft 4¼in above rail level. The engine weighed 28ton 15cwt. The outside inclined cylinders were 14in by 20in. The cab consisted of a canopy supported on four pillars, fronted by a skimpy facing plate and flanked by small side bunkers. The engines had dumb buffers and sometimes were to be seen with dumb-buffered tenders attached. They were destined to spend their working lives moving at speeds of 5mph or less. It was quite a sight to see them waddling back to their depots after a day's work at a reckless 10mph.

LOCOMOTIVE MATTERS 1880–1903

For heavier shunting duties and short haul goods work Holmes designed his 795 Class 0-6-0 tank. These engines weighed 45ton 5cwt, and had 4ft 6in driving wheels and 17in by 26in cylinders. When an order for 20 was placed with Neilson Reid & Co early in 1900 the firm—which seemed to be short of work at the time—offered to build 20 additional tanks 'or ordinary goods engines' at attractive rates. They also undertook to speed up delivery of all 40 engines. The offer was rejected, but in 1901 the NB ordered a further 20 of the class from Sharp Stewart & Co Ltd.

The Holmes 18in 0-6-0 first appeared in 1888 and in the next 12 years 168 engines of the class were built all of them at Cowlairs except for 15 built by Neilson and a like number by Sharp Stewart & Co Ltd. They were uncomplicated, reliable locomotives, wonderful revenue earners not only for the NB but for the LNER and BR. They had the same grate area as the 17in engines, but the heating surface was increased from 1,059sq ft to 1,235·13sq ft. The tractive effort of the earlier engine was 16,000lb and that of the new engine 17,220lb. The weight of engine and tender of the 18in design was 72ton 4cwt, that of the 17in design 70ton 8cwt. The engines were to be seen all over the system doing all sorts of work from mineral to passenger.

The second Holmes bogie express engine—the 633 Class—appeared in 1890. Twelve engines were turned out from Cowlairs in anticipation of an increase in traffic following the opening of the Forth Bridge. They differed in several respects from the first Holmes express engine. The boiler pressure was reduced to 140psi (from 150psi) giving a reduction in tractive effort from 12,790lb to 12,860lb. The total heating surface, however, was increased from 1,126sq ft to 1,262sq ft. The 7ft driving wheel gave place to wheels of 6ft 6in in the new engine. Twelve additional engines of the class were built at Cowlairs in 1894 and 1895. These had a boiler pressure of 150psi and a tractive effort of 13,800lb. Nos 633-5 and 642 were allocated to Perth when new; 262-3, 312, 401 and 211-2 went to Aberdeen, 213-16 to St Margarets and 217-8 to Carlisle. The St Margarets engines were among those which took over from the NE engines on the Edinburgh–Berwick run in 1897.

The West Highland line, with its unprecedented operating problems, resulted in Holmes designing a scaled-down version of his main line express engine. The West Highland bogie was designed to run at moderate speeds on 75lb rails over a curving course where long, rising gradients were endemic. It had 5ft 7in driving wheels and 18in by 24in steam-jacketed cylinders. The total heating surface was 1,235·13sq ft and the tractive effort 14,800lb. The engines weighed 43ton 6cwt. It was the first class to be fitted with clasp brakes, the only Holmes engine to have lever reversing gear and the only passenger engine not to have the sandboxes incorporated in the splashers. Because of unexpected delays in the construction of the West Highland line the engines were built before the railway was ready to receive them, and were stored for a time at Cowlairs. Twenty-four engines of the class were built at Cowlairs between 1893 and 1896.

In 1898 there came a more powerful version of the Holmes main line express engine—the 729 Class. It exhibited most of the Holmes features and dimensions. Variations included the cylinders, which were 18¼in by 26in, and the boiler pressure was raised to 175psi. The total heating surface was 1,350sq ft and the tractive effort 16,400lb. Engine and tender weighed 86ton 5cwt.

Experience during the summer of 1901 showed that the brand new 633 Class could not cope single handed with the greatly increased loads on the Aberdeen and Waverley routes. Accordingly Holmes was asked to produce a suitable engine. His drawings were submitted to the board on 21 November 1901 when the following minute was recorded:

> The general manager submitted drawings of proposed new express passenger engines, and recommended that 12 of these be built to replace engines wearing out, also that the excess cost (£800 per engine be debited to capital. This was agreed to, the engines to be fitted with 19in cylinders, and the locomotive superintendent was instructed to report to next meeting as to the practicability of a more powerful type of engine.

Holmes presented his revised design to the board on 13 March 1902 and 12 engines were authorised. This, the 317 Class, was Holmes' last design. They were the first NB engines to have steel boilers and carry a pressure of 200psi. The 19in by 26in cylinders had piston valves. The cab was of the square design that was to become standard on future NB classes. There has been speculation over the reason for the departure from the well-established round cab. Holmes was in failing health and W. P. Reid had been appointed to assist him; it has been suggested that Reid put forward or himself designed the square cab. However, Reid was not appointed until December 1902, nine months after the engines had been authorised, and they must have been in an advanced state of construction when he arrived at Cowlairs. Moreover, Reid was specifically appointed *outdoor* assistant. He was not a design man. If anyone other than Holmes altered the design or suggested an alteration the most likely person to do so would have been Robert Chalmers.

The 12 engines were completed in 1903. Nos 317-22 went to Aberdeen, 325-6 to St Margarets and 327-32 to Carlisle. Holmes did not survive to see his final class in action. One of his own engines hauled his funeral train from Lenzie to Haymarket. The editor of the *St. Rollox and Springburn Express*, a future Secretary of State for Scotland, had this to say of him:

With the passing away of Mr Matthew Holmes Glasgow and particularly Springburn, is the poorer. Of a quiet and unobtrusive nature Mr Holmes was a gentleman every inch. He did much good work in his sixty odd years, and he always did it without placing a trumpet to his mouth. To the humblest workman he was always accessible and a patient hearing was always afforded whether the complaint was groundless or the reverse. Men in his position do not act so. The imperious tyrant had no part in the life of Matthew Holmes who was beloved by the men under him, and no better compliment perhaps can be paid an overseer than that in the discharge of a sacred trust he evinced humanity of the kindest pattern. In every sense of the term he left the railway world better than he found it. He is another example of those captains of industry who have risen from the ranks, and to the last was an example of affability and kindness of heart.

CHAPTER 5

East Coast Occasions

A QUASI PARTNERSHIP

It has been fashionable to represent the East Coast combine as a shoulder-to-shoulder alliance dedicated to combating West Coast aggression. The truth is rather different. The race to the north took place against a background of bitter conflict between the NB and NE. Over the years the East Coast companies intrigued with and against each other like Balkan princelings and were much given to washing their dirty linen in the Court of Session, the Railway and Canal Commissioners Court and the House of Lords.

The NB alleged that slipshod work south of the Border prejudiced the efficiency (and therefore the profitability) of the route. The English companies suspected that the East Coast trains were badly handled once they passed out of southern control. The English partners were irked by the fact that the NB resolutely refused to share in the expense of advertising East Coast trains although claiming a say in the form the advertisements were to take. Above all there was suspicion in London and York that the Scottish company was channelling down the Waverley route to the Midland traffic which rightly belonged to the East Coast. A legal document referred to the East Coast group as 'a quasi partnership'. Bearing in mind that one of the dictionary definitions of quasi is 'in appearance only' the description was an apt one.

An observer who stood by the side of the NB main line, say at Dunbar in the 1890s, could have been forgiven for thinking that he had stumbled across a North Eastern main line over which the North British exercised modest running powers. He would have seen all the great Anglo-Scottish expresses passing by in charge of NE engines and crews leaving only four humdrum locals and the goods trains to NB engines. This state of affairs had its origin in an Act of 1862 by which the NB, in return for a free hand in the taking over of the Edinburgh, Perth & Dundee Railway and entry into Newcastle via Hexham for its Border County trains, gave the NE the right to haul the Anglo-Scottish through trains between

Berwick and Edinburgh with its own engines and crews. Running powers accorded to English companies over Scottish lines were nothing new. The NE had running powers over the NB to Glasgow, Perth and Arbroath and from there over the Caledonian to Aberdeen. The GN had similar powers except that it did not have the right to run between Berwick and Edinburgh. Midlands trains were entitled to run over the NB from Carlisle to Edinburgh, Perth, Dundee and Arbroath, as well as over the Caledonian all the way from Carlisle to Aberdeen, a privilege it shared with the LNW. If the English companies had exercised their running powers their trains would have swamped the indigenous Scottish services. But only the NE claimed its rights.

It was in 1865 that the NE first intimated to the NB that it proposed to exercise its running powers to Edinburgh, but it was not until February 1869 that the NB was given a firm date for the commencement of the running-power trains. The company was further instructed to provide standage at Edinburgh for 10 NE engines and to make certain services available. In April a delegation from the NE inspected NB facilities and found them wanting. The shed site which the NB had allocated at Leith Walk was rejected out of hand, the NE men claiming a more convenient site at St Margarets. The delegation left for York leaving the NB a list of demands which had to be satisfied before they would deign to trust NE engines on NB metals. These included a certain amount of rerailing, alterations to station platforms, the provision of coke loading facilities and water cranes, and the raising of existing cranes to suit the larger NE tenders.

The first NE-hauled train reached Edinburgh on 1 June 1869. Some said the NB had sold its birthright; in fact the arrangement was a sensible one and it worked well. The GN brought the trains up to York (188 miles) and the NE took them on to Edinburgh, $204\frac{1}{2}$ miles with an engine change at Newcastle. To have developed Berwick as a railway frontier station would have meant a further change of engine for a journey of only $57\frac{1}{2}$ miles.

The NE organised its plant and re-deployed its locomotives on the basis of a through run from Newcastle to Edinburgh. The southern companies made it their policy to keep the management of the trains in their hands. They steadily developed the route adding more trains and speeding up the service. In 1870 the NE handled four Anglo-Scottish expresses each way between Berwick and Edinburgh and one each way on Sundays. By 1880 the service consisted of six up and eight down trains with two each way on Sundays. In 1890 the up service was unaltered, but there were nine down trains with two up trains and one down train on Sundays. Five years later, while the up service remained the same, the down service had increased to 13 trains.

The NB, of course, retained control of the local trains and goods trains. In 1895 there were 21 up goods on the route, 11 of which were worked through to Tweedmouth with NB engines. In the down direction 25 goods trains originated at or passed through Berwick on weekdays. One through passenger train was worked to Berwick by an NB engine—by accident! It had begun life as a fish train to which a few passenger vehicles had been added. As more carriages were added to meet demand the fish vans were gradually dropped and the one time fish train became a passenger train. Apparently its change of status was overlooked, for the NE never claimed it.

In the NB working timetable the NE trains were designated 'North Eastern running power trains', but in the public timetable they appeared as 'North Eastern trains'. The NB never publicly admitted that they were running-power trains. They took the view that they hired NE engines to haul NB trains. The NE on the other hand always claimed that they were their running-power trains.

In 1881 there was an accident involving a double-headed running-power train at Abbeyhill just outside Edinburgh. According to Railway Clearing House rules when a running-power train was involved in an accident on a foreign line the owner of the train was responsible for damages. The NB was in a cleft stick over the matter. If it claimed that the train in question was a running-power train it would lose face, but if it recognised that the train was its own the company would be faced with damages. The upshot was that the NB placed the liability for damages on the NE on the grounds that its crew was responsible for the accident, as indeed they were. The NE on the other hand maintained that the train once it had crossed the Border was an NB train and therefore the NB was responsible for its running.

After a long acrimonious exchange of letters the NB bowed to the fact that the NE would not accept liability. The secretary informed his NE opposite number, 'We must therefore in the meantime be content to charge the amount against your company in our books'. To this the NE secretary replied, 'It is no use your debiting the amount to this company as we shall certainly not pay it'.

The NB undertook to make the Dunbar station pilot available to assist NE trains from Dunbar to Grantshouse on request, and the NB also agreed to provide engines for through special trains from Edinburgh to Berwick if NE engines were not available. The Dunbar pilot did not work on Sundays and it was the custom for the NB engines to double-head the NE engines on the two night expresses from Edinburgh to Grantshouse. On weekdays the Dunbar pilot did a trip to Drem just at the time the 2.30 dining car express from Waverley was due and this train also was allowed NB assistance all the way to the summit. The agreement allowed pilot assistance if the load exceeded 15 vehicles with an NE 901 Class engine or 16 vehicles with a 1463 Class engine.

In 1891 the NB became aware that the NE was abusing the privilege of taking a pilot. In August of that year Holmes complained to Worsdell that an NE driver had claimed pilot assistance with a 14-coach train. Worsdell confirmed that the driver had not been entitled to a pilot and assured Holmes that the man would be disciplined.

Two years later Holmes again complained that the 2.30 diner was regularly taking NB pilot assistance with a load of 14 vehicles. Apparently forgetting the incident of 1891 Worsdell claimed that his driver was within his rights in asking for a pilot. Holmes gleefully confronted Worsdell with the earlier correspondence. In a frank reply the NE locomotive superintendent admitted that his engines were not up to the task he had set them. 'The loads mentioned,' he confessed to Holmes, 'are in excess of what the engines can actually do and keep time.'

The reply from Holmes must have provoked anger at Gateshead, 'I am of the opinion that you should provide engines that will keep time with loads specified in your letter of 1 September 1891 and you should pay extra for pilot assistance short of this load, otherwise the agreement will have to be revised'.

The 2.30, of course, was the prestige dining car express from Edinburgh to London. It was an ordinary train, and as such was not covered by the agreement on piloting. It was a very bad timekeeper which accounted for the NE's desire to secure a pilot. On one occasion, when two Glasgow coaches were attached to the

2.30 at Waverley without notice, Gibb complained to Conacher, 'It seems to me that when the train has been working so badly as it has been doing a change of this sort should be the subject of previous consultation between the passenger superintendents'. Conacher asked Inspector McLaren for his comments and his explanation was that the train had been full and the two extra carriages had been put on to accommodate the waiting passengers. At the foot of his letter McLaren urged Conacher to ask Gibb why four NE carriages had been put on the down dining car express at York a few days earlier. It was nursery school stuff, but Conacher complied. Gibb's answer was that the four carriages were required to carry NE shareholders to Newcastle after a meeting at York.

The trouble with the 2.30 persisted. McLaren complained that on 5 September the train left with only 13 carriages yet its driver claimed an NB pilot. 'If the North Eastern company cannot run the train with one engine', he told Conacher, 'they had better take off their engine and allow us to find an engine which will do it'. Conacher was indiscreet enough to express this view to Gibb who replied:

> It appears to me that the last paragraph of your letter is one which ought not to have been written. I am told by Mr Worsdell our locomotive superintendent that an assisting engine was obtained on the day in question for the purpose only of getting up the gradient at Cockburnspath bank as the train consisted of 13 vehicles including the two dining cars and the kitchen cars. As you are aware we are entitled under our agreement with you to have the assistance of pilot engines, a service for which we pay.

When McLaren was shown this letter he again pointed out that under the agreement pilot assistance was due to NE trains only at Dunbar, and additional engine power was to be provided only for fish trains and specials. He continued:

> I therefore hold that the 2.30 pm being an ordinary train the North Eastern company are bound to provide two engines for it at Edinburgh if the Dunbar pilot from any cause should not be available and if one North Eastern engine is not able to take the train throughout. In the latter event a satisfactory solution of the question would be for the North Eastern company to withdraw their engine from the 2.30 train and leave this company to find one which will work it through to Berwick as I believe our locomotive superintendent is prepared to do.

If the NE was willing to accept NB pilotage it was not willing to return the compliment. On learning that an NE engine returning light from Edinburgh to Gateshead had been attached in front of an NB goods train, Worsdell issued the following instructions:

> I beg to inform you that on 22nd ultimo our engine No 1910 was stopped by NB signalman at Inveresk when running light from Edinburgh to Gateshead and the driver was instructed to couple on to NB engine No 655 which was working on a goods train and proceeded with it to Burnmouth where the latter stopped to attach some wagons. I have given instruction that our men must not couple on to any NB engines in future.

WHOSE ENGINES?

Early in 1894 the NB declared its intention to run the East Coast expresses between Edinburgh and Berwick with its own engines. Oakley and Gibb were aghast. 'I say that no railwayman in his senses having the power to reach Edinburgh would stop at Berwick', protested the general manager of the GN. Efforts by the English officers to soothe the NB failed and on 6 June Conacher informed Gibb, 'My directors have definitely resolved to maintain this company's undoubted right as owning company to work the principal through trains between Edinburgh and Berwick and we are prepared to take immediate action to have our right legally determined'.

The NB decision split the East Coast alliance apart, and precipitated one of the longest legal battles in the history of British railways. It took four years and 11 tribunals, including two appearances at the House of Lords, to produce some semblance of an agreement. Meanwhile the NE remained in possession. Successive dreary actions in the Court of Session, the Court of the Railway and Canal Commissioners and the House of Lords at which the same witnesses produced the same evidence were relieved by highlights when one or other of the parties took, or threatened to take, the law into its own hands. One such highlight occurred at the end of 1895.

One of the interminable NE–NB actions had been concluded in December but the result would not be announced until early in the new year. To complicate matters the arrangement by which the NB paid the NE $7\frac{1}{4}$d per mile in respect of NE engines hauling passenger trains on NB track was due to expire on 31 December and the NE had intimated that thereafter the charge would be raised to 1s per mile. On the afternoon of Christmas Eve Conacher, with a fine disregard for English social custom, wired Gibbs:

> We will not pending a final decision in our action permit your engines to come on to our line except in accordance with engine mileage agreement. You must therefore take this message as notice that on 1 January we will take the trains from and to Berwick unless present arrangement is further extended.

Matthew Holmes was told to produce engine diagrams, and all arrangements were made for the pending NB takeover.

Gibb, writing on 28 December from the Westminster office of the NE, replied to Conacher in a letter that began, 'I have just come up here from Aldeburgh, very reluctantly as it was rather hard to have my holiday broken into by a matter which might have been raised earlier than by a telegram on the afternoon of Christmas Eve'. He urged Conacher not to use force when the decision of the court was only days away. For the time being commonsense prevailed, and the NB held its hand.

Randolph Wemyss, a director of the NB, startled his own board by saying that were he an NE director he would have acted just as they had done. He pointed out that the NB was in low water when the original agreement was made and the fact that the company was now prosperous was no reason for the agreement to be breached. He was all for leaving the NE in possession, but he suggested that the NB should develop its goods and passenger traffic via the Waverley route and the Midland. His theory was that if they played the Midland against the NE York would be more inclined to offer them better terms.

Conacher seized on the Wemyss suggestion with enthusiasm, and he called a meeting of his officers for 8 January 1896 to discuss ways of implementing the scheme. Conacher was a practical railwayman, not a strategist, and he did not see the dangers inherent in the proposal. Walker would not have made this mistake. Fortunately D. McDougall, chief officer of the company in Glasgow, was present at the meeting to advise him. 'I have no hesitation,' he said, 'in stating that in my opinion to adopt such a policy would be a distinct blunder on our part. If it was discovered what we were at (as discovered it most assuredly would be) it would be much to our prejudice for them to retaliate and

Page 85:
(above) *Invitation to opening of the Forth Bridge, 4 March 1890*; (below) *Cantilever tower of the Forth Bridge under construction*

Page 86:

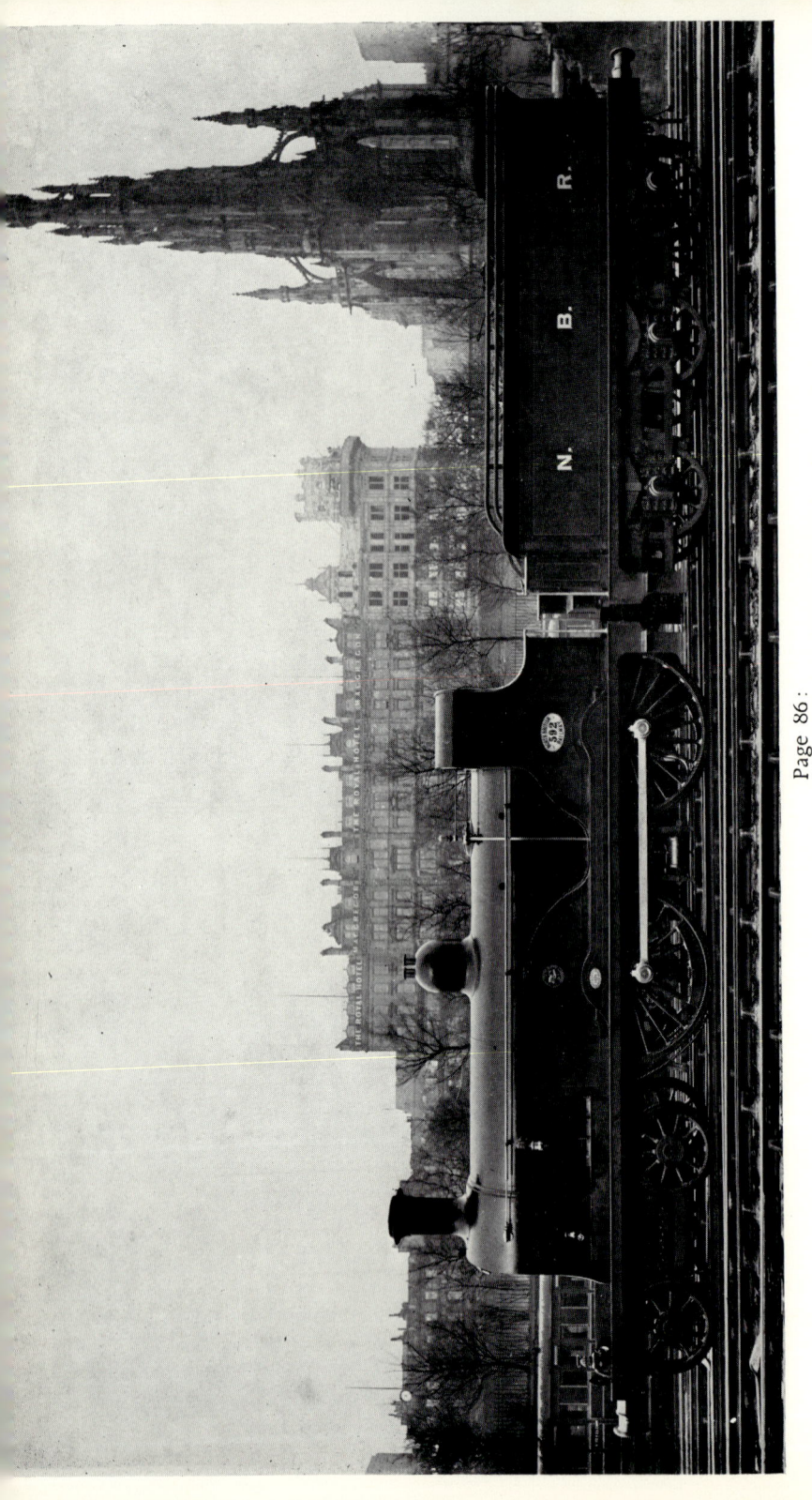

Holmes 4-4-0 No 592 posed against an Edinburgh background. This engine was exhibited at the Edinburgh International Exhibition of 1886 and subsequently carried a commemorative plaque

work with the Caledonian company to Scotland via Carlisle.' The plan was dropped.

On the day after the meeting the following letter was received by Conacher from Gibb:

> Will you be kind enough to let me know, for the information of my directors, whether your directors would entertain any objection to the North Eastern Company running some trains to Perth in exercise of their running powers under the North British and Edinburgh and Glasgow Amalgamation Act of 1865? A good many arrangements in regard to matters of detail would have to be made if we commenced running but our first object is to ascertain what would be your attitude towards a proposal to consider the question.

Here indeed was fuel for the furnace. The NB replied coldly to the effect that it could not consider the proposal until current differences between the companies had been satisfactorily settled.

What had come to be known as 'the case' drifted on from one tribunal to the next with neither party satisfied with the results. While the battle was at its height Gibb and Conacher met socially at the Liberal Club in Edinburgh. Gibb had an idea for a new-style East Coast poster-timetable with an attractive pictorial heading, and he discussed it at length with the NB general manager. Conacher expressed interest, and Gibb got the impression that the NB, contrary to its usual practice, would be willing to share in the cost of the poster.

In due course a proof copy of the poster was sent to Edinburgh. Conacher objected to it on the grounds that neither picture nor text did justice to the NB, and he withheld his formal permission for its exhibition. Oakley and Gibb pleaded with him to release the poster since there was insufficient time in which to have it reprinted before the timetable came into effect. Conacher agreed on condition that the offensive matter would be adjusted at the end of the currency of the timetable. When he was presented with a bill for £48 7s 6d, this being the NB's share of the cost, he refused to pay on the grounds that he had made no promise to share the expense.

In December 1896 'the case' was in much the same state as it had been in the previous December. Another round at the courts had been concluded on 14 December and the dispute had been passed to the Railway and Canal Commissioners. Because of the incidence of the Christmas holidays in England and New Year holidays in Scotland the matter could not receive the attention of the court until at least mid-January 1897. In the meantime both parties undertook to observe the status quo for a month from 14 December. The agreement was binding for one month. But what would happen after 14 January?

The NB announced that on 14 January it would eject the NE from its territory lock, stock and barrel, and this time it meant what it said. The NE countered with a statement that it would continue to exercise its full running powers after 14 January. Gibb clarified the NE position in a letter to Conacher on 22 December:

> You may put aside any idea that you can by taking advantage of the vacation in the Commissioners Court obtain by force what you cannot obtain by right. We cannot submit to that. The only effect of your taking such an extreme step would be that the through East Coast service would be dislocated and stopped and it is I think an essentially unfair position because we are not seeking in any way to prejudice your contention but merely to tide over the holiday period without prejudice to either side and without inconvenience to the public. It would be absolutely impossible to institute a new system of engine working for a short period without much inconvenience and loss. There is no available accommodation for engines at Berwick and your proposal would absolutely deprive us for a time of the running powers you now admit we possess.

Conacher hotly denied that he had ever admitted that NE exercised running powers over the NB. He again affirmed his view that the NB hired engines from the NE. On Gibb's threat to enforce running powers he wrote, 'In other words you claim the right to capture between Edinburgh and Berwick our whole existing through services and to practically oust us from our main line, confining us to local traffic'.

On 1 January 1897 Gibb wrote:

> I am sorry you should show so little appreciation either of the desirability of settling our legal differences without resort to what are practically methods of force or of the interests of the East Coast route. However, as my appeal to you has failed we must seek some restraining influence from the court by whom our differences fall to be settled.

But the only court that could deal with 'the case' was not in session, and the NB was at liberty to go ahead unchecked with its plans for the takeover. Conacher was confident that his company would make a good job of the Berwick–Edinburgh trains. Gibb was equally confident that there would be chaos.

It was no simple task for Holmes to find express engines to handle the new traffic, and men were a problem too. Many NB men were strangers to the Berwick road and only a handful of crews had experience of running over it at express speed. Conacher had guaranteed to run the trains to the existing timetable in spite of the Berwick stop. The two down night expresses and the up night express which did not stop at Berwick posed the biggest problem. The 2.53 down train from Berwick, the fastest on the route, was timed at an average speed of 51mph. To stop the train at Berwick and effect an engine change would, Conacher calculated, cost 7min, and to get the train into Edinburgh on time would call for locomotive working of a very high order. At a meeting between Conacher and Holmes on 11 January it was decided to allow the NE to engine the three non-stop trains. The offer was presented to Gibb as a concession. He rejected it contemptuously. On the matter of retaining the 'flyers' he replied, 'There does not appear to be any necessity for our doing so if you carry out the undertaking given by your counsel that these trains will be run by you between Berwick and Edinburgh so as to maintain the timing at Edinburgh and Berwick respectively notwithstanding the stop at Berwick'. Gibb was content to let the NB stew in its own juice.

Worse was to come. At the end of his letter Gibb wrote, apparently as an afterthought, 'I presume you have made yourself acquainted with the boundary between the two systems and in the enforcement of the strict legal rights on which you are engaged no attempt will be made by you to pass your engines on to any part of the line which is owned by the North Eastern company'.

That paragraph was full of menace. The boundary between the NE and NB was at the south end of Berwick station. NB permanent way ended at the Royal Border Bridge, and the crossover was on the bridge safely in NE territory. Gibb implied that he would deny NB engines access to the crossover. Conacher dispatched an urgent telegram to York:

> Am I to understand from the last paragraph of your letter that your company are temporarily to throw difficulties in the way of our utilizing as we have hitherto done and are now doing the cross-over road immediately south of the station in taking our

engines off south-going trains? Please wire reply now. I am advised that if you decline to continue to allow our engines to use the cross-over you will be acting illegally and in contravention of your obligation to us to work the East Coast through trains in full efficiency and to give us all possible facilities at Berwick.

Back came the uncompromising reply from York:

You cannot expect us under the circumstances to allow you to trespass on our property and I must ask you to carry out your arrangements without doing so.

To that Conacher replied:

For any delay caused in exchanging engines at Berwick by our having through your action to adopt an unusual method of exchange your company will, pending our taking the necessary proceedings to vindicate our rights, be held responsible.

Gibb retorted:

I am not aware of any agreement or arrangement or statute which gives the North British the power to use any part of the North Eastern line, and I am advised that a right to use the North Eastern line as a means of access from your running line to your sidings cannot be claimed as a facility either under the agreement of 1862 or under any general statute.

I protest against your seeking to use the North Eastern line to aid you in your project of putting all our East Coast working at risk on a purely technical ground, just between the period of the 14th and the settlement of the terms by the Railway Commissioner. In our view the action of the North British in this is neither reasonable nor fair, and although we shall, of course, do our utmost to work the trains punctually to and from Berwick we are not inclined to grant you the right to use a piece of line which you have no right to use. I trust therefore you will find some way of disposing of your engines on your own line.

On 12 January when news was received that the NE would not engine the non-stop trains Conacher wired Holmes:

North Eastern declines our offer to let them run three non stopping trains. You must, therefore, be ready to run them also, and they must be double engined. Have your complete scheme for taking over all the trains ready for discussion here tomorrow.

Up to that time no definite time had been announced for the

takeover. First thing on the morning of the 13th the NE wired Edinburgh for information on that point, but none was forthcoming. NB headquarters was in a state of confusion and even Conacher did not know when he would be in a position to engine the trains. During the course of that hectic morning Deuchars arrived at Conacher's office with the news that the resident NE inspector at Waverley had just told him that he expected NB engines to take over *that night*. At 11.14 the general manager wired Holmes to have the engines prepared immediately. At 1.10 he ordered the locomotive superintendent to come to Edinburgh to report. At 1.47 a further telegram arrived from Gibb:

> Still no information from you as to first train you intend to work. Please wire immediately to York so that arrangements can be made.

A conference of NB officers began at 2 pm, the delegates still not knowing whether or not the company was to engine the trains that night. Holmes joined the meeting at 3.30. Among the engines allocated to the Anglo-Scottish trains were Nos 633, 634, 639 and 640 of the 6ft 6in Class 4-4-0s of 1890-1, and 595, 596, 598 and 603 of the 7ft 4-4-0s of 1886. Some of the old Drummond 4-4-0s including 477, 479 and 486 were enlisted to help with the double heading. The engine diagrams in some cases provided for the engines doing a return journey from Edinburgh to Glasgow or Perth in addition to their Berwick stint. At 4.20 another telegram from Gibb somewhat relieved the tension of the meeting:

> We are proposing to engine trains tonight and tomorrow as usual. Wire me first train you propose to engine from Berwick and from Edinburgh.

At least the NB did not have to provide engines for that night's trains.

It was late in the afternoon before Conacher was in a position to furnish Gibb with the information he had so persistently demanded:

> I note you will continue to engine trains tonight and tomorrow as usual. The first trains we will take are the 2.53 ex Berwick and the 10 am ex Edinburgh on Friday morning. We will bring the 11.15 up on Friday night at 12.21 and make every effort to hand you all the other trains at the booked times. I trust you will do all you can to bring all the down trains into Berwick at their present booked

times and instruct your drivers to detach their engines as quickly as possible.

Gibb let Conacher know what he thought of NB administration:

I am in receipt of your letter of yesterday confirming your telegram informing me of the first train on which you intend to substitute NB engines for NE engines. As you are aware one of our departments thought you were to commence on the morning of the 14th while another thought the evening or morning of the 15th. In withholding from me any communication of your intentions with, as I cannot help thinking, a singular lack of the courtesy and consideration used in business relations, you have left me quite in the dark as to what your intentions really were. However your telegram of yesterday repairs that omission.

The last NE engine left Edinburgh non-stop to Newcastle at 11.15 on 14 January. By the time it had cleared Berwick the fateful Friday 15th had broken and the NB was master in its own house. It was a stormy night with strong winds and driving snow squalls —not an occasion for setting railway records. The 8.15 from King's Cross reached Berwick on time shortly after 2 am behind one NE engine. An NB inspector watched as the two waiting NB engines moved in to replace the English engine. The changeover was accomplished smoothly and presently the train pulled out, the drivers intent on recovering the time lost by the unaccustomed stop. The NB mastered the rising gradient from Berwick to Grantshouse in 22min; the NE with two engines had taken 24min on the previous Friday morning. The next down train, the 11.20 from King's Cross was handled with equal dispatch. The climb to Grantshouse was accomplished in 20min compared with 23min taken by one NE engine on the same train a week earlier. It was a promising start for the NB.

The first up train was the 10 am from Waverley. It was an event to see two NB engines at the head of *The Flying Scotsman*. This train was allowed 72min for the $57\frac{1}{2}$ miles and no difficulty was experienced in getting to Berwick on time. What happened then was straight from the swashbuckling pioneer days of railways. The NE refused to allow the NB engines on to the disputed cross-over. There was a flurry of activity among the watching inspectors as the train was hastily set back and the engines run round on NB territory. The train was then pushed on to the waiting NE engine. This was done according to an NE observer 'by men riding on the buffers and holding the brake pipe'. A second up train was similarly handled in the course of the morning.

Sir Henry Oakley learned of the Border incident in the early afternoon. Realising that a continuance of the process would only result in a spate of late trains reaching the GN he urged Gibb to declare an armistice, and he agreed. He had demonstrated who was the real master at Berwick. When the 2.30 diner arrived the engine change took place on the NE crossing. That night's 11.15 climbed from Innerwick to Grantshouse in 9min. On the previous Friday the single NE engine had taken 14min and had lost a total of 11min in the run up to Berwick.

During the next fortnight the NB achieved some exhilarating running—at a price. Conacher had to achieve results, for he knew that in a matter of weeks he would have to justify his company's action in court. Gibb's prophecy of doom did not materialise, but the NE general manager was not dismayed. He convinced himself that the NB would not be able to sustain the pressure when the summer timetable was introduced and trains were running in duplicate and triplicate.

The NB was at special pains to deliver the 11.15pm to the NE with time to spare. On a typical night this train with a 213-ton load passed Dunbar ($29\frac{1}{4}$ miles) in 28min 58sec, and then capped that performance by climbing to Cockburnspath ($4\frac{3}{4}$ miles) in $6\frac{1}{2}$min. The train was in Berwick in 58min 49sec. Running in the down direction was just as impressive, especially when a late departure from Berwick inspired a spurt by the NB men. On one such occasion the distance was run in 57min 49sec, the final $23\frac{1}{2}$ miles including 3 miles at 1 in 78 being covered in 22min 1sec. On another occasion *The Flying Scotsman* with one 633 Class locomotive was stopped for $3\frac{1}{2}$min at the foot of the 1 in 78 climb leading to Waverley and still managed to arrive 7min early. The NB men really were trying.

On 26 January 1897, only 12 days after gaining possession of his main line, Conacher was defending his right to continue hauling the East Coast trains in the Court of the Railway and Canal Commissioners. He based his case on the superiority of NB engines over NE engines. He explained that NB engines were based on a design of the company's former engineer Dugald Drummond and that a similar design for the Caledonian railway was currently achieving great success on that company's heavily-graded main line between Carlisle and Glasgow. He drew attention to the excellent timekeeping of the NB engines between Edinburgh and Berwick during the last two weeks.

Counsel for the NE, well briefed by NE inspectors who had travelled in the trains, demolished Conacher's case with a devastating opening question. 'In how many cases within the last fortnight', he asked, 'have you run from Berwick to Edinburgh either way with two engines?' Conacher fumbled with his papers, but could not produce an answer. 'Assume from me,' went on counsel, 'that during the last fortnight you have run 80 trains with two engines. Have you information how that compares with what was done by the North Eastern in the corresponding fortnight last year?' Conacher professed not to have the information. 'Assume from me,' continued counsel, 'that in the corresponding fortnight last year the North Eastern had only two engines on 11 trains and that this year your company ran 80 trains with two engines; how do you account for that?' The answer all too plainly was that the NB required two engines to do the job that the NE for the most part required only one.

The Court divided the East Coast services between the two companies, but the judgment was not implemented until March 1898. In February a reconnaisance party of NE officers came to Edinburgh to plan the re-occupation of NB territory, and Worsdell sent drivers north to have a look at the new signalling which had been installed at Waverley since the NE withdrawal. NB officials took a jaundiced view of the visitors. Holmes inquired of Conacher, 'I shall be glad to know if we are to perform the shunting of trains at Edinburgh and also provide engines to assist their trains?' He added, 'I would strongly recommend that they be required to perform these duties with their own engines and men'. Conacher agreed. Two days before the return of the NE he informed Gibb, 'Each company will have to put its own trains from and to Edinburgh in position and take them away to storage sidings. Please do not omit to let your people clearly understand this'.

The NE treated its cold reception at Edinburgh with disdain. The company established its own ticket office at Waverley and refused to convey on its trains Edinburgh–Berwick passengers who had bought their tickets at the NB booking office. Requests from passengers for special stops at stations between Berwick and Edinburgh were ignored unless they were made to York. When four through trains were added to the timetable in the summer of 1898 the NE claimed all of them. There were NB protests about that, but by 1900 the NE had again ousted the NB from its main line and was providing engines for more trains than ever before.

THE DINING CAR DISPUTE

In 1898 the West Coast added a dining car to its morning Glasgow–London service, so it was no surprise when an East Coast conference recommended the provision of a dining car on *The Flying Scotsman*. The proposal was not received with enthusiasm by the NE which looked with disfavour at the prospect of losing the revenue accruing to its hotels department from the train's 20min stop at York. Nevertheless, Gibb agreed to the introduction of the dining car provided that the 20min saved at York was deducted from the overall time of the Edinburgh–London journey. A first class row blew up in 1900 when *The Flying Scotsman* operated with dining cars and the NB and GN refused to a speed-up of the train.

The argument put forward by London and Edinburgh was that the companies could not run the train to time on the existing schedule so there was no point in speeding it up. It was also pointed out that when the West Coast had put dining cars on its morning trains and eliminated the 20min stop at Preston the time had been used to absorb lost minutes and there had been a commendable improvement in timekeeping. East Coast timekeeping was shocking. During the whole of July, August and September 1900 the second portion of the up *Flying Scotsman* (10.7 am from Waverley) achieved only five on-time arrivals at King's Cross. The timekeeping had gone from bad to worse as the season advanced. In July the average late arrival was 10·27min, in August it was 22·15min, and in September it rose to 33·84min. Over the three months the train had 1,711min recorded against it.

The NB was particularly sensitive about the late arrival of NE-hauled trains at Edinburgh. Scottish internal services were geared to arrivals from the south, and the departure of the connecting trains from Edinburgh could not be delayed for more than a few minutes without incurring serious delays on three main lines (Edinburgh–Glasgow, Edinburgh–Perth and Edinburgh–Aberdeen) and associated branch lines. In practice internal trains were dispatched on time and special trains were put on to cater for passengers delivered late by the NE. Between 1 July and 31 October the NB ran 10,752 miles with specials to accommodate passengers who arrived late in NE trains. The cost of the extra working was not recoverable from the English company.

Deuchars complained that NB local traffic was impeded by northbound NE trains stopping for water at stations between Berwick and Edinburgh, although the NE had agreed not to stop for water on NB territory. In fact the engines were so stretched with heavy loads and long non-stop runs that they were forced to stop, sometimes not far short of Edinburgh. A Deuchars' report tells of a double-headed NE train having to stop at Longniddry where both engines took water.

Gibb attributed the reluctance of the GN to co-operate in the speeding up of the 10 am to that company's inability to produce locomotives capable of the higher speeds required. In a somewhat snide letter to Charles Steel of the GN he more than hinted that the alleged deficiencies of Doncaster should not be allowed to stand in the way of York's plans for faster service.

> I gather that the real difficulty in your mind arises from a doubt whether the trains can be run punctually at the proposed speeds. On this point Mr Worsdell assures me that we need be under no misapprehension and as this goes to the root of the matter I would suggest that you and Mr Jackson [of the NBR] and I should have a meeting with the three locomotive and passenger superintendents on as early a day as possible. I quite agree that if the proposed speeds are not practicable with the proposed weights of the trains the scheme must fall to the ground at least so far as the Great Northern is concerned, although you would, I presume, in that event, co-operate in altering the timing of the train so as to enable the North Eastern to accelerate on their line where we do not doubt it can be done without difficulty.

Deuchars' attitude to the matter was, 'A plague on both your houses'. The following report submitted to the general manager in December 1899 is typical of many:

> With reference to previous correspondence I am sorry to say that the down East Coast trains are still keeping very unsatisfactory time whereby our local working is being seriously dislocated and our mileage bill largely added to by the running of duplicate trains between Edinburgh and the west and north. I beg to enclose the conductor's journals for two recent cases, viz. the 11.30 pm ex-King's Cross on the 13th and 14th instant and perhaps you will

again take up alike with the North Eastern and Great Northern companies. Of course, the North Eastern company will urge exceptional causes such as the breakdown of an engine but if it is not one thing it is another, and one thing at least is quite clear—the southern companies are apparently not prepared to maintain the running time between the various points. Both should be pressed to provide adequate engine power and take other measures to secure punctuality. The engines we have to use to cover deficiences might be more profitably employed otherwise with working the goods traffic which is being greatly hindered through shortage of engine power.

Deuchars wrote several official and private letters to Burtt on the subject of bad running. In one such letter he said, 'You will excuse me for saying it but I am not drawing conclusions from isolated or exceptional cases. It is a fact as I will endeavour to show you that your trains both up and down not infrequently lose time from point to point through the slow running of your engines.' Again referring specifically to the controversial 10 am he wrote, 'Again yesterday this train lost about 20 minutes while in your company's hands. The bad working of this and other trains —see recent correspondence—hardly points to any immediate prospect of acceleration'.

Throughout the period of the 1900 summer timetable *The Flying Scotsman* ran with dining cars but to the old timing. In October Gibb intimated that his company would not be willing to operate the diners unless the train was accelerated with the introduction of the winter timetable on 1 November. He reckoned that the NE could gain 15min between York and Edinburgh and the GN 15min between London and York giving a 6 pm arrival at the termini compared with the current 6.30 arrival.

The reason for the extreme reluctance of the NB and GN to take part in Gibb's acceleration plan had nothing to do with locomotive power. The fact is that the companies had a profound fear of creating a 'race' situation. When the West Coast had refrained from speeding up its trains while cutting out the lunch stop it was merely observing to the letter an agreement entered into with the East Coast concerning the overall times between London and Glasgow and Edinburgh.

In a letter to his general manager Deuchars spoke of the dangers of 'enlarging the principle of racing which we are so anxious to avoid' and he went on,

It is to be regretted that Mr Gibb adheres to the proposed acceleration of the up and down day expresses for that will simply be a reintroduction of the racing element which is highly objectionable and dangerous at any time and particularly during the winter months when we have adverse weather conditions and heavy goods and mineral working to contend with.

The NB solicitor was instructed to 'get quietly from Steel' whether he would support Gibb. Steel left no room for doubt about the attitude of his company. To Gibb he wrote, 'I may say at once that this company's directors are very strongly opposed to any acceleration of speed unless we are forced into it by a competing company'.

During October the GN kept Euston informed of every move in the dispute, and the NB did likewise with the Caledonian. William Paterson of the Caledonian was entirely sympathetic. He wrote, 'All fighting and racing has been expensive, not wanted by the travellers and in the end led to arrangements between the competing routes. Accelerations and fast running are expensive and have not in my experience led to increased traffic or receipts'. Nevertheless, Deuchars was told to anticipate a Caledonian acceleration and plan steps which could be taken by the NB to counter it.

On 9 October Harrison of the LNWR convened a meeting of the East Coast and West Coast companies at Euston, but no agreement was reached. Gibb defied the efforts of the four companies to achieve peace. The new NE winter timetable issued on 30 October showed the down *Flying Scotsman* booked away from Berwick at 5.1 and arriving in Waverley at 6.15. The NB and GN timetables issued on the same day showed the train leaving Berwick at 5.13 and reaching Waverley at 6.30.

On the first day of the new service—1 November—the NE was in racing fettle. Worsdell's No 2010 covered the 67 miles between Newcastle and Berwick in $69\frac{1}{2}$min to achieve a $1\frac{1}{2}$min early arrival. But the NE did not control the signals at Berwick. The NB signalman kept the train standing for $18\frac{1}{2}$min eventually letting it go at its NB booked time. The NE driver had to get to Edinburgh with his 275ton train in 62min to meet the demands of his company's timetable. He ran to such effect that at Inveresk, only 5 miles from Edinburgh, he had gained 12min. But from that point on he was checked at every signal and ran into Waverley 14min late by the NE timetable, 1min early by the NB timetable.

The newspapers, scenting blood, made the most of the situation. *The Times* was vigorously pro-Gibb. 'The action of the North British Railway company in preventing a shortening of the time for the journey between London and Edinburgh is an action of which none but the North British Railway company is capable.' The *Glasgow Herald* thought *The Times* had made an 'egregious mistake'. Its sober opinion was, 'The public have had enough of railway racing. The North Eastern has embarked on a mad career of competition for the saving of minutes on a whole day's journey'.

Faced with the combined opposition of its partners and the West Coast companies the NE had no choice but to abandon its unilateral attempt to create a race situation.

CHAPTER 6

Conquest of the West

THE ROAD TO THE WEST

The hardest political blow suffered by the Caledonian in all its history was its defeat by the NB in its bid to take over the Edinburgh & Glasgow in 1865. Had it won that battle it would have dominated Edinburgh and the east and in time swamped the NB. But the boot was on the other foot. By winning the E & G the NB got to Glasgow, the Lanarkshire coalfields and the Clyde Coast, places in which its rival thought it had no right to be.

By consolidating its magnificent Bridges Route the NB established a near monopoly of the east from the Border to Aberdeen, and the improved services which it offered won it public acclaim. Soon after the opening of the Forth Bridge a deputation of the Town Council of Aberdeen waited on the general manager and presented a memorial inviting the NB to build an independent line to a station of its own in Aberdeen. A similar deputation from Peterhead wanted the NB to push on into Buchan. The general manager assured the memorialists that he would give the matter attention. But the NB had no intention of embarking on the costly round of Parliamentary battles that the proposed northwards extension would provoke. Its immediate plans centered in the west. Its aim was to create an independent route stretching all the way from Inverness to Carlisle which would be complementary to the grand route already established in the east.

The west of Scotland was so different from the east that it might well have been hundreds of miles away in another country. The broad estuaries and flat, fertile coastlands of the east gave way to serried mountain ranges and deep gloomy glens. When the first railway promoters went into the West Highlands in 1845 the clan chiefs set their henchmen on the surveyors. Half a century later, in building and operating a railway into those regions, the NB had to fight feudalism so rampant that a stationmaster at a West Highland station who wanted to house a summer visitor had to seek permission, not from his employer but from his feudal superior.

The artery leading from the NB headquarters to the west was the Edinburgh & Glasgow Railway main line. Because it linked the two principal cities of Scotland it was the most important line in the country and the busiest on the NB. The E & G had engineered it beautifully as a level, high-speed route—except for the last $1\frac{1}{4}$ miles. The NB's basic ambition was to run a train every hour between the cities with the best trains completing the journey in an hour. With the locomotive power available in the 1890s such a timetable should have been possible but for the extraordinary operating hazards which the line presented.

A rope-worked incline was a crippling handicap for any main line to have, especially when it started at the platform ends of one of the termini. To gain entry to Glasgow from the high ground at Cowlairs the E & G had been obliged to take its line under the Forth & Clyde canal and not over it as had been planned. This meant that the railway had to be dropped on a 1 in 42 gradient, partly in tunnel, to Queen Street station.

From 1842, with the exception of a brief three-year period, all trains had been rope assisted from Queen Street to Cowlairs. When a departing train was ready to begin the ascent a messenger rope was secured between the haulage rope and the front coupling of the engine, the coupling being inverted. A bell signal was then sent to Cowlairs and the ponderous winding engine was set in motion. The climb was slow. When the train breasted the summit steam was shut off momentarily, the now slackened messenger rope fell off the inverted hook and the train was able to proceed on its way without stopping.

All incoming trains stopped at Cowlairs where the engine was removed and replaced with two or more special brake trucks, depending on the weight of the train. These vehicles were heavily built, entirely open, and each was manned by a brakeman. The station pilot, or sometimes the train engine after it had run round, pushed the train to the crest of the slope from which point it made its way cautiously to Queen Street by gravity.

Cowlairs incline was as costly to operate as it was cumbersome. The ropes lasted from 12 to 16 months. Their periodic replacement took a whole weekend. A special staff of enginemen, brakemen and splicers was required to maintain and operate the rope and winding engine.

In 1892 John Conacher carried out an investigation into the

working of the incline. He found that the process of changing from locomotive to brake haulage at Cowlairs habitually caused a traffic build up on the down line at peak periods, with resultant late placing of stock at Queen Street and delayed departures. He saw no way of increasing the traffic flow using existing equipment and methods. He carried out tests with locomotive-hauled trains and the success of these encouraged him to advise the board to dispense with rope haulage. Conacher realised that, with ever-increasing traffic, the abandonment of the rope alone would not fully solve his problem. Accordingly he recommended to the board that the main line be quadrupled from Bishopbriggs to Queen Street. This proposal involved the widening of a deep rock cutting between Bishopbriggs and Cowlairs and the driving of another tunnel between Cowlairs and Queen Street—both difficult and expensive operations. The board talked over Conacher's proposals but nothing was done for six years, by which time the traffic blocks were chaotic and seemingly insoluble. Then on 22 September 1898 the board resolved 'to adopt the scheme recommended by the general manager for the provision of a new access starting at Bishopbriggs station and for the discontinuance of the working by stationary engine and incline rope and to include the scheme in the Parliamentary programme for the ensuing session'.

The line never was quadrupled, and 10 years were to pass before rope haulage was abandoned. The directors could not rid themselves of the spectre of a train running amok on that fearsome gradient and dashing itself to destruction in the cramped confines of the terminal station. In the event a train did get out of control coming down the incline and dashed into a crowded Queen Street station on a Saturday afternoon. The train was the 1.5 express from Edinburgh in charge of Holmes 4-4-0 No 595. Nobody was seriously hurt but the runaway engine demolished the bar. Thereafter No 595 was known to NB men as Carrie Nation, that being the name of a contemporary American temperance reformer.

Once the Edinburgh-bound trains had cleared Cowlairs incline their troubles were far from over. The inviting easily-graded, smoothly-curved 46 miles of road that lay ahead were more often than not so encumbered with speed restrictions that sustained bursts of speed were impossible. There was a dark side to the mineral traffic receipts which enhanced the half-yearly accounts. As millions of tons of coal, fireclay and oil shale were extracted

Page 103:
David Deuchars, superintendent of the line and key figure in organising the Race to the North

Page 104:
North Eastern engines on NB metals: (above) Waverley station East End with London express double-headed by NE engines about to leave; (below) Holmes '729' class No 740 as rebuilt by W. P. Reid piloting an NE Atlantic on an up East Coast express near Ayton

over the years a web of underground workings formed under the railways threatening their stability. When a working was about to pass under a line the practice was for the mineowner to notify the railway company and railway and mining engineers surveyed the site. Sometimes the railway company simply told the mine-owners to keep it informed of the progress of the working so that the line could be built up as it sank. More often it was decided to leave pillars of coal in situ under the line. These 'stoops' sometimes contained thousands of tons of coal which had to be paid for by the railway.

The E & G main line had the misfortune to cross successive beds of coal, fireclay and shale. The underground tentacles tended to strike at the most vulnerable parts of the railway. The NB bought a block of fireclay costing £1,350 to safeguard Castlecary Viaduct and within a few months was negotiating with Young's Paraffin Light Company for the purchase of a shale bed under the Seven Arch bridge near Ratho. The Saracen Coal Company required the purchase of 300 tons of coal under a bridge in the Cowlairs area and a signalbox threatened by an advancing seam was saved by the purchase of a stoop costing £473 7s—much more than the box had cost to build. The 1880 extension to Cowlairs works was built on 12½ acres of coal which cost the NB from £50 to £60 per acre. Yet the main line got off lightly. In 1882 the NB paid £6,375 to Messrs Baird 'to secure the stability of the viaduct carrying the railway over the river Clyde at Bothwell'. Eight years later when Baird's main seam was approaching the viaduct the NB was obliged to buy 39,320 tons of coal at a cost of £5,900. And again in 1894 the company paid £10,500 for 105,000 tons of coal to prevent the Split and Virgin seams from undermining the viaduct. £22,775 spent on coal the NB would never see made Bothwell Viaduct an expensive structure.

TO CARLISLE

In 1889 the NB took the drastic decision to build a direct line from Glasgow to Carlisle. It was drastic because both the Caledonian and G & SW had long-established lines linking the cities. It was a measure of the NB's frustration at the performance of its own Waverley route. The NB route from Glasgow to Carlisle via Edinburgh and the Waverley route was 145¼ miles compared with 101 by the Caledonian and 115 by the G & SW. Traffic between the Midlands and north of England and the industrial Clyde valley was heavy but the NB got very little of it. The NB problem was expressed in a letter written by Walker to George Findlay of the LNWR in 1884:

> It appears to me unaccountable that although our route from Carlisle which practically gives us access to every place in Scotland has been opened for upwards of 20 years your people continue to entertain the notion that the only route is via the Caledonian and ignore any instruction to the contrary. If so be the case, as I am informed, that the LNWR book of routing instructions shows only one route for traffic to Scotland, that via the Caledonian Railway, I venture to express the hope that it will be further supplemented and show that via the NBR as well.

There had been discontent with the Waverley route in the NB boardroom ever since its opening. There were those who thought that it never should have been built at least beyond Hawick and there had been a move to close it or sell it to the Midland. Traders would not use the line for through traffic because the time taken by the route was too long. Passengers from Waverley route stations to Glasgow claimed that the trains always ran late and that connections at Edinburgh were missed.

Details of Midland route timekeeping in the summer of 1880 were not flattering to the owning companies. In July the late arrivals of the morning express from St Pancras to Edinburgh totalled 1,352min of which the NB was responsible for 688min. The mid-day train accumulated 58min of lost time up to Carlisle and the figure increased to 117min at Edinburgh. With the night train the NB managed to reduce the Midland deficit of 685min at Carlisle to 576min at Edinburgh. The three trains between them lost 2,345min of which 835 were lost on the NB. The corresponding up trains lost 2,565min during the month, 1,099 on the NB.

The late running of NB trains was a favourite topic of conversation in Border towns and in the correspondence columns of the local papers. The main complaint of through passengers to Glasgow was of missed connections. The trouble arose through the fact that many Edinburgh–Glasgow expresses were East Coast 'facility' trains, and the NB was under an obligation to its partners not to delay these trains for the Midland connection.

Mr T. Lindsay Watson was a champion of the disgruntled Waverley route travellers. Walker wanted to please him over the

Edinburgh connections, but he could not see a way of doing so without rousing the ire of the East Coast companies. At length he made a secret agreement with Watson, the gist of which was that Glasgow trains would be held at Edinburgh if Galashiels telegraphed to say that there were Glasgow passengers on the Waverley route trains. Watson's jubilation was such that he printed the 'secret' information on postcards and had them distributed in the Border towns. Walker wrote, 'If one of these cards gets into the hands of the East Coast companies our object will be defeated'.

Meanwhile Walker negotiated with the Midland for an acceleration of the service. When news of the pending negotiations reached Watson he was on the point of delivering a public address in a Border town, and he asked Walker for details of the impending improvements so that he could make the news the climax of his speech. Walker replied, 'If it were prudent to give you materials for a splendid speech on Tuesday I should be very pleased to oblige you. But it is not and therefore you must just wait and allow me to bring about what you desire in my own way'.

The outcome of the negotiations was hardly earthshaking. All the NB and Midland could achieve between them was a 5min cut in the journey time between the capitals. However, the East Coast companies agreed to the departure times of the Glasgow 'facility' trains being put back 5min, and the new timetable gave Waverley route through passengers to the west a 15min margin in which to catch the connection at Edinburgh. But Oakley added a rider that the Glasgow trains must not be held beyond booked time to make the Midland connection.

Early in 1889, in the course of a board discussion on the Waverley route and its problems Walker told his directors, 'We cannot compare with the Caledonian Railway and the Glasgow & South Western Railway and therefore are not in the running'. It was then that he asked W. R. Galbraith, the Glasgow civil engineer who had a long association with the NB and who had recently surveyed the Glenfarg line, to find a direct route to Carlisle. Galbraith surveyed a route which left the NB in the neighbourhood of Hamilton and joined the Waverley route at Longtown. He pointed out, in presenting his report, that the line was feasible but that it would be very expensive. The best routes and all the worthwhile towns in the area had already been secured by the Caledonian and the G & SW and the NB line at best would merely serve as a corridor leading to the riches of England. Walker took the project seriously and, fearing East Coast displeasure, he made a special trip to London to explain the significance of the new line to Oakley. He also put Thompson of the Midland in the picture.

A few weeks later when Walker was at Westminster on Parliamentary business he was stopped in a lobby by Thompson and a G & SW director named Nicholson and asked, 'How would it do for the NB to acquire the G & SW?' It was no idle question. Plainly the two men had discussed the possibility. The prospect of such an amalgamation raised exciting visions. With the G & SW in the bag the NB would have not only a ready-made route to Carlisle but rich new territory stetching from the Clyde to the Solway and embracing the Ayrshire coafields and the ports of Greenock, Ardrossan and Ayr. Where would the Caledonian be then?

The bill for the amalgamation of the two railways was presented and gained considerable support from the G & SW board. But the Sou' West was essentially a Glasgow company run by Glasgow men who saw the stigma of its Edinburgh origin on the NB. That other great Glasgow concern the Caledonian for once brought up its big guns in support of the G & SW. The amalgamation attempt failed.

The NB had to suffer its Waverley route. Fortunately the opening of the Forth Bridge brought more than the expected increase in traffic by the Midland route to stations north of Carlisle. The receipts from passenger journeys originating in England, which were £44,619 for June, July, August and September 1899, rose to £72,673 for the corresponding months of 1890. The increase in revenue was £6,809 5s. But that did nothing to solve the problem of traffic to the west.

THE WEST HIGHLAND

The NB failure to secure a route to Carlisle from Glasgow was its second major defeat in the west within a decade. In 1883 it had been within sight of taking Inverness when the powerfully-backed, splendidly-engineered Glasgow & North Western Railway came close to getting its Act. The line was to have left the NB on the north side of Glasgow and run 177 miles via Loch Lomond, Crianlarich, Glen Coe, Fort William and the Great Glen to Inverness. The NB was to work the line. It was to have served a great tract of railless country in the West Highlands and because of that it received widespread support from a public that had become travel conscious. But the Highland Railway which had built a line across the Grampians to Inverness at great cost and was still struggling to make it pay, successfully opposed the G & NW. The promoters of the G & NW saw no prospect of making the line pay without the Inverness terminus and the whole scheme was abandoned.

Shortly after the failure of the G & SW amalgamation proposal the NB heard of a new attempt to get a railway through the West Highlands and it expressed interest. The railway was the idea of two Lochaber men, Mr Boyd and George Murdoch, who were dismayed and frustrated at the failure of the railway entrepreneurs of the south to provide their district with modern transport. Lochaber and its capital, Fort William, were shut off from the rest of the country by mountain barriers. The main road out of the town, a poor one, got round the mountains by passing down the shore of Loch Linnhe and threading its way through Glen Coe eventually to reach Crianlarich, Loch Lomond and Glasgow. The hazards and discomfort of the long coach trip did not encourage people to travel. Another road ran east through Glen Spean and by Loch Laggan to Kingussie on the Highland Railway 50 miles away. Passengers arriving by train from the south faced a $6\frac{1}{2}$hr coach journey before they reached Fort William. However, since the opening of the Callander & Oban Railway in 1880 it had been possible to travel to Oban by rail and complete the journey to Fort William by steamer.

Up to this time the only railways in the West Highlands were the two cross-country routes, the one reaching out to Oban from the central belt and the other running west from Dingwall to Strome Ferry. There was no lateral trunk line through the West Highlands. Boyd and Murdoch proposed to build one 100 miles long through terrain more difficult by far than anything so far tackled by railway builders in Britain. It was a breathtaking venture. The men of Lochaber proposed to get round the Ben Nevis massif by taking the railway east through Glen Spean to Tulloch. From there the line was to turn south to cross 33 miles of roadless wilderness.

There could have been nothing less attractive to railway promoters than what lay in that gap. On leaving Tulloch the line was visualised climbing steeply up the mountain face above the east shore of Loch Trieg to reach a 1,350ft summit on the Moor of Rannoch. From there the promoters had to look for a path across the 400 square miles of quagmire and outcropping rock that made up the Moor. Comparative civilisation was reached at Bridge of Orchy, from which place the railway was to wind down through Tyndrum to Crianlarich where it would cross the Callander & Oban line. Then it was seen plunging deep into Glen Falloch to reach Ardlui at the head of Loch Lomond. By Loch Lomondside it made its way to Tarbet and then by Loch Long and the Gareloch to a junction with the NB at Craigendoran on the Clyde.

Boyd and Murdoch included in their plans a westward extension of the line from Fort William to Roshven. This was considered essential to the economic success of the railway for a port would be created on the western seas through which the lucrative fish traffic, then the perquisite of Strome Ferry and Oban, would be channelled to the south.

It was not immediately clear why the NB backed a scheme—it was to be called the West Highland Railway—so fraught with difficulties and with no certainty of even a modest reward. Some years after the railway was completed *The Financial Times* reflected, 'The West Highland is a relic of those days when the North British and Caledonian railways cared less for their shareholders' interests than they did for cutting into each other's districts to provide two lines where one would hardly earn a livelihood'. Fear of a Caledonian assault on the territory certainly was one of the motives for the NB taking the West Highland under its wing. The Highland Railway had no doubt that the NB's real intention was to use the West Highland as a stepping stone to Inverness. Both the Caledonian and the Highland opposed the West Highland Bill. But there was a feeling abroad that the people of Lochaber had been neglected too long by successive governments, and the improvement of communication was long overdue. Once the Highland had been given assurances (which it received with reservations) that the NB had no designs on Inverness, the West Highland got its Act. But there was a significant deletion. The western extension ended on the Caledonian Canal at Banavie, only 2 miles from Fort William. The abandonment of the Roshven sea terminal had been forced by Professor Blackburn of Glasgow University whose house was 400yd from the proposed pier. The preservation of the view from a retired academic's window was

NORTH BRITISH RAILWAY.

Excursions on Saturday, Monday, and Tuesday, 16th, 18th, and 19th July.

TO FORT-WILLIAM, TYNDRUM, CRIANLARICH, SPEAN BRIDGE, ROY BRIDGE, TULLOCH, RANNOCH, & BRIDGE-OF-ORCHY,

By the West Highland Railway.

GOING.		CHEAP RETURN FARES. Third Class.	RETURNING.	
STATIONS.	Train Leaves.		STATIONS.	Train Leaves.
				P.M.
		4/6	FORT-WILLIAM... ,,	3 20
			SPEAN BRIDGE ,,	3 38
	A.M.		ROY BRIDGE ... ,,	3 47
QUEEN ST. (HIGH LEV.) at	7 13	4/-	TULLOCH ... ,,	4 1
COWLAIRS .. .. ,,	7 25		RANNOCH ... ,,	4 40
MARYHILL.. .. .. ,,	7 31	3/6	BRIDGE-OF-ORCHY ,,	5 10
		3/-	TYNDRUM ... ,,	5 27
			CRIANLARICH ... ,,	5 47

Similar Tickets will also be issued from Hyndland, Partick, Yorkhill, Finnieston, Charing Cross, Great Western Road, Maryhill, Lochburn, Possilpark, Springburn, Barnhill, Garngad, Alexandra Park, Duke Street, Bellgrove, Bridgeton Cross, Gallowgate (Central), and College, by trains in connection.

Excursionists going on 16th may return on 18th, those going on 18th may return on 19th, and those going on 19th may return on 20th July by any of the Ordinary Trains on payment of one-fourth of the Excursion Fare (plus fractional parts of a Penny) at the Booking-Offices before returning.

TO INVERGARRY, FORT-AUGUSTUS, GLENFINNAN, LOCHAILORT, ARISAIG, AND *MALLAIG.

By the West Highland Railway.

GOING.		CHEAP RETURN FARES. Third Class.	RETURNING.	
STATION.	Train Leaves.		STATIONS.	Train Leaves.
	A.M.			P.M.
		5/-	FORT-AUGUSTUS at	3 35
			INVERGARRY ,,	3 56
QUEEN ST. (HIGH LEVEL) .. at	5 50		*MALLAIG ... ,,	2 15
		4/6	ARISAIG ... ,,	2 38
			LOCHAILORT ,,	2 58
			GLENFINNAN ,,	3 21

Similar Tickets will also be issued from Hyndland, Partick, Yorkhill, Finnieston, and Charing Cross by train in connection.

Passengers may remain until the following day and return by any of the Ordinary Trains on payment of One-fourth of the Excursion Fare (plus fractional parts of a penny) at the Booking-Offices before returning.

* Passengers for Mallaig can break the journey at any Station between Fort-William and Mallaig.

Glasgow Fair West Highland excursion announcement 1904

considered by the relevant court of inquiry to be more important than the economic welfare of a depressed community.

By mid-summer 1894 the West Highland Railway was a reality. From Craigendoran on the Clyde to Fort William on Loch Linnhe the line was 100 miles long, and there was a short branch in the making from Fort William to Banavie on the Caledonian Canal. During July staff came up from the south and settled down to a new life in surroundings that must have seemed very strange to them. The first engines came from Cowlairs—they had been waiting for a year for the opening of the line—and drivers went out on training trips over a route the like of which they had never dreamed. On 7 August the first passengers traversed the line and enjoyed an experience new to railway travellers in Britain. They looked down on Loch Long as their train crawled round a shelf cut out of the rock 450ft above the water. They marvelled at the Horse Shoe Curve and the desolation of the Moor of Rannoch seen before only by the most intrepid of travellers. Later there was the thrilling passage of Monessie Gorge, where roaring waters sent spray as high as the carriage windows.

For the first few weeks the trains travelled cautiously. On the climb from Bridge of Orchy to Gorton passing place on the Moor of Rannoch speed was limited to 20mph and all the way across the moor trains were not allowed to exceed 15mph. The average speed throughout the 100 mile journey was 25mph. Not until the engineers were satisfied that the line was thoroughly consolidated did they allow a relaxation of the restrictions.

That winter the West Highland was given its baptism of fire. The worst blizzard of the century swept across Scotland filling the cuttings, burying railway equipment and piling up against the station buildings and the little railway cottages. On the Moor of Rannoch the line was obliterated. Then came the great frost which solidified the snow. It had to be hacked out of the cuttings piece by piece. For many weeks traffic was interrupted. The bill for snow clearance amounted to £2,680 2s 8d. When spring came and the snow at last melted it was found that damage to the line demanded the imposition of 13 speed restrictions ranging from a few chains to three miles.

The very fact that the West Highland Railway was *there* brought new hope to the islanders. That a western extension of the line was needed was no longer in doubt. The vital questions were, where would the western terminus be sited and how would the railway be financed? A government commission agreed that such a railway was necessary, but conceded that its construction and operation was outside the scope of orthodox railway finance. A government subsidy would be necessary.

The most promising spot for a terminal seemed to be Mallaig Bay, where a pier could be constructed to serve the steamers that would ply to Skye and Stornoway and there would be shelter for the fishing fleet. Between Mallaig and the existing railhead at Banavie lay 39 miles 54 chains of very difficult country.

Two bills were presented to Parliament. The West Highland Railway (Mallaig Extension) Bill was the normal measure required for the construction of any railway. The West Highland Railway (Guarantee) Bill provided for the subsidising of the construction of the railway and harbour, and of the subsequent operation of the railway. The first bill became an act in 1894 after only token opposition. The second bill provoked a political storm which raged at national level for two years. The Tories saw nothing wrong in subsidising a railway when everybody agreed that it could not be run as a commercial proposition. The Liberals abhorred the idea of taxpayers' money being used to bolster the finances of a railway company. The NB directors were portrayed as rapacious capitalists. In the welter of party political strife the welfare of the islanders was forgotten. John Aird lost patience and withdrew his plant and men from the area.

It was not until 1896 that the controversial act was obtained and the WHR was free to make its Mallaig Extension. The contract went to Robert McAlpine, the promoters acknowledging the magnitude of the task he had taken on by giving him $5\frac{1}{2}$ years to complete just under 40 miles of railway. A confident McAlpine thought he could do it in $3\frac{1}{2}$ years. He did it in a little over 4.

A layman looking at unbroken ground might have wondered where a railway could have been put. McAlpine had to make 100 cuttings and 11 tunnels through hard, splintery rock. He drew world attention to himself by his imaginative use of mass concrete for bridges large and small. The bridge over Borrodale Burn had a span of 127ft, the largest concrete span in the world up to that time. The graceful Glenfinnan Viaduct had 21 spans each of 50ft.

At daybreak on 1 April 1901 the steamer *Clansman* from Stornoway sailed into Mallaig harbour and delivered to the waiting train the first islanders to use the new railway. At long last the much dreamed of iron road to the isles was a firm line on the map.

THE BEER LINE

In 1893, a year before the West Highland was opened, the NB wolf shed its sheep's clothing and, in spite of its promise to the Highland Railway, announced its intention of building a railway from Fort William to Inverness. The Highland countered by promoting a line from Inverness to Fort William. Both companies were financially winded at the time and neither pressed its case. But in 1894 the NB came back with a new scheme to reach Inverness. Before long there were six different railway projects on the go for lines between Fort William and Inverness. It was a sort of Great Glen railway mania and was to prove as destructive as the 1845 prototype.

The only scheme that succeeded in getting rails on the ground was the Invergarry & Fort Augustus Railway, a purely local project—or so it seemed on paper. The line left the WHR at Spean Bridge and ran by Loch Lochy and the bank of the Caledonian Canal to Fort Augustus at the south end of Loch Ness. It was said to have been conceived only to meet the needs of the local people. But the local population along the line's 24 miles could be numbered in hundreds rather than thousands, and few of them had much cause to travel.

The railway was engineered by Formans & McCall and substantially built. There were imposing rock and earth cuttings along the route. Although only a single line was laid, enough land was taken to provide for its doubling when traffic had sufficiently developed. But where was the traffic to come from in this remote, sparsely populated area? The two intermediate stations—Invergarry and Aberchalder—were substantial structures extravagantly provided with siding accommodation. The village of Fort Augustus stood on the east side of Loch Ness. Passengers alighting at the station could have walked to the steamboat pier by crossing the canal and the river Oich on existing road bridges. But the I & FA took its line beyond the village to a new pier, in the process building a new swing bridge over the canal and a large viaduct over the Oich. This extension swallowed almost a quarter of the cost of the whole line. Why did a small local company spend all that money to reach a pier to which passengers could have walked in a few minutes? The Highland Railway quite simply saw the I & FA as a dagger pointed at Inverness and the extension from the village as a first step in the creation of a line along the west shore of Loch Ness. The I & FA might be a small independent company but the NB only had to acquire it and that much feared company would be half-way to Inverness. Had the Highland but known, the NB board had had a special meeting at which 'it was agreed to recommend that the North British and West Highland railways should jointly promote a line from Roy Bridge to the Invergarry & Fort Augustus Railway with powers over the I & FA and extension to Inverness'. In other words the NB planned to build a line up Glen Roy to join the I & FA which it would use to reach Fort Augustus whence it would build its own route to Inverness. The NB visualised having its own station at Inverness, with running powers into the Highland station which it was prepared to enlarge at its own expense.

The principal progenitor of the I & FA was Lord Burton. Much of the administration was done at the Burton-on-Trent premises of Bass Radcliffe & Gretton and more than half the finance came from that source. (That was why the irreverent called it 'the beer line'.) In a way it was a rich man's toy. So much was spent on construction and on litigation against rival schemes that there was no money left with which to buy engines and rolling stock. If the line was to open one of the large companies would have to be invited to work it. The North British, through the WHR, offered to work the line for £3,000 per half year, whereupon the Highland stepped in and offered to do the job for £2,000. The Highland's object was to gain possession of the line and so remove the threat to Inverness.

On 22 July 1903 the I & FA was opened for traffic. It had cost £344,000 to build. In the first half-year the total revenue was £907. By that time the folly of having built the line at all was only too apparent. The clamour to build a railway through the Great Glen subsided as quickly as it had arisen and never was to be revived. Three years after it had been built the expensive extension to the pier was abandoned. With Inverness secure the Highland lost interest in its ailing foster child and withdrew its engines in the spring of 1907. The NB took over and worked the line for four years before withdrawing. It lay derelict until 1913 when the NB bought it for £22,500 and added it to its system as a branch.

In 1908 the NB absorbed the whole of the WHR undertaking. The 165 miles comprising the original West Highland, the Mallaig Extension and the Fort Augustus branch were to delight generations of railway travellers. The Fort Augustus branch inevitably was an early casualty and the 42 chain Banavie branch did not survive the withdrawal of the Caledonian Canal steamer service. But the 142 miles of the main stem survive, with the original atmosphere of the old West Highland remarkably unimpaired in spite of three changes of ownership.

CHAPTER 7

The Clyde and Loch Lomond

THE CLYDE, ARDRISHAIG & CRINAN RAILWAY

The NB's brash entry into the already overcrowded and fiercely competitive Clyde steamboat trade in 1866 met with near disaster. That was no surprise to the experienced private steamboat operators who had witnessed the failure of every railway attempt to establish a Clyde fleet. But the NB retained a toehold on the Clyde with small steamers running short trips from a base at Helensburgh.

Beyond the Clyde were the tourist territories of Argyll and the West Highlands as yet untapped by rail except for the cross-country Callander & Oban Railway, a Caledonian preserve.

In 1887 the NB backed an integrated rail and steamer venture in the west that nearly came off. The most famous service on the Clyde was David MacBrayne's Royal Route from Glasgow and Greenock to Ardrishaig in Loch Fyne via the Kyles of Bute. The NB joined forces with MacBrayne to support a rail and steamer route to Ardrishaig. The Clyde, Crinan & Ardrishaig Railway saw the light of day in a lawyer's office in Lochgilphead and was given the Royal Assent on 8 August 1887.

The line of communication envisaged in the act was complex. Steamers were to leave the NB base at Craigendoran near Helensburgh and sail to Ardnadam pier in the Holy Loch. From that point the first stage of the railway was to run 8 miles 5 furlongs by Loch Eck to Newton Bay on the east shore of Loch Fyne. Ferries were to take passengers and goods across the loch to Furnace, and the second stage of the railway was to continue the route 15 miles 4 furlongs down the loch shore to a terminus at the Canal Office, Ardrishaig. Ardrishaig, of course, was a key point on the Royal Route. Steamers arrived there from the upper Clyde and the service was continued by canal boat to Crinan where a steamer was waiting to carry passengers on to Oban and Fort William. The NB was to work the railway and MacBrayne was to have access to all the piers, special attention being given to the development of new circular tours involving trains and steamers.

A tourist route had been in operation via Loch Eck for nine years. Coaches starting from Dunoon pier plied to Inverchapel at the south end of the loch where the passengers transferred to the steamer *Fairy Queen* for the sail up to Locheckhead. The next stage of the journey, to Strachur on Loch Fyne, was accomplished by coach, and a steamer took passengers across to Inveraray. The buildings and plant, coaches, horses, harness, the *Fairy Queen* and piers and slipways associated with the Loch Eck route were owned by the Glasgow & Inveraray Steamboat Company, and the act provided for the acquisition of these assets by the Ardrishaig Railway. Provision was also made for the purchase of Crarae quarry, a valuable property on the line of the second stage of the railway.

The Ardrishaig Railway's publicity material was well spiced with the extravagant claims beloved by small railway promoters. 'Our proposed line,' explained the company secretary, 'traverses one of the best tourist districts of Scotland, and will be a great feeder to the North British and East Coast English lines especially with regard to tourist, fish, cattle and sheep traffic. The importance of our line to railway companies was shown by the vigorous opposition of the Caledonian Railway Company to our agreement with the North British.' Of course, the Caledonian opposed anything the NB did on principle. The Caledonian was then building the extension from Greenock to its new pier at Gourock and the Ardrishaig promoters interpreted this as a Caledonian attempt to get closer to the new company's railhead in the Holy Loch!

The NB certainly took the Ardrishaig Railway seriously. The general manager induced Oakley and Tennant to meet the Ardrishaig secretary at Edinburgh on 11 October 1887. The CAC wanted the English companies to pay to it 25 per cent of the receipts derived from traffic originating on the CAC and bound for the GN and NE and a like percentage on traffic from the English lines to the CAC. This rate was to be continued until the Ardrishaig Railway shareholders secured a dividend of 4 per cent on their capital of £180,000. In spite of pressure put on them by the NB the English managers 'came to the conclusion that it was not necessary for either the NE or the GN to come under any obligation to this railway'. The NB guaranteed 25 per cent of receipts but was never called on to pay. The Clyde, Ardrishaig & Crinan was not built.

DR INGLIS AND THE NB BOATS

With the opening of the new rail-connected pier at Craigendoran, a mile east of Helensburgh, in 1882 the NB maritime venture took on a new lease of life. The new generation of swift, comfortable paddle steamers with their red funnels with white bands and black tops and their romantic names from the novels of Sir Walter Scott became a familiar feature of the Clyde estuary. Because of shallow water round Craigendoran the NB boats were of necessity smaller than the rival vessels of the Caledonian Steam Packet Company but that did not hinder them from challenging the 'auld enemy' for the rich commuter trade and the holiday and excursion traffic.

Dr John Inglis played a significant part in the development of the NB fleet. As proprietor of A. & J. Inglis, shipbuilders and engineers and builder of many of the boats, he had a hand in their design and as a director of the NB he had a say in their operation. The shipyard of A. & J. Inglis was established on the left bank of the Kelvin just above its confluence with the Clyde on ground owned by the NB. The railway company charged a rent of only one shilling per year on condition that Inglis routed all his freight over the NB. In Dr Inglis's office hung a large photograph of NB Atlantic *Aberdonian* as well it might for the doctor, as chairman of the locomotive committee, had persuaded the NB, much against the grain, to embark on the big engine policy that produced the Atlantic. When new additions were being considered for the fleet the board invariably invited tenders from half a dozen or so Clyde builders and just as invariably Inglis got the job. The firm built everything after *Redgauntlet* of 1895.

In the opening years of the twentieth century the Clyde steamboat war reached a climax with the rival railways rushing trains at ever increasing speeds to the railheads and increasingly powerful vessels taking the passengers on to their respective piers. The traffic was at its most hectic at the morning and evening rush hours. This was a contest the NB could not ignore. The rail route along the north bank had been improved by the doubling of the Dalreoch–Cardross section in 1896 and the establishment of a loop line by the extension of the Yoker line to the main line at Dalmuir. Every weekday afternoon NB and Caledonian trains left Glasgow about the same time and raced down opposite banks of the Clyde to their respective railheads. The G & SW was in the contest too, but the NB regarded the Sou' West as an ally fighting a common foe. Indeed, the NB and the G & SW had held talks with a view to building a common-user boat which would be used as a relief boat by either company as required. When at one stage the Caledonian put a 4-6-0 built for the Anglo-Scottish expresses on the boat trains the NB countered by putting an Atlantic on the 4 pm Glasgow–Craigendoran. It was a ludicrous choice for such a service and such a line. The Atlantic did the journey only once and in one direction.

Dr Inglis complained that the engines of the boat expresses roaring over the viaduct above his shipyard were spraying his premises with sparks and causing fires. He invented a spark arrester and urged the board to fit it to the engines hauling the boat trains. He asked for a list of numbers so that he could watch the trains from his office and see if his instructions had been obeyed.

The racing was money-wasting and the effort won nothing for the contestants. One boat could have carried all the passengers instead of the three available. The inevitable peace conference led to a sensible traffic sharing agreement.

There were minor brushes between Caledonian and NB boats. There were joustings for the Holy Loch piers, and *Talisman* and *Kenilworth* gave the Caledonian boats a run for their money on the Rothesay route. There was an interesting interlude when a Volunteers company chartered a Caledonian boat to take them from Rothesay to Craigendoran where they intended to board a special NB train to take them to their summer camp in Kinghorn in Fife. I. H. Gilchrist, manager of the NB fleet, asked Deuchars if he should allow the Caledonian boat to berth at Craigendoran. Deuchars told him he should, otherwise the Caledonian would take the passengers to Gourock and run them by Caledonian train to Edinburgh before handing them over to the NB and the company would lose mileage.

When the opening of Rothesay Dock at Clydebank was pending it became known that a Clyde steamer would be used to convey the official party, which included royalty, from Glasgow to the new dock, and there was much jockeying in the railway offices to secure the honour of providing the official ship. The NB and G & SW conferred on the question of whether the ship should be offered at a reduced charter fee—only to find that the Caledonian had offered a vessel free. The NB had the consolation of providing a vessel to act as a floating restaurant.

Talisman and *Kenilworth* became firm favourites on the Rothesay route; the public regarded them as the NB twin sisters. But W. F. Jackson, perusing the steamboat accounts at the end of one season, noticed that more coal had been delivered to *Talisman* than to *Kenilworth*. He took the matter up with Gilchrist who explained:

> The increase in the consumption of coal in the *Talisman* during September last was occasioned by the piston rings being worn so that steam was passing from side to side in the cylinder; hence more steam was required to get the work done.
>
> The mileage of the two boats is practically alike. They were both on the Rothesay run and were taking the same run alternately i.e. the *Kenilworth* was, say, on No 1 run today and the *Talisman* on No 2 run; next day the *Talisman* was on No 1 run and the *Kenilworth* on No 2. The *Kenilworth* was built on the same lines as the *Talisman* but has always proved to be a more economical boat than the *Talisman*.
>
> It must also be kept in mind that owing to its foul condition the bottom of the *Kenilworth* was scraped and coated with composition in July whereas *Talisman* ran the whole season without having been slipped.

Typically, Jackson was not satisfied with Gilchrist's explanation and he passed his letter to Dr Inglis for comment. Inglis replied:

> Mr Gilchrist's explanations are quite sufficient. I do not remember if new rings were made for *Talisman's* pistons. Metal is cheaper than steam. The two steamers are not exactly alike—a slight change was made in the form of *Kenilworth*, hardly noticeable, but the men have found it out evidently. I know the average speed must include calls, but those would average out and the *Waverley* would show a higher speed than *Lucy Ashton*. We found in *Talisman* that the degree of fouling produced in the Kelvin reduced the maximum speed by one knot, and at that reduced speed involved an extra expenditure of about half a ton of coal per hour.

On 18 September 1914 the NB board decided to scrap the veteran *Lucy Ashton*, built in 1888 and oldest boat in the fleet, and at the same time tenders were put out for a replacement. Inglis undertook to have a conventional paddler ready for 1 May 1915. Alas! the new vessel, *Fair Maid* was requisitioned by the Admiralty and lost on war service.

H

Lucy Ashton remained on the Clyde to provide the wartime services on the upper firth. Surprisingly she continued to ply through the inter-war years when she was to be seen paddling leisurely between the quiet Gareloch piers. At the end of the 1939 season she received her second death sentence, and once again a war won her a reprieve. Again she provided passenger services on the upper firth during hostilities. In 1946, due to the shortage of vessels—many ships of the Clyde fleet had failed to return—*Lucy Ashton* was refurbished and placed in passenger service from Craigendoran. She survived to wear BR colours and was retired finally in 1948, 34 years after the first order to scrap her had been given. In 1949 the stripped shell of her hull cavorted briefly on Clyde waters, propelled in a welter of noise and spray by jet engine in some uncouth experiment.

LOCH LOMOND

The NB, somewhat outclassed in the battle of the Clyde took steps to gain the upper hand on Loch Lomond. By 1890 Scotland's premier tourist attraction was an NB monopoly. The company had just purchased the loch's privately-owned steamer fleet. Rail access to Balloch pier at the south end of the loch was exclusively NB, and the West Highland Railway then taking shape would give NB trains a foothold at the northern end of the loch. The WHR tried to purchase Ardlui pier but failed to get the requisite powers.

The monopoly was short lived. Soon the Caledonian came rushing to Loch Lomond with its sleeves up, bent on taking the loch in a pincer movement. The Glenfalloch Railway was promoted to link the Callander & Oban at Crianlarich with Ardlui by means of a line taken down Glen Falloch parallel with the West Highland. The eight-mile glen housed only a handful of people. Two railways in such a place would have been a monument to supreme foolishness of railway rivalry. Fortunately the Glenfalloch bill was not proved. At the same time a scheme was produced for a Caledonian-controlled line from Glasgow through Dumbarton and down the Vale of Leven to the south shore of the loch, to run parallel with the existing NB line. Furthermore the Caledonian announced that it would operate its own steamer fleet from an independent terminus at Aber Bay. The scene was set for an all-out Caledonian-NB war on the placid water of Loch Lomond.

In those days Loch Lomond was more than a tourist attraction. Roads round the shores were poor or non-existent and the all-year-round steamer service conveyed mails, merchandise and livestock to the lochside villages. Both the Caledonian and the NB well knew that the loch could not support two full scale and exactly parallel transport operations. There was no enthusiasm in the boardrooms for a repetition on Loch Lomond of the fierce steamer war then raging on the Clyde. The outcome was that the rivals agreed to share the steamer fleet on the loch and the rail approach to Balloch as far back as Dumbarton, but the independent Caledonian line from Glasgow to Dumbarton proceeded under the aegis of the Lanarkshire & Dumbarton Railway. The Dumbarton & Balloch Joint Line Committee was to come into effect on the day that the L & D opened and was to have control of the line from Dumbarton East to Balloch pier and of the steamers on the loch.

The L & D was a difficult line to construct and it was not until the autumn of 1899 that it approached completion. By mid-September there still had been no announcement about its opening and the NB printed and issued timetables showing the Loch Lomond service as usual. Then on 26 September the Caledonian announced that the L & D would begin operating on 1 October. Moreover, the Caledonian published a timetable that showed scant regard to the existence of NB trains on the joint section of the line. It was not an auspicious start to the partnership, but after hurried inter-company talks a workable timetable was produced in time for the opening day.

The Lanarkshire & Dumbartonshire began operations on 1 October 1899. When travellers disembarked from the steamers at Balloch under the new regime they found not one but two trains awaiting them. The NB train ran as before to Glasgow Queen Street via Dumbarton and the Helensburgh line, while a brand new Caledonian train waited to take passengers to Glasgow Central (Low Level) via Dumbarton and the L & D. As far as Dumbarton tickets were interavailable, but beyond Dumbarton each company honoured only its own tickets. Passengers joining the trains at stations in the Vale of Leven had to be careful to specify whether they wanted a Caledonian or an NB ticket, and they had to make certain that they caught the appropriate train. While there was no scope for steamboat racing on Loch Lomond the companies competed briskly for the associated rail traffic and something like a race to Loch Lomond ensued.

During the first year of joint operation NB trains ran 90,549 miles on the joint line compared with 53,132 miles by Caledonian trains. The Caledonian steadily stepped up its services. By 1917 the NB figure was 96,517 miles, the Caledonian 78,473 miles. In 1922 Caledonian trains ran 76,039 miles against 61,870 run by the NB. The rival companies fought vigorously for the traffic. By means of posters and other publicity the companies extolled the virtues of their respective routes, although the competing trains at times ran within sight of each other. At one time the NB advertised a through carriage between Balloch Pier and King's Cross. The 1913 timetable showed this vehicle leaving Balloch at 7.45 and running via Bathgate to join the 10 am from Edinburgh. The down departure was 11.25 am from King's Cross the through vehicle being taken forward by the 8.15 pm Edinburgh–Balloch.

It was too much to expect that all would be sweetness and light in the enforced coalition between the ancient rivals. When the time came to renew the Loch Lomond fleet the NB and Caledonian disagreed over the steamer policy to be adopted. The NB wanted relatively small vessels that could be built on the Clyde and towed up the River Leven to the loch. The Caledonian on the other hand was determined to put large steamers like those of their Clyde fleet on the loch, the vessels to be prefabricated and assembled at Balloch. The companies failed to resolve their difference and the issue was submitted to a ponderous and expensive process of arbitration. The NB won, and two paddle steamers *Prince George* and *Princess May* were laid down at the Pointhouse yard of A. & J. Inglis, the traditional builder of NB boats.

Inter-railway bickering extended to the day to day operation of the fleet. Peter Parlane, the carpenter of the Loch Lomond boats, was classed as a seaman and was paid accordingly. Once a week in summer he acted as mate, and occasionally he had functioned as master. His counterpart with the CSP Clyde fleet was regarded as a joiner and classed as a railway shopman. As such he was paid 40s per week compared with the 31s paid to Parlane. The Caledonian thought the Loch Lomond man should be paid at the same rate as his CSP opposite number; the NB thought otherwise. 'If he is to be paid as a shopman,' pleaded the NB general manager, 'this will invoke additional expense and at the present rate of wages would place the carpenter in a much better position financially than the masters of the steamers.'

On 11 July 1910 the Joint Line committee decided to build a larger vessel than usual, but one that would be able to sail up the Leven. She was to be ready for the 1911 season. The new vessel *Prince Edward* was a paddle steamer of 304 tons, 175ft long and 22·1ft wide. She proved to be a tight fit for the Leven. In announcing the vessel's addition to the fleet in January 1912 the NB chairman explained, *'Prince Edward* was launched from Messrs Inglis yard on 20 March 1911 and taken from the Clyde to Kirkland in the river Leven in May and from there to Balloch Pier, Loch Lomond at the beginning of November last'. An intriguing tale emerges from the missing months May to November.

During the passage of the Leven *Prince Edward* stuck fast between Renton and Alexandria. Attempts to move the vessel using horse teams and traction engines failed, and an intriguing situation arose. *Prince Edward* was still the property of the builder who had taken out an insurance policy to cover the movement of the vessel up the river—normally a passage of several hours. The Caledonian wanted to use brute force to get the ship into the loch; the plan was to lift the hull using pontoons and then tow it forward. Inglis consulted his policy and concluded that it did not cover him for any damage that might be sustained during the lifting process. The NB general manager telegraphed Mathieson of the Caledonian:

> Engineer Steel reports Leven falling rapidly making it necessary to lift steamer one foot. It is feared that this involves the serious risk of damage probably not covered by insurance. In the circumstances this company are against attempting to float the steamer up the river on barges and we are also against incurring any considerable expenditure in attempting to get the steamer up the river. Rather that any risk or that any expense should be incurred we are of the opinion that the steamer should lie where she is until there is a natural rise in the river.

The NB was reconciled to the fact that barring a very wet summer the vessel would remain stranded until the winter rains came. Writing to Inglis, the general manager said, 'We can if necessary do the work on the loch this summer without the steamer'. The NB was in a strong position in that Inglis was a director of the company and the management of the hull had been entrusted to Gilchrist, the NB marine superintendent. Inglis dealt exclusively with the NB half of the potential ownership; for him the Caledonian did not exist. His concern for the ship was shown when he wrote to Jackson on 31 May, 'I hope someone is looking after the decks this hot weather. They should be wetted after sundown'. Jackson assured him that awnings had been erected over the decks.

A telegram sent by Jackson to Gilchrist on 13 June spoke of trouble from a new quarter: 'Am informed *Prince Edward* is to all intents and purposes being used as a promenade by all and sundry. Arrange for protection'. The stranded vessel was indeed proving a big attraction to Vale of Leven residents who flocked to the site especially on Sundays and on the fine summer evenings. Interest fell away after a week or two but Mr Parback of Dillichip Print Works, at the bottom of whose garden the hull was lodged, complained strongly to Jackson of 'a nuisance'. The suggestion was that ladies were being entertained aboard *Prince Edward*. The case was placed in the hands of Detective Shepherd of the railway police, who in due course furnished a report headed 'Irregularities on board vessel *Prince Edward*'. Among other matters it related how Sergeant Finlay of Alexandria had boarded the vessel and been introduced by the day watchman 'to his two sisters whom he said had come from Glasgow to spend the day with him'. The report considered the night watchman to be blameless, he being 'a very old man and not likely to be bothered with anyone'. The nuisance seems to have been resolved for on 23 June Jackson was assuring Inglis, 'whatever may have been the position so far as the past is concerned I have no doubt the steps which have been taken will prevent anything of the kind occurring in future'.

Prince Edward reached Loch Lomond in November 1911, was fitted out at Balloch and entered regular service on 1 June 1912. She ran her official acceptance trials on 4 July. The passage up the Leven had cost £721 for traction and repairs to the hull. When during the 1914-18 war the vessel was commandeered by the Admiralty the D & B offered delivery at Balloch and was told it might as well offer delivery in the kingdom of heaven.

THE LURE OF THE TROSSACHS

The Trossachs, that enchanting corner of western Perthshire

with its mountains, woods and ribbon lochs, found a superb publicist in Sir Walter Scott. But when the tourists came in the wake of *Rob Roy* and *The Lady of the Lake* they found the country difficult of access. So also did the railway companies. The Trossachs remained railless, but the NB, after establishing a railhead on the fringe of the area, built a toll road into its heart. A Caledonian attempt, through its subsidiary the Callander & Oban Railway, failed to carry through the Trossachs Railway because it could not rouse the interest of the largest feudal landowner, the Duke of Montrose. The NB, in its drive towards the Trossachs, through its subsidiary the Strathendrick & Aberfoyle Railway, saw to it that His Grace had a seat on the board.

The Blane Valley Railway was opened in 1866, left the Lennoxtown branch of the NB at that town, and ran for eight miles through the valley serving the hamlets of Campsie Glen, Strathblane and the small village of Blanefield. The original promoters had a grand scheme for taking it on to the Trossachs but they ran out of money when the railway reached the turnpike road a mile or two beyond Blanefield. They planted a station at their involuntary terminus and called it Killearn although the village of that name was nowhere in sight. There the railway stuck for 15 years.

James Keyden, a lawyer and promoter of small railways, was the man behind the Blane Valley. It was in his office on 16 September 1879 that the Strathendrick & Loch Lomond Railway was first mooted. It was to be a continuation of the Blane Valley westward to Aberfoyle and on to Inversnaid on the east shore of Loch Lomond. It was grandly described as 'the new route to Loch Lomond'. The Duke of Montrose did not like the idea so 'it was resolved that the meeting should be adjourned and that a future meeting should be called when His Grace is satisfied as to the Line'.

The parties met again in a month to consider a revised version of the project. The railway now was to be constructed in two parts. The first part was to run from its end-on junction with the Blane Valley to join the existing Forth & Clyde Junction Railway (Stirling–Balloch) near Gartness. The second part was to leave the F & CJ at Buchlyvie and cross Flanders Moss to Aberfoyle where it would terminate. The extension to Inversnaid was abandoned, but the company hoped to operate a coach service on the road to Loch Lomond. The new line would therefore, with the NB and

Blane Valley and the Forth & Clyde, provide a direct rail link between Glasgow and Aberfoyle. A key part of the plan was for the railway company to build a private road across the mountains to Loch Katrine in the heart of the Trossachs. His Grace approved of the new railway, now renamed the Strathendrick & Aberfoyle Railway, and the NB and BV offered support. Present at the meeting were John Forman, engineer of Glasgow, and Provost Hugh Kennedy of Partick, a contractor by profession. Forman was invited to be engineer of the line and Kennedy the contractor.

NORTH BRITISH RAILWAY.

Excursions on Monday and Tuesday, 18th and 19th July 1904.

To ABERFOYLE.

GOING.		CHEAP RETURN FARE.	RETURNING.	
STATIONS.	Train Leaves.	Third Class.	STATION.	Train Leaves.
QUEEN ST. (HIGH LEVEL).. at	A.M. 9 30	2/-	ABERFOYLE at	P.M. 6 55
COWLAIRS .. .. .. "	9 38			

Similar Tickets will also be issued from Jordanhill, Whiteinch, Hyndland, Partick, Yorkhill, Finnieston, Charing Cross, Great Western Road, Maryhill, Lochburn, Possilpark, Springburn, Barnhill, Garngad, Alexandra Park, Duke Street, Bellgrove, Bridgeton Cross, Gallowgate (Central), and College, by trains in connection with Excursion Train from Queen Street.

NOTE.—Passengers from and to all Stations, except Cowlairs, change carriages at Queen Street in each direction.

Passengers may return by any Ordinary Train on the following day on payment of One-fourth extra at the Booking-Office, Aberfoyle, before returning.

Glasgow Fair Aberfoyle excursion announcement 1904

Forman's estimate of the cost of the line was £51,947. Nine months after the first meeting Keyden had collected £7,534, but that did not deter him from putting out tenders. Kennedy undertook to build the line for £29,682 3s 9d. The meeting held to allocate the contract was actually in progress when Kennedy learned that a rival contractor had put in a bid for £28,521 0s 7d. He burst into Keyden's office and told the board that he had left the preparation of the contract to his son and that he had made a mistake in his calculations. The correct price, it appeared was £28,435 16s 9d. 'If you have any difficulty in getting the stock taken up I might take a little more,' Kennedy told the board. He got the contract, but not before he had parted with £1,000 in payment for a block of S & AR stock.

When Wieland of the NB heard that the contract had been let before the full capital of £50,000 had been subscribed he ordered Kenyon to cancel it. The board embarked on another vigorous round of canvassing. Directorships were offered for cash and potential subscribers were promised stations in front of their doors. Kennedy contributed another £20,000. When the Duke of Montrose failed to pay the £500 he had promised for Parliamentary expenses it was Kennedy who footed the bill, and he let it be known that a further £7,000 would be forthcoming if he got the contract. A grateful board not only gave him the contract but elected him a director in place of the Duke of Montrose who had resisted all blandishments to take up shares other than those he had been given for his land.

When permission to start construction was given the Strathendrick's troubles were by no means over. The company had expected to build the line to the same standards as the Blane Valley and the Forth & Clyde, but Wieland insisted that the more exacting standards of the NB must be observed. That put another £2,500 on the bill. No serious engineering problems arose, except that the contractor had difficulty in finding a solid bottom on parts of Flanders Moss. In the summer of 1882 Carswell, the NB civil engineer, inspected the partly completed line and produced a scathing report in which he accused Kennedy of having failed to construct the railway according to specification. Wieland duly informed the S & AR board that the NB would on no account work the line unless it was completed in all respects in accordance with the contract. Poor Kennedy was becoming disenchanted with his role. When his periodical professional fees became due he found that he was paid the agreed amount less sums due as 'calls' on his shares. On one occasion when the account due was £3,541 10s he received only £1,053 1s 6d. 'I only accept the instalment as made out under protest,' he told the board.

By the middle of 1880 Kennedy considered that he had completed the line to the satisfaction of all and the board arranged for the opening. When Maj-Gen Hutchinson inspected the line on 27 July he found it unfit to accept traffic of any kind and gave the company a month to put matters right. In particular he insisted that a tablet apparatus be installed at Killearn station where the Strathendrick linked up with the Blane Valley. The company had proposed to save money by having the section extend from

Lennoxtown at the east end of the Blane Valley to Gartness Junction at the west end of the first part of the Strathendrick and on the Forth & Clyde. The section, in other words, was to extend along the route of two contiguous, independent railways and end on a third—a most peculiar arrangement. Tablet apparatus was hurriedly obtained for Killearn and the staff trained in its use. The line was opened on 1 October 1882. The special train promised by the NB for the occasion failed to turn up.

The service which opened the line ran from Queen Street station Glasgow to Aberfoyle. The trains, which were worked throughout by the NB, traversed the metals of four different companies in 34 miles which led to difficulties in the accountant's department when they came to dividing the revenue between the participating companies. The Strathendrick described the first timetable imposed on it by the NB as 'most unsatisfactory and disappointing' but agreed to put up with it for one month. There was traffic in the area but the line was not equipped to handle it. Livestock came down from Glenfinlas to the new station at Aberfoyle but there was no siding for the cattle trucks nor was there a crane capable of dealing with the stone traffic from the local quarry. Kennedy installed one of his own. There was timber on offer at Gartmore but, again, no crane.

Troubles abounded for the S & AR. There were no lineside fences on Flanders Moss. Kennedy had made do with ditches which he thought would serve the same purpose, but sheep fell into them and there were claims for compensation. It was said that the trains frightened horses where the line bordered the turnpike near Aberfoyle and Kennedy was obliged to plant a screen of trees between the railway and the road. A landowner insisted that his grouse were killing themselves by flying into the railway telegraph wires, so the wires had to be fitted with grouse scarers. The Strathendrick named its first station Killearn, which was the name of the last station on the Blane Valley. Passengers kept getting out at the wrong station even after the Strathendrick station was renamed New Killearn and the Blane Valley station Old Killearn. The BVR station was later renamed Dumgoyn Hill and then Dumgoyne. When the Strathendrick tried to improve the amenities of Aberfoyle station by building a small refreshment room, Wieland informed the board that 'until I am assured that it is not intended to have a place for the sale of intoxicating liquors but merely for temperance beverages' he would not sanction the refreshment room.

The Strathendrick failed to establish a coach link with Inversnaid. The Aberfoyle–Loch Lomond road was little more than a farm track and the local authority refused to bring it up to coach standard. But the toll road to Loch Katrine was completed, the cost being shared by the North British, the Duke of Montrose and the proprietor of the Aberfoyle quarry. At an early date Mr Cook discovered this new route into the Trossachs and trade flourished. Unlike the railway the road paid its way. Regularly a credit entry appeared against the item 'Trossachs Road' in the company accounts.

In its first month of operation the Strathendrick earned a total revenue of £138 14s 10d, and for the next two months the figures were £88 17s 11d and £82 14s 4d. These dismal results did not prevent James Keyden from promoting another railway in the area. This was the Milngavie, Strathendrick & Port of Menteith Railway which was to cut diagonally across the territory already served by the Blane Valley, Strathendrick and Forth & Clyde. 'It is directly antagonistic to our interests and bound to abstract a large amount of traffic,' complained a director of the BVR. At the next meeting an outraged board sacked Keyden. He had the interesting experience of sitting in his own office recording his own dismissal in the minute book. After the entry he added 'intimating at the same time as he did so [resigned] solely to meet the wishes of the board he would require the usual payment in lieu of notice which he was advised was a year's salary'. The board approved the minute 'with the exception of the paragraph beginning with the word *intimating* and ending with the word *salary*'.

The next meeting of the BVR board took place of necessity in the NB boardroom, a Mr James Houston being in attendance in an adjoining room. In due course he was called before the board and informed that he was privileged to be appointed company secretary at a salary of £50 per annum. He was further informed that he would be required to provide a boardroom free of charge and pay his own clerk.

The Clyde, Loch Lomond and the Trossachs could be explored by leisurely day outings from Glasgow and Edinburgh, and the NB took advantage of the fact to establish what became the two most successful day tours in the West of Scotland. Passengers leaving Glasgow for the Trossachs Tour travelled to Aberfoyle by rail and from there to Loch Katrine by the toll road. A steamer took them on to Stronachlachar at the western end of Loch Katrine where a coach was waiting to convey them to Inversnaid. The homeward journey was by steamer to Balloch and train direct to Glasgow. For Edinburgh passengers a through carriage was run to Stirling via the Forth Bridge, transferred to the Stirling–Balloch train, and transferred again to the Glasgow–Aberfoyle train at Buchlyvie. The passengers then followed the same route as the Glasgow passengers. Or the tours could be completed in the reverse direction.

The Three Lochs Tour embraced Loch Long, Loch Goil and Loch Lomond. The steamer sailed from Craigendoran and cruised by Loch Long and Loch Goil to Arrochar, tracing the path pioneered for the NB by *Lady Rowena*. The passengers walked across to Tarbet where the Loch Lomond steamer was waiting to take them to Balloch thence home by rail.

On 1 August 1891 the BVR and S & AR were absorbed by the NB. Eleven days later the BVR directors met for the last time and before he closed the minute book the secretary recorded, 'In regard to the sanitary arrangements at Blanefield station the directors, while feeling their office officially terminated, desired the secretary to urge the NB secretary to get the water at once introduced to the station and house and to look after the drains'.

CHAPTER 8

Here and There

FIFE

The Kingdom of Fife was the NB's treasure chest. Its pits produced 9,000,000 tons of coal in their peak years and all but a fraction of it was carried by the NB. Fife coal was the company's life blood.

The NB had inherited Fife from the Edinburgh, Perth & Dundee Railway in 1862. In 1880 the main trunk line ran diagonally across Fife from Burntisland, the ferry terminal on the Forth, to Tayport on the Tay where a ferry provided a connection to Broughty Ferry and Dundee. From Ladybank on the main line a long branch reached out through Abernethy and Bridge of Earn to reach Perth via Hilton Junction on the Caledonian. The approach from the east was from Stirling through Alloa, Dunfermline and Cowdenbeath to Thornton on the main line. A secondary west-east route left the Stirling–Dunfermline line at Alloa and, following a more northerly course via the Devon Valley and Mawcarse, met the main line at Ladybank. From Thornton a line was built in stages round the coast through Leven and Anstruther eventually to reach the university town of St Andrews in the East Neuk. In the coalfields a network of branches meshed the pits as they developed.

The keystone of NB policy was to keep Fife inviolate. The natural barriers of the Tay and the Forth which had proved so difficult for the railway to conquer also served to deter prospective invaders. The vulnerable frontier was in the east and that was where the NB was specially vigilant against the Caledonian aggression it knew must come.

In 1879 the Alloa Railway Company was authorised to build a bridge across the Forth at Alloa and make a railway 3 miles long from the Caledonian's South Alloa branch across the river to the town of Alloa. The Caledonian put up two-thirds of the capital for the Alloa Railway and undertook to work it. Since no provision was made to link the new railway with the NB's Stirling–Dunfermline line at Alloa the NB viewed the Alloa Railway as a stalk on which eventually an eastward extension into Fife would be grafted.

The Caledonian attack came in 1883 with the publication of a Bill for the construction of the Alloa, Dunfermline & Kirkcaldy Railway. This line was to run from Alloa 29½ miles through Fife to Kirkcaldy. Plans to build a dock at Kirkcaldy were deleted from the bill at the last moment, but the NB had no doubt that the Caledonian's ultimate intention was to create its own coal port in Fife. The company viewed the AD & K as 'a hostile and aggressive scheme for the purpose of placing in the power of the Caledonian Company the means of invading Fifeshire district and diverting traffic to the Caledonian system'.

The Caledonian had friends in Fife and for that state of affairs the NB, with its monopolistic take-it-or-leave-it attitude, poor services and high fares, had only itself to blame. The new line received vigorous local support, but the NB pleaded successfully that it had staked many thousands of pounds in the future of Fife by deciding to reconstruct the Tay Bridge, and build the Forth Bridge and associated lines in Fife. Nothing more was heard of the AG & K.

In 1891 the Caledonian was again at the gates of Fife this time secure in the knowledge that there was a substantial Trojan horse of merchants, and traders within waiting to welcome the invaders. The new line was to start at Larbert and reach Fife by means of a tunnel under the Forth. The destination as before was Kirkcaldy and a large dock was included in the scheme. There was no doubt that Fife had a raw deal from the NB and the public showed its displeasure by giving the Caledonian massive support. The local MP, a noted NB-hater, spearheaded the attack. The NB pleaded that the new Bridges Route and other contemplated improvements were on the point of transforming transport in Fife and the project was defeated.

In 1889 the NB strengthened its position in Fife by purchasing from Randolph Erskine Wemyss, one of the largest coal owners in the district, Methil Dock and the private railway connecting it to the Wemyss pits. Wemyss was given a seat on the NB board. To prevent recurrent threats from outside, the company made a pact in 1896 with 28 Fife coal owners, including Wemyss, whereby the coalowners agreed that for a period of 21 years they would not support any scheme for a new railway in Fife (other than NB promotions) and that they would not build new railways themselves. In 1897 Wemyss announced that he was about to build a new railway to Methil which would operate in direct opposition to the railway he had sold to the NB. Here was a bizarre situation in which a director of the NB blatantly decided to go into business against his own company and this in spite of a pact only recently entered into. The resulting row brought about the departure of Lord Tweeddale and Sir Charles Tennant from the chairmanship and vice chairmanship of the company and of John Conacher from the management. It was to lead to the branding of the NB as a pariah by railway managements throughout the land.

DROPPING THE PILOT

Two quotations illustrate graphically the gulf in temperament between Conacher and Wemyss. A neighbour wrote to Mrs Conacher:

> When I heard that a *Christian* gentleman was to succeed the late Mr Walker I remarked that one of two things would happen; either there would be a revolution in the management of the company or Mr Conacher's stay there would be a brief one.

The following is an extract from a letter from Carswell the NB engineer to Walker:

> My inspector reports that on 10th inst. when the foreman surface-man was going over his length between Cameron Bridge and Thornton he met Mr Wemyss of Wemyss Castle riding along the railway on horseback, and it seemed to the foreman that all the huntsmen and hounds which accompanied him had also been on the railway it was so marked and the fences broken down. On the foreman challenging Mr Wemyss he told him who he was and said that he might report him.

The key to the situation in which the NB found itself lay with George Wieland. As a young man he had come from Euston to be the NB secretary and by the 1890s he was the most powerful man in the NB hierarchy. When he resigned the secretaryship, ostensibly on the grounds of ill health, he was given a handsome present and a seat on the board. Once in the boardroom he formed a cabal with Wemyss and another director, Grierson, to seize control of the company.

Wieland, when he had sponsored Conacher's appointment had wanted a railwayman purely and simply—a man who would run the railway and not interfere in the politics of the boardroom.

And Conacher did run the railway. He guided the affairs of the company at a critical stage of its development. The Scottish traders came to trust him and respect him as their Welsh counterparts had done when Conacher was on the Cambrian. He gave Fife the best service it ever had and succeeded in breaking down the deep-rooted antagonism of the local merchants. But Conacher was not a man who could condone what he considered to be malpractices in high places. When he spoke out against the action of Wemyss, Wieland was angry. He cautioned his general manager:

> I would strongly urge the desirability of your devising some means of appeasing Mr Wemyss who is in a bad way about his case, and if not appeased will inevitably give us a great deal of trouble and probably be the occasion of further losses to us in Fife.

Conacher wrote a conciliatory letter to Wemyss pointing out that when the shareholders got to know of his action they would turn against him. Wemyss was unimpressed and continued to demand what he regarded as his rights. The company tried to appease him by offering him a toll on all his traffic passing over the NB which would have gone by the new railway. Wemyss retorted that his price for not building the railway was £3,000 a year for 30 years.

Crisis point was reached when the cabal succeeded in deposing Lord Tweeddale and Sir Charles Tennant and installing Wieland in the chair. Sir Charles wrote to Conacher, 'It is a great relief to me to be out of the disturbed atmosphere of the NB boardroom'. And Tweeddale assured the general manager, 'I do not think the steps we have taken will result in any injury to your position and prospects for the reason that you are *indispensable*'.

But Conacher was not indispensable. The cabal insinuated that he had been guilty of dishonest practices in connection with certain accounts. It was a cruel accusation to make against such a man. He resigned.

The railway world was aghast at the turn of events. The press spoke of 'the evil triumvirate' in the NB boardroom. Oakley, who had played a key role in having Conacher appointed, was shocked and bewildered. 'Unless,' he told Conacher, 'there are hidden springs of a personal nature or some prejudices akin to the Scottish mind I cannot conceive why they let you go. When the facts are

Page 137:
Atlantics on the Waverley Route: (above) *NB Atlantic No 901* St Johnstoun *in a setting of Border hills, 1917;* (below) *No 875* Midlothian *at Galashiels on an up express*

Page 138:

The West Highland Railway: (below) Fort William station around the World War 1 period

(above) Two Glens hard work in LNER day (centre) West Highla[nd] Railway device

known light may appear but, in any event, my confidence in you is not impaired nor my faith in your powers and conduct lessened.'

George Younger, the Edinburgh brewer and a director of the NB, told Conacher that he had thought of resigning in disgust but had decided to stay on and avert as much evil as possible. 'Time will revenge you, and 91-99 will some day be recognised as the golden days of the North British.' James Addie a Glasgow trader thought, 'the magnificent traffic you have so successfully built up will, I fear, go back to the state it was in when you took command'.

It was the custom for general managers of railway companies to exchange passes and when Conacher departed he routinely returned those passes he held for lines throughout the country. Many companies showed their displeasure at the board's action by returning the passes to Conacher for his private use. When the NB secretary returned Conacher's Metropolitan District Railway pass to the issuing company to have it re-issued in the name of his successor, the Metropolitan general manager sent it to Conacher instead with the comment, 'The only satisfaction I have in receiving it is to return it to you and ask you to keep it'.

Conacher was as much loved as his late employer was despised. He was offered many posts and accepted one in the electric supply industry. On 7 March 1900 *The Financial Times* reported, 'If capable management can do anything to secure good service to consumers of electric light the customers of the Metropolitan Electric Supply Company ought to have less reason to complain in future'. But railways were Conacher's world. Soon he was back at Oswestry as chairman of his beloved Cambrian with his son as general manager. Frequently in the closing years of his life he was consulted by railway managements with problems on their hands and undertook commissions in England and Ireland. But he would have nothing to do with Scotland. In 1904 when he was asked to advise on the Newburgh & North Fife Railway he explained:

> I am obliged for your letter and would have been pleased to have rendered you the desired assistance if the case had not been a Scottish one, but on my coming to London after giving up the management of the North British Railway I made it a rule not to take up any one relative to railways in Scotland and to this rule I have adhered.

I

John Conacher had turned his back on his native land.

No one had done more for the NB than David Deuchars and he seemed to be the obvious successor to Conacher. But the appointment went to a relatively obscure rating clerk, William Fulton Jackson, a Wieland man. We first met Jackson as the persecutor of poor John Currie over the matter of the privilege ticket. He was a man who could write to his superintendent of the line, 'The 6 pm from Glasgow yesterday had only two lights burning in the first class carriage. Has the guard noted this in his journal?' His pungent letters became a byword throughout the system. At least it could be said of him that he kept everyone on their toes.

Jackson held his post for over 20 years. The NB's fortunes revived in 1905 when Wieland died and a reconstituted board under the chairmanship of the Earl of Dalkeith took command.

SUBURBAN TRENDS

In 1880 the upsurge in Glasgow's suburban traffic was causing embarrassment to the NB. Nine years earlier the company had opened a suburban terminal station in the High Street and named it College in recognition of the fact that it occupied the former site of the University of Glasgow. College received traffic from suburban stations east of Glasgow, from Coatbridge, Airdrie, Hamilton, Bothwell and from Edinburgh via Bathgate. If the station had a fault it was that it was some distance from the city centre. And the fact that it had no connection with Queen Street station made the interchange of passengers difficult.

Traffic from the Clyde coast, the Vale of Leven and the western suburbs came into Queen Street and had to run the gauntlet of Cowlairs incline. There was no prospect of increasing line capacity. To cater for the impending increase in suburban traffic the NB considered building a second suburban terminal, a counterpart of College that would accept traffic coming in from the west. A site was chosen at the corner of Hope Street and Bothwell Street but the company had second thoughts when an alert shareholder pointed out that the NB would be handing passengers on a plate to the Caledonian whose Central station was just across the road from the proposed NB terminal.

It was a this point that the company took the bold step of deciding to link College station in the east with its lines in the west by means of a new railway passing under and through the heart of Glasgow. The line was to pass directly under Queen Street station where low level platforms would be built. All traffic from east and west would flow through the new station bringing much needed relief to Cowlairs incline, and main line and local services would be concentrated at one point.

An independent company, the Glasgow City & District Railway, formed to promote and build the railway got its Act in 1882. As with all schemes promoted in urban areas preliminary expenses were heavy. The company spent £53,478 in legal expenses and £395,305 on property before the first sod was turned. The project involved the construction of 3·123 miles of line, of which 1·758 miles were underground. The cost of the underground section was £588,163, or £334,000 per mile.

In burrowing under the city the engineers encountered running sand, boulder clay, a mixture of boulder clay and rock, sandstone, solid rock, soft mud and shale. Cut and cover methods were used where practicable, elsewhere the tunnels were excavated from shafts sunk from the surface. Care had to be taken at all times to ensure that there was a minimum of interference with the normal business of the city. At the peak of operations work was proceeding at 22 faces.

Kent Road was troublesome. This thoroughfare, under which the railway was to be made by cut and cover was built on running sand for the whole of its length and was flanked on both sides by tall dwelling houses. When the contractors dug an experimental trench at the north side of the street the sand ran out from under the buildings and the walls showed signs of cracking. The trench was abandoned and a new technique was employed based on the principle that dry sand occupied the same bulk as wet sand. The problem was to let the water flow into the drains leaving the dry sand behind.

Two rows of sheet piling were driven into the sand on opposite sides of the street 35ft apart. The surface of the street down to the top of the arch was excavated, then the excavation was shaped to the form of the proposed arch. The next step was the concreting of the arch. When the arch had set, cavities were excavated where the side walls of the tunnel were to be, the digging being done slowly to prevent an outflow of water and sand. The escaping water was passed into a sump before being siphoned into the drains thus ensuring that any sand in the water was retained.

Concrete was then poured into the cavities to form the tunnel walls. When the operation was finished the contractor found himself with a concrete shell enclosing a solid core of sand rather like insulation covering a cable. The workmen then dug out the sand, bricking up the walls and the arch as they advanced.

The dwelling houses on either side sent sewage pipes into the middle of the road at the level of the tunnel. A new main drain had to be constructed below the tunnel and the sewage pipes led into it.

The new low level station below Queen Street was excavated without unduly obstructing traffic in the station overhead. This was done by dividing the station into strips each 45ft long and 110ft wide (the width of the low level station) and excavating each strip in turn, the surface of each strip being reinstated before the next was begun. The job took two years to finish. About a mile west of Queen Street the tunnel widened out for a distance of 102yd to accommodate Charing Cross station. College station was re-sited on the new line at the east end of High Street tunnel and at a lower level than the original.

One day Henry Lamond, secretary of the GC & D, received a letter from John Walker in which reference was made to a station at Hyndland Road. This puzzled Lamont for neither the board nor himself knew of any such station; indeed the line did not go near the proposed site. When he sought elucidation Walker explained that he had decided to make a branch line from the GC & D near Partick. 'Mr Simpson the engineer is cognisant of the matter,' explained Walker, 'and will be able to point out the site to you.' Thus did the NB treat its subordinate companies. Hyndland was described in the relevant correspondence as a 'temporary station'. The ultimate intention was to take the line on to a terminus on Great Western Road opposite the Botanic Gardens, but this extension was not made.

When the GC & D opened on 15 March 1886 it was the first underground railway in Scotland and only the fourth in Britain. It transformed the traffic pattern on the north bank of the Clyde. Trains from Edinburgh via Bathgate instead of terminating inconveniently at College now gave a service not only to Queen Street but to suburban stations west of the city centre. Hyndland was now the terminus for the Edinburgh trains and for some of the east-west shuttle services. The new line also made possible, with the City of Glasgow Union Railway, a complete circular service embracing Queen Street, Partick, Maryhill, Bellgrove and back to Queen Street.

The NB had a half share in the CGU with the G & SW. The line was opened in 1875 to provide a goods link between Shields Junction on the G & SW and Springburn on the NB. Although it passed through the inner suburbs in the east and north its passenger potential was not at first exploited. When the GC & D opened there were only two stations on the CGU's portion of the circle—Duke Street and Alexandra Park. However within nine months of the opening of the GC & D three stations, Springburn, Barnhill and Garngad, were opened on the eastern flank of the circle. The CGU operated its own service between Springburn and Glasgow (St Enoch) superimposed on which was the GCD circle service. When the CGU was partitioned between its owning companies in 1896 the Springburn service became wholly NB.

More than 200 trains a day passed through the tunnels. The efficiency of the new system, compared with its only competitor the horse tram, was not in question but the patrons of the new railway soon found that there were disadvantages in travelling by underground steam railway. The new Queen Street low level station quickly became a dark sulphurous cavern where passengers were apt to be engulfed in swirling sooty smoke. Charing Cross was worse. The line approached the station from both directions on rising gradients and the tunnel was seldom clear of smoke from labouring locomotives. Great gusts of smoke and steam displaced by trains approaching simultaneously from opposite directions belched from the tunnel mouths making it difficult at times for passengers to see the platform edges. One man in fact stepped off the platform and fell on to the track. Mr Carswell, the company engineer, tried to improve the travellers' lot by introducing a novel system of electric lighting in the carriages, the current being picked up from conductor rails fixed to the tunnel walls. But the system succumbed to the all-pervading pollution.

There existed a long standing feud between the Corporation of Glasgow and the NB mainly over the condition of the city stations. Charing Cross was a gift to the anti-NB lobby. Bailie Bilsland, leader of the agitation, told a Corporation meeting, 'There is no doubt that the conditions under which the public use Charing Cross station are simply scandalous'. A colleague, Mr Alexander, added, 'It really is in a very abominable condition; in fact one is hardly able to get into a train with comfort or without danger'. A clause in the GC & D Act obliged the railway company to ventilate the tunnels to the satisfaction of the Corporation and the magistrates were bent on enforcing the requirement.

The first shots in the campaign were fired only months after the opening of the underground line, but produced no reaction from the NB other than formal letters stating that the matter was being looked into. For three years the topic was debated at Corporation meetings and the words 'scandalous' and 'outrageous' were freely bandied about. It was not until 1889 that the NB produced a plan for the ventilation of the tunnel between Queen Street and Charing Cross by means of shafts driven from the surface. The idea of despoiling the atmosphere of a prime residential district and impeding important thoroughfares drove the Corporation into a frenzy. The plan was rejected out of hand.

Maj Marindin of the Board of Trade was called in to advise on the problem and infuriated the corporation by concluding that the NB scheme for making a shaft was acceptable. The city fathers wanted the smoke removed from the tunnel but did not want it in the streets. It was suggested in all seriousness that the company be allowed to make a shaft to let fresh air in but not let the smoke out. In the end the roof was removed from Charing Cross station, but not before thousands of pounds had disappeared into the pockets of the lawyers who for seven years pursued the case through various courts.

A feature of the Glasgow suburban service was the mass movement of workmen morning and evening. Special trains conveyed workmen from stations in the northern and eastern suburbs to the Singer Manufacturing Company's works at Clydebank—then the largest factory in Scotland. The specials ran to and from private platforms at the works. The men travelled in old unlit four-wheeled carriages so crammed that at times the frames were known to have sagged down on to the rims of the wheels, the resulting friction sending showers of sparks cascading through the floorboards. At least the patrons of the 'Singer workmen' enjoyed the privilege of travelling at the cheapest fare ever offered on the NB—0·17 of a penny per mile.

Jackson complained that carriages on the workers' services were being vandalised, although it is difficult to see what they had in them to vandalise. He made an arrangement with William Beardmore, whose works in the Dalmarnock area were served by NB trains, whereby volunteer vigilantes recruited from the workers kept an eye on their fellow travellers. Jackson was so pleased with the result of the experiment that he extended the principle generally to workers' services.

Spitting in carriages annoyed the fastidious Jackson. He personally devised notices for exhibition in smoking compartments throughout the system. There were two versions of the notice. One for use in working class areas was strongly worded, the other aimed at the more sedate regions simply said 'Please do not spit'. He instructed Deuchars, 'When the notices have been in use for some considerable time you will, of course, report the results. Your inspectors should be instructed to watch the matter closely during the time the experiment is in operation'. Deuchars duly reported that the most voluminous expectoration was to be witnessed in the Hamilton trains.

How dependent employers were on the NB is shown in a letter which was written by the general manager of Messrs Kennedy (Carntyne) Ltd to the general manager of the railway company:

> As we find Carntyne station extremely handy for our workers, there is a train leaves the western districts of Glasgow, that is to say Jordanhill, at 7.44 and gets here about 8.10 we find very suitable for starting time. We have therefore altered the starting time in our works to suit the train, and we trust for next year this train and the time of it will be continued, and our purpose in writing is to ask if you would be kind enough to do so.

Macfarlane Strang & Co, which had a factory in a northern district of Glasgow not served by public transport, paid the whole cost of constructing a station at Lochburn on the circle line between Maryhill and Possilpark.

In 1880 when the GC & D was first suggested Sir Thomas Bouch was engineering the Edinburgh Suburban & Southside Junction Railway. It was his last railway; he died before the act was obtained. The line was very different from its Glasgow counterpart. It was not designed primarily as a suburban passenger railway but as an avoiding line that would provide a route for goods traffic passing between the north and west lines and the East Coast and Waverley routes, thereby relieving congestion on the line through Haymarket and Waverley. It was hoped that the passenger traffic would build up as the southern suburbs expanded.

The new line left the Glasgow line west of Haymarket and describing a left hand arc passed through Gorgie, Morningside Road, Blackford Hill, Newington and Duddingston before joining the Waverley route at Niddrie North Junction. Trains following the route could return to Waverley via Portobello. Or the direction could be reversed. The Suburban circle was opened on 1 December 1884.

There was no Edinburgh equivalent of the 'Singer workmen', although there was considerable worker traffic to the docks and factories around Leith. The distance was $3\frac{1}{2}$ miles and the return tickets were sold in bundles of 12 at 1s 3d, 0·19 of a penny per mile. Workers on the other side of the Forth complained that they were charged 0·38 of a penny per mile between Kinghorn and Kirkcaldy. The Suburban circle too carried some worker traffic. When the service was cut following a coal strike the proprietors of three breweries at Duddingston wrote to the NB complaining that they would have to close down unless their workers' trains were restored.

One of the numerous documents that stationmasters were required to send to headquarters at intervals was one giving returns of income from various items of platform furniture. Many stations augmented their receipts with revenue earned by weighing machines, chocolate machines, name-stamping machines and football game machines. At one period the Suburban line stations of Morningside Road and Newington were equipped with peepshow machines of the what-the-butler-saw genre. For the price of a penny slipped surrepticiously into a slot the douce Victorian citizen on his way to business could treat himself to a glimpse of scenes then thought to be salacious. A variation of this machine delivered photographs to take away. A letter written by Walker to the manager of the Photo Vending Machine Company in the 1880s has a twentieth century ring about it:

> The attention of the company has been called to certain photographs exposed for sale in the automatic machines. I have obtained copies of the photographs which are said to be objectionable and they are the following, viz. Miss Devine, Miss Irene Woodward and the Misses Vernon. I think they rather tend towards indecency and it would be well to avoid anything that would be likely to offend the public taste.

On 1 July 1903 the NB strengthened its hold on Leith by opening a short, direct line to a terminus at Leith Central. A spur from Lochend Junction to the new line enabled trains to run direct to and from the Suburban line thus putting the southern suburbs in communication with the Leith industrial complex. Leith Central was also used as a terminus for certain Glasgow trains and at busy periods for holiday trains serving a variety of destinations. In the previous year a short branch had been taken from Haymarket West Junction to a new terminus at Corstorphine and this station too was used as necessary by long distance trains. The outer residential areas were served by trains running to Musselburgh, Glencorse, Macmerry, Dalkeith, Polton, Penicuik, Gullane and North Berwick. Elite of the Edinburgh residential trains was *The Peeblesshire Express*. This train left Peebles at 8·44 am each weekday and stopping at Leadburn to pick up a portion from Broomlee on the Dolphinton branch was due in Edinburgh at 9·37. The down train left Waverley at 4·32 pm arriving in Peebles at 5·30 pm except on Saturday when the times were 1·33 pm and 2·28 respectively.

With the coming of the electric trams to Glasgow the suburban railways lost ground. Large numbers of passengers deserted the grimy city-centre stations for the new vehicles with their frequent services and very low fares. In Edinburgh the cumbersome cable car system was less of a menace but many people took surface transport rather than face the long flights of stairs or the inclined roads that led from the Waverley platforms to street level.

THE EDINBURGH HOTEL

It had always been a sore point with the NB that it had not been able to build in Edinburgh a station that would be worthy of the capital. Visitors could walk along Princes Street without being aware that Waverley station was there. Anyone who took the trouble to find a vantage point from which the station could be glimpsed saw what appeared to be several rows of low-roofed sheds. The NB was not responsible for this sad state of affairs. The Bank of Scotland, which stood like a castle high on the south hillface overlooking the station, invoked the law of servitudes and ancient lights to prevent the railway company from erecting a structure more than 30ft high. The NB could not even erect a signal without first obtaining the permission of the bank. On one occasion the company built a lowly signalbox at the west end of the station without leave of the bank. From the lofty pinnacles of the bank it must have looked like a dog kennel. Nevertheless, from the autocrats of the bank came a letter requiring the NB 'to submit a proposal for compensating us in respect of the erection of a signal box, signal bridge and platform indicator at the Waverley Bridge without our consent'.

It was the age of the great railway hotels. Many companies had learned that hotels brought them profit and prestige. So the NB decided to have a hotel. Its own offices at the corner of Princes Street and George IV bridge occupied one of the finest sites in Edinburgh. Although it overlooked the station and the valley it had the merit of not being in line with the hallowed windows of the Bank of Scotland. The NB decided to knock down the offices and in their place erect the grandest of grand hotels, a building that would dominate Princes Street and would be a permanent symbol of North British supremacy. That the Caledonian had similar designs for the opposite end of Princes Street only added piquancy to the proceedings.

The board's first task was to investigate the mysteries of hotel management. The newly formed hotel committee under the chairmanship of George Wieland first sought inspiration from the Metropole Hotel in Brighton, then considered to be one of the most spectacular hostelries in the country. But the Metropole management was firmly of the opinion that railwaymen should stick to running railways and leave hotels to hoteliers. Wieland was sent away with a flea in his ear.

Nothing daunted the chairman and three of his committee members set off in 1895 on a grand tour of the great hotels of Europe, the party staying in turn at the Hamburgher Hof in Hamburg, the Central, Savoy and Bristol in Berlin, the Imperial and Bristol in Vienna, the Hotel Hungaria and the Royal in Budapest as well as hotels in Cologne, Munich and Lucerne. At the end of his European hotel crawl—undertaken, of course, at the expense of the NB shareholders—Wieland presented a report which must rank as a curiosity to students of catering history.

The committee was much taken with the gilt and glitter of the Royal, Budapest and especially by the £2,500 worth of gilding in the ballroom. Wieland strongly advised that 'if the new Waverley Station Hotel is to be made a success no false economy should be exercised in such matters'. Lavish banqueting halls, he thought, would bring winter business. But he did not think much of Continental kitchens. In one of the most ostentatious hotels the committee had swept through a glittering dining-room into a dark, cavernous, over-heated kitchen where food was cooking on huge coal furnaces and everywhere there was dirt and dust. 'In no case,' went on the report, 'was apparatus to be seen approaching in efficiency and economy the apparatus which may be seen in this city [Edinburgh] in the new kitchens of Charles Jenner and Company.

With the finer points of the European hotels in mind the board embarked on the task of building its super hotel. The site was mostly on hard rock. When work started in January 1897 Hamilton Beattie the architect described what happened: 'To facilitate the removal of the rock blasting was tried but I had to stop it as the first night's work broke £25 of glass in the General Post Office and rendered the old buildings in Princes Street insecure'.

The heavy rock excavations which in places went 20ft below the level of the railway had to be made by hand. Among the old buildings affected was the NB head office at 2 Princes Street. The staff was hurriedly evacuated to the Waterloo Hotel and the business of the company was conducted henceforward from its bedrooms. High retaining walls were built to safeguard Princes Street and North Bridge. Meanwhile, the general manager was pressing to have the south wall of the hotel built up to the level of the station roof; it was needed to support the station roof girders.

As originally planned the hotel was to have had shops at ground floor level in Princes Street and the NB offices were to have been on the ground floor opposite North Bridge. Thomas Cook staked a claim to the shop on the right of the main door; he was asked to submit an example of the 'discreet lettering' he would use to advertise his establishment. The committee, mindful of its European experience, ordered two marble columns for the entrance hall with marble pilasters and dado and alabaster slabs for the walls. Acting on the principle that one certain way to make people look at a building was to put a clock on it the board ordered an elaborate timepiece which it was proposed to mount in a massive stone tower.

Hamilton Beattie died in 1898 and the work was carried on by his brother George. The hotel took four years to build and cost

£559,055. The finished building differed only in detail from the original design. The shops and offices on the ground floor were dispensed with and the alabaster and marble concoction gave way to a more functional entrance hall. When the fabric was complete the committee devoted its energies to fitting out the interior of the building in lavish style. Mr Towle of the Midland, the doyen of railway hoteliers, was employed to advise the committee. Everything for the hotel was of the best. Professor Barr of Glasgow University was commissioned 'to design, specify, schedule and superintend the erection of the whole apparatus, fixtures and fittings required for the supply and distribution of electrical energy for all purposes'. The canny NB instructed the professor to devise the circuits in such a way that only one light at a time would go on in the bedrooms no matter how many switches were pressed.

At almost every meeting of the committee salesmen paraded wares ranging from soap to champagne. Curtains, carpets and samples of linen were put on display along with designs for maid's dresses and special luggage labels for the guests. A Mr Waddell offered to fit out darkrooms for amateur photographers. Among the items purchased were 37,650 cigars, two dozen foot baths, two dozen hip baths, 75 bath thermometers, 70 vines, 70 clematis and the associated trellis work. Welcome visitors to the committee meetings were the wine merchants intent on stocking the hotel cellars. George Wieland himself selected the whiskies, brandies, Hocks and Moselles—a task for which he was eminently fitted by taste and temperament. Wieland had begun the task of building up the cellars as early as October 1900 when he purchased 12 gross casks of 1895 vintage brandy at 7s 6d per gallon. When samples of seven brands of proprietary whiskies had been proferred and tasted at one committee meeting the comment minuted at the end of the day was 'consideration thereof continued'. Wieland decided that the hotel must serve a special blend of NB whisky and four blending vats, two of 800gal capacity and two of 400gal were set up in the basement. The resulting liquors were dispensed at 6d and 9d per glass. The North British Hotel opened its doors on 15 October 1902, more than a year before the rival Caledonian hotel was in a position to accept guests.

The NB was proud of its new hotel and rightly so for it was one of the most impressive buildings in Edinburgh. At last the NB had an architectural showpiece in the capital. Trade was brisk enough to keep the two reception desks busy, keys being shot from one desk to the other through a Lampson pneumatic chute. But it was not long before the NB ran into the realities of hotel keeping. 'We are astonished,' reported the hotel committee, 'at the number of accounts incurred by persons who left the hotel without paying their bills.' At one meeting the ethics of placing an advertisement for the hotel in *The Highlands by Road* was debated. At another meeting a discussion on a weighty problem produced the following minute: 'The committee approved of the name on the door of the present ladies' lavatory on the ground floor being altered so as to convert it into a lavatory for gentlemen'. The NB had bad luck with its lavatories. On the day that the company's hotel in Glasgow was reopened after its rebuilding it was found that the lavatory doors had no bolts and a member of the staff was sent out to buy 100 bolts and sockets at 10d each.

CHAPTER 9

Locomotive Matters 1903–1923

REORGANISATION

With the departure of Matthew Holmes from the scene in 1903 there was no doubt as to who was the key figure at Cowlairs—Robert Chalmers. As chief draughtsman and locomotive superintendent he had served the company continuously for 28 years. His friend, former associate and near contemporary Dugald Drummond was in command at Eastleigh and had nine vigorous years ahead of him as locomotive superintendent of the LSWR. It was logical to think that Chalmers would slip into the vacant NB chair. But that was not to be. The appointment went to the new boy at Cowlairs, William Paton Reid.

In 1903 the NB was firmly controlled by the cabal that had dimissed Conacher. George Wieland was chairman, and his make-do-and-mend policy was reflected in the locomotive department. He would rather patch up an old engine than build a new one. In the vital opening years of the century when many railways were entering a new locomotive era with the building of 4-6-0s and Atlantics Cowlairs was in the doldrums. To complicate matters Reid was not completely master of his own house. He was a probationer, his appointment being for six months only. He did not have the foreign line passes and other perquisites that went with senior appointments. At the end of his first six months his appointment was continued for a further six months on a temporary basis, and it was not until 2 June 1904 that he was permanently appointed.

In the first three years of Reid's reign only one new design came from Cowlairs. It had been initiated by Holmes although the completed drawings were not submitted until 11 February 1904. The engine was a close-coupled 0-6-0 dock tank with 15in by 22in outside cylinders, 3ft 9in driving wheels and a boiler pressure of 130psi. Six were completed at Cowlairs between December 1904 and January 1905. Reid had estimated their cost at £1,500 each; the actual cost was £1,771 3s 4d. Six more engines were put in hand in January 1905 and by 1912 the class numbered 35, all of which had been built at Cowlairs.

There was an echo of Drummond at Cowlairs only a few weeks after Reid took office. One of the locomotives on show at the Glasgow exhibition of 1901 had been a T9 4-4-0 of the LSWR fitted with the designer's patent water tube boiler. The Drummond boiler was the subject of comment in the technical press and the performance of engines fitted with it was watched with interest by railway managements. On 30 July 1903 the general manager of the NB submitted a plan and specification of the Drummond boiler 'fitted with cross water tubes, casings and doors', explaining to the board that the boiler was said to result in a saving of fuel. He was authorised to obtain tenders for the boiler from the North British Locomotive Co, Kitson & Co, the Yorkshire Engine Company, and Robert Stephenson & Co Ltd. At the same time Reid was told to make enquiries about the reported efficiency of the boiler. The tenders and Reid's report were available at the locomotive committee meeting of 27 August. Reid's report was inconclusive, and the general manager was instructed to delay purchase until the efficiency of the boilers had been established. That was the nearest the NB came to employing Drummond water tube boilers.

With the death of Wieland in April 1905 the grip of the ruling clique was loosened. The new chairman, the Earl of Dalkeith, knew that all was not well in the locomotive department and he placed in charge of the locomotive committee a director who was singularly fitted for the post. He was Dr John Inglis whom we have encountered already in this narrative as head of the shipbuilding and engineering firm of A. & J. Inglis. The change in the fortunes of the department was dramatic.

So chaotic had things become that no one at Cowlairs could say with certainty how many engines the company owned, or in what condition they were in. Inglis ordered a census to be taken of locomotives and rolling stock. The task occupied five months and the result disclosed that there were 847 engines on the active list and 80 on the duplicate list. There were 664 tenders on the books but only 647 could be found. Inglis ordered another census of rolling stock and when this failed to produce the missing tenders he concluded that the company records were wrong. Investigations revealed that many years previously when 17 tender engines had been replaced with tank engines the books had not been altered. The records listed 3,760 carriages but the census accounted for only 3,492. A second count located most of the missing vehicles, but the following had vanished without trace:

No	Description	Year built	Value
806	3rd class	1884	£452 11s 4d
530	Brake 3rd	1872	£275 15s 11d
576	Brake 3rd	1872	£275 15s 11d
130	Passenger van	1872	£229 15s 11d
45	Carriage truck	1868	£55 17s 0d

The first four vehicles were written off and the carriage truck was replaced from revenue.

During the census 44 engines were found to be unfit for the work on which they were engaged. Inglis devised a system of regular inspection which ensured that the mechanical condition of all old engines would be known. Each half year Reid was required to furnish a certificate for every engine over 35 years old and every boiler 25 years old.

THE ATLANTICS

The construction of new passenger locomotives had barely kept pace with the increase in traffic. The Holmes engines had been built in small batches and their total number was insufficient to cope with the heavy summer demands for power. Too much reliance had to be placed on older engines and on rebuilds. Inglis held that a rebuild was no match for a new engine and that money was being squandered on a rebuilding programme. He insisted that only a bold policy of new construction would retrieve the company's fortunes and, not without difficulty, he brought the board round to his way of thinking.

In the autumn of 1905 Cowlairs began casting about for ideas for a new engine. The NB liked what was currently happening on the Midland and the first design produced was for a Smith compound that was openly referred to as 'the Midland express engine'. The construction of 14 such engines was authorised, but the decision was cancelled a fortnight later. Inglis visited Crewe and Eastleigh in search of ideas while Jackson sought inspiration from the North Eastern. Inglis meanwhile got information on the

Port Carlisle possesses a railway, perforce –
Where the sole locomotive's a commonplace horse,
And in all merry England there's surely none other
Train system with so little danger or bother, –
So here's to the creature that's useful and handy,
Success and renown still attend "the old Dandy".

Page 155:
Horse Power on the NB: (above) *The Port Carlisle Dandy;* (below) *The NBR coach which operated between Musselburgh and Levenhall in connection with the trains*

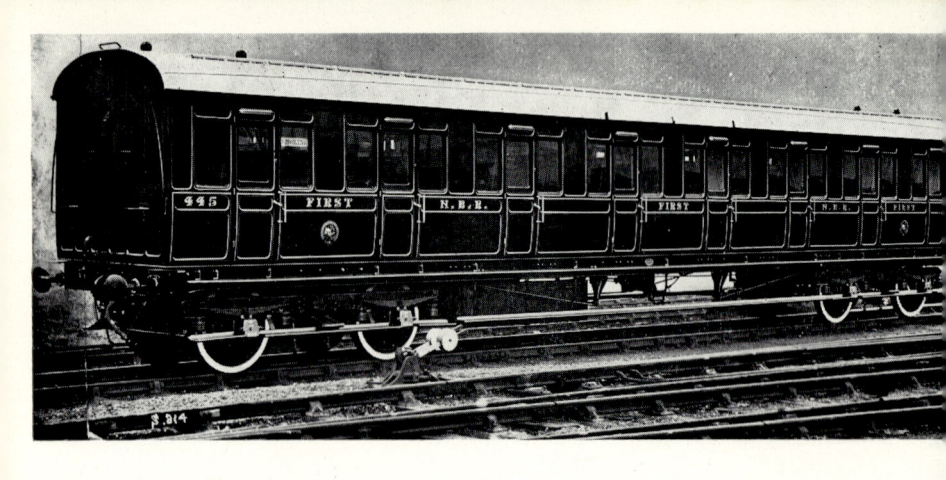

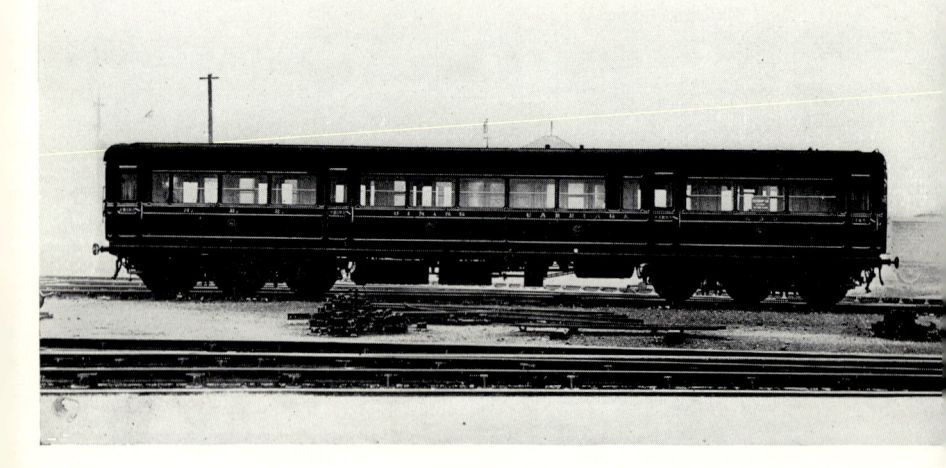

Page 156:
Carriages: (top) *First class compartment carriage;* (centre) *West Highland Railway first class saloon;* (bottom) *12-wheeled composite dining carriage*

financing of a locomotive building programme from J. F. McIntosh of the Caledonian.

The design eventually accepted was for a very large Atlantic and 14 of these engines were built at the Hyde Park works of the North British Locomotive Company in 1906. They were massive, impressive machines. Their huge boilers and the necessarily squat mountings gave them a hunched appearance—an appearance of power. Engine and tender weighed 119ton 16cwt. The outside cylinders were 20in by 28in, the driving wheels were 6ft 9in. The boiler pressure was 190psi. The tender carried 7 tons of coal and 4,240gal of water. Features new to the NB were the steam reverser, drop grate, Belpaire firebox and the large, double-windowed cab.

There has been much speculation about the origin of the Atlantic design. 'Pure Great Central' is the epithet most commonly applied to it, one account going so far as to say that NBL, which had just completed a batch of GC Atlantics, used the GC drawings as a basis of the NB design. The similarity of the NB to the GC Atlantic is obvious, but there is no official record of the GC locomotive department having been consulted by Cowlairs. There is clear documentary evidence that the drawings were prepared at Cowlairs and that NBL had no hand in the design. It is, however, known that Robinson of the GC was a close personal friend of the Chalmers family. When Robinson and Robert and Walter Chalmers met the talk would be of locomotives, and it is reasonable to assume that the Chalmers father and son team would be influenced by first hand information about Atlantic design and performance imparted by the locomotive superintendent of the GC. That private contact might well explain the apparent GC influence in NB design. In 1908 when Cowlairs produced an 0-8-0 design the result was surprisingly like a GC 0-8-0 (LNER Q4). See page 174.

The Atlantics were intended to eliminate expensive double-heading on the Waverley route and on the Edinburgh–Aberdeen line, but from the start they ran into trouble. The engines were delivered late and the peak of the 1906 summer traffic was over before they came into service. There was not a turntable on the system that could accommodate them, and that led to operational difficulties. The engines did not reach Aberdeen at all in the first six months of their career.

On the very first Sunday on which an Atlantic was available the engine was sent to the Arbroath–Montrose section of the Aberdeen route for permanent way tests. James Bell, the civil engineer, concluded that all the bridges in the section would have to be strengthened or rebuilt to make them safe for the Atlantics. Bell was suspicious of the Atlantics, his feeling towards them perhaps being influenced by the fact that he had not been shown the drawings. When his district inspectors began to report finding broken rails and spread track in the wake of Atlantic-hauled trains a classic civil engineer versus locomotive superintendent confrontation flared up. Bell demanded the withdrawal of the engines from the Waverley route and the imposition of a top speed limit of 55mph over the whole system, and the board yielded to his demands. When Cowlairs failed to solve the problem of the rough-riding engines Ivatt was called in as a consultant, and when his recommendations were rejected by the board Vincent Raven was consulted. The NE assistant locomotive superintendent conducted a series of tests with the NB Atlantics including a trial run with one of the class on an East Coast express from Edinburgh to Newcastle and back using the NE dynamometer car. He suggested certain alterations, none of them major, and some were put into effect by the NB board.

The travail of the Atlantics lasted for nearly two years. Then the storm in Mr Bell's cup suddenly subsided. David Deuchars, the man whose job it was to run the trains on time, found that the engines were doing good work. Indeed, he was of the opinion that he could do with more Atlantics and he told the board so. Before a decision was taken the board sponsored comparative tests between an Atlantic and Midland and North Eastern compounds on the Waverley route, and between an Atlantic and an LNWR Experiment Class over Shap. The NB directors saw nothing in the results of these tests to convince them that their faith in the Atlantics was misplaced. Six engines were added to the class in 1911 and a further two in 1921. They proved to be splendid performers, especially after they were superheated, and for many years after the NB had ceased to exist as a separate company they hauled the heaviest trains over some of the most difficult routes in the country.

In his pursuance of his dictum of 'more power for a modern train' Dr Inglis induced the company to build goods engines which would do for the increasingly heavier goods trains what the

Atlantics were expected to do for the passenger trains. Two classes were turned out in 1906. The first design was for a powerful 0-6-0 and 10 of the class were built by the North British Locomotive Co and delivered just before the first of the Atlantics, two more coming from Cowlairs before the end of the year. These engines weighed 66ton 15cwt. They had 18½in by 26in cylinders, 5ft driving wheels, and boiler pressure of 180psi. The engines remained the standard goods class until the introduction of the first superheated goods in 1913. A total of 78 was built, 54 being fitted with the Westinghouse brake for passenger working.

The other 1906 goods type was the 4-4-0 Intermediate Class. This engine, intended for the light, fast fish trains from Aberdeen, proved in practice to be an excellent mixed traffic engine. It worked trains of all types except the heaviest goods and passenger traffic. The cylinders were 19in by 26in, the driving wheels 6ft and the boiler pressure 160psi. Twelve of the class were built at Cowlairs in 1906 although the last four did not enter traffic until January 1907.

RETRENCHMENT

As a result of the Inglis policy the NB by the end of 1906 was the happy owner of 14 brand new express engines and 24 goods engines of unprecedented power and versatility. The engines alone cost £135,350 and there was a parallel output of new passenger and goods rolling stock. The adventurous programme precipitated one of the NB's recurring financial crises. By March 1907 the company was scouting round to raise short term loans to tide it over the bad patch. As on previous occasions customers of the company rallied to its assistance. J. & P. Coats, the thread spinners, gave £150,000 at ½ per cent less than Bank of England rate, and the Tharsis Sulphur & Copper Co gave £350,000 on the same terms. Dr Inglis contributed £30,000.

In that same month of March drastic economies were introduced. Jackson was instructed 'to devote his primary attention and best energies during the remaining period of the current half-year to a detailed investigation of the expenditure in the locomotive, engineers and traffic departments'. When the relevant half-yearly report showed ever-climbing costs Jackson was told in the plainest terms that his officers had failed to appreciate the gravity of the situation or take adequate steps to meet it. He was ordered to impress on departmental chiefs 'the extreme necessity for the strictest economy in the interest of the company and the need for a further and substantial curtailment of services'.

The board recognised that its troubles were partly due to the unending struggle to keep up with the Caley. The Caledonian, equally conscious of the wastefulness of competitive traffic, readily agreed to the formation of a joint committee

> for the purpose of restricting competition, of reducing the train service, and otherwise lessening the expenditure of the companies, with the special instruction that the board desire that the reduction in the train service and expenditure should be considered from the point of view of the benefit of both companies and on the lines of what might reasonably be expected to follow a complete amalgamation of the companies.

On the NB 107 trains, ranging from the prestige, Atlantic-hauled Edinburgh–Aberdeen expresses to Edinburgh suburbans were deleted from the timetable. Sunday services were withdrawn in most areas. Stations were closed. The Cowlairs working week was cut from the normal $5\frac{1}{2}$ days to 4 days and a special working committee was set up to find ways of economising in the locomotive department.

The bugbear was light engine mileage. In the current half year passenger light engine movements accounted for 356,300 miles, which was 8 per cent of the total passenger mileage. A special check made over a four-week period showed that light engine mileage was 42,370. The cost in wages, coal and engine and track wear was prodigious. Three-quarters of the total light engine mileage resulted from unbalanced ordinary train workings, and some curious examples came to light as a result of the investigations. For instance 384 miles per month were incurred in running an empty train from Buchlyvie to Stirling to satisfy a trader whose annual traffic amounted to only £610. Again on Mondays the 9.2 am arrival at Glasgow Queen Street from Edinburgh was preceded by a relief express due at 8.50, although the traffic offered justified only one train. The relief train had been put on as the result of a memorial presented by passengers who insisted that they had to reach Glasgow before 9 o'clock.

Light engine mileage between Eastfield shed and Queen Street station, a distance of two miles, accounted for 20,300 miles in the four-week period. The position had been aggravated by the discontinuance of rope haulage on the incline. Engines which formerly had been detached at Cowlairs now took their trains down the incline to Queen Street. Every engine, including tank engines, had to go back up the incline to Eastfield to be turned. The board suggested that a turntable and water column be provided at Queen Street. That, however, would have meant the removal of two roads from an already inadequate goods station, and the matter was dropped when the goods manager protested. The problem remained with the NB and its successors until the arrival of DMUs in the 1950s.

Considerable light engine mileage was incurred by engines which had doubled-headed trains over part of a route returning to base. There was for example much traffic in light engines between Falahill and St Margarets and Whitrope and Hawick. The investigating committee found that some trains were being double-headed when the load was within the limit prescribed for one engine, and drivers were urged to seek assistance only when absolutely necessary. Engines returning to shed from outer termini which did have locomotive sheds accounted for additional light engine mileage. For instance, the engine which worked the Craigendoran–Arrochar service at the south end of the West Highland Railway had to run light from Helensburgh to Arrochar to work the first up train in the morning, and return light from Arrochar at the end of the day. This light engine mileage was eliminated by providing an engine pit at Arrochar and stabling the engine in the open at night.

The halt in spending resulted in an interesting building programme for 1908 being cancelled. The proposed 0-8-0 mineral engine was not proceeded with, nor were proposals for a large 4-6-0 for the Waverley route and a smaller engine of the same wheel arrangement for the West Highland.

The lull in building was short-lived. On 15 October 1908 Dr Inglis presided over a committee which met to consider a new engine programme. The pressing need was for a sound, bread-and-butter 4-4-0 more powerful than the existing engines of the type. Again, the company was facing increasing competition from rapidly expanding electric tram networks, and a passenger tank capable of fast running on outer suburban services was urgently required. And the abandonment of Cowlairs rope incline meant that a suitable banking engine was required.

The 'new engine' committee recommended the construction of 100 engines over a four-year period at an estimated cost of £286,220. One of the directors, Mr Howard, proposed that none of the engines be built at Cowlairs and that, indeed, all new engines should be supplied by private builders. Howard's view was that if Cowlairs concentrated on repairs, and left new construction to outside firms, a great deal of money would be saved. The matter was discussed at several successive meetings of the board. On 17 December 1908 the directors decided that in future only six new engines would be built at Cowlairs each half year 'and that otherwise no new work should be undertaken at Cowlairs except such as will enable full advantage to be taken of the men and tools there'. The decision was not implemented largely because it was found that Cowlairs could build engines cheaper than outside contractors.

A STRIDE FORWARD

Four new classes appeared in 1909. Between July and September the North British Locomotive Co delivered six of the large new passenger 4-4-0s. They weighed 105ton 16cwt with tender, had 19in by 26in cylinders and 6ft 6in driving wheels. The boiler pressure was 190psi and the tractive effort 18,434lb. One engine was named *Sir Walter Scott* and the other five were given colourful, romantic names of characters in Scott's Waverley novels. The engines took up service on the Waverley and Edinburgh–Perth routes.

While NBL was building the Scott Class Cowlairs had a 6ft version of the engine in hand. In most respects these engines—the Intermediate Class—were similar to the Scotts. The main differences, apart from the driving wheel diameter, were the boiler pressure which was 180psi, and the tractive effort which was 19,800. The engines did not carry names. Twelve Intermediates were delivered between October 1909 and January 1910.

Between April and June 1910 a Scott and an Intermediate took part in exhaustive comparative trials between Edinburgh and Perth and, after studying the subsequent report, the board authorised the construction of six additional Scotts. NBL was offered the contract at not more than £3,000 per engine, but the company refused to build them at that price. Cowlairs built the engines within the stipulated price. This episode marked the beginning of a break in the NB's 45-year continuous relationship with the Glasgow builders. Henceforward tenders from England were taken seriously.

The board seemed to have lingering doubts about the building of a 4-6-0, for an Intermediate was tested against a Highland Railway Castle Class 4-6-0 between Blair Atholl and Dalwhinnie on the Highland line and between Perth and Kinross Junction. The tests convinced the directors of the wisdom of pursuing their 4-4-0 policy.

The 12 0-4-4 passenger tanks delivered by NBL in September 1909 resembled the Holmes tanks, but they had larger boilers. The driving wheels were 6ft 6in, the cylinders 18in by 26in. The NBL-built 0-6-2 tanks had 18in by 26in cylinders and 4ft 6in driving wheels. They were fitted with a slip coupling operated from the cab by a rope and pulley arrangement, and spent their working lives banking trains on Cowlairs incline.

With the completion of the 1909 programme the value of the locomotive stock stood at £2,153,604 19s 7d. The year was a landmark in NB locomotive history. That the new classes gave satisfaction was shown by the fact that the company did not deviate from the basic designs in future building. The 0-6-2 tank eventually formed a class 114-strong and were to be seen on shunting and mineral duties all over the sytem. They were a familiar sight in Fife working coal trains in pairs.

In 1911 Cowlairs produced a design for a 4-4-2 passenger tank and an order for 30 was placed with the Yorkshire Engine Co, the first being delivered in December. The class had the usual 18in by 26in cylinders, 5ft 9in driving wheels and boiler pressure of 175psi. They were the first NB tanks to be dual fitted with vacuum as well as Westinghouse brake equipment. At first they were put on the semi-fast trains between Edinburgh and Glasgow via Bathgate but because of their small tank capacity (1,900gal) they were soon withdrawn from that service. They did their best work between Glasgow and the Clyde coast and Loch Lomond. The drivers complained that they were forced to drive in a standing position because the tanks extended back into the cab at full height.

The last of the engines ordered or begun in 1909 were nearing completion when the company embarked on its first experiment in superheating. On 9 February 1911 Schmidt superheaters were ordered for two Scotts then under construction, No 400 *The Dugal*

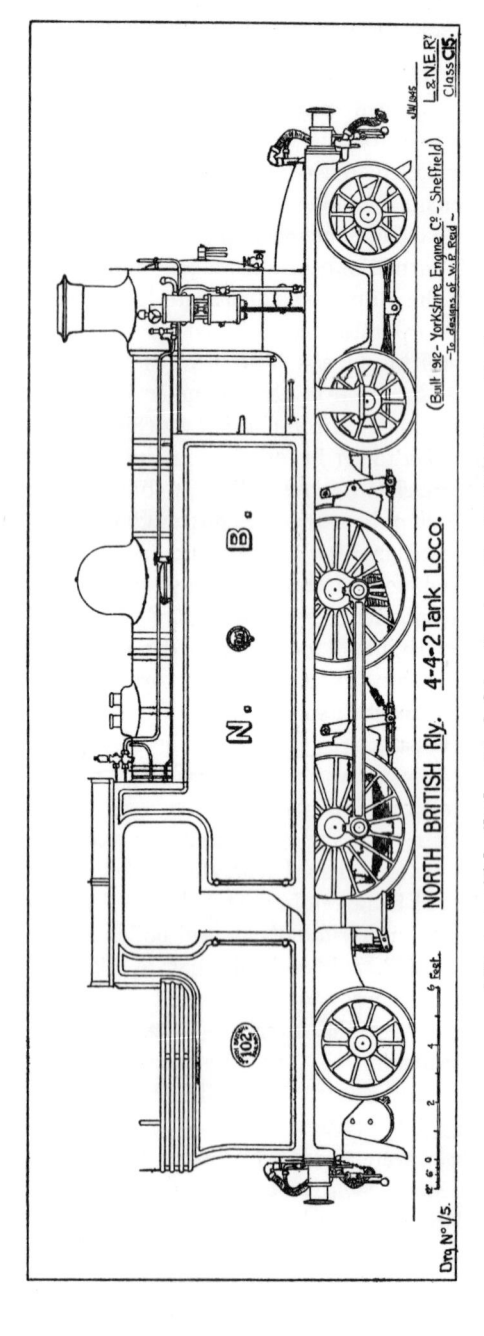

NB 4-4-2T built by Yorkshire Engine Co (LNER Class C15)

Cratur and No 303 *Hal O' the Wynd*. A month later, on 9 March, an agreement was signed with the New Superheater Co Ltd for the supply of fittings for the test of a Phoenix superheater. The apparatus was installed in No 887 *Redgauntlet,* the engine being fitted with an extended smokebox to receive it. On 8 August 1912 it was reported that 'agreement with the New Superheater Company Limited has turned out unsatisfactorily'. Meanwhile tests had been made with the Robinson superheater as a result of which 'the Superheater Corporation Ltd offered to grant a licence to the North British to fit Robinson superheaters to engines built or caused to be built by them to 21 December 1915 at a royalty of £40 each on condition that the company fit no other superheater and with a reduction to £35 each if 40 engines are fitted'.

The superheater trials on the NB as on other railways proved highly successful and in 1913 the board confidently ordered a batch of superheated Scotts and a batch of superheated Intermediates. These engines were ordered as Intermediates and referred to in official correspondence as such but by virtue of being given the names of West Highland glens they became known as the Glen Class. They proved to be excellent engines for the West Highland line, although they worked successfully all over the system.

The next logical step was the designing of a powerful superheated goods engine. This was the S Class 0-6-0, the first of which was completed at Cowlairs in 1914. It had 5ft driving wheels, a boiler pressure of 165psi and a tractive effort of 25,211lb. The engines were put on long distance goods, notably Cadder to Aberdeen and Carlisle to Dundee.

Some of the new superheated engines had been delivered and building of others was in full swing when, on 4 August 1914, World War I broke out. The NB had a foretaste of what was to come when, on 16 August, 70 troop trains passed through Waverley station. In the first four months of 1914 the NB and NE had exchanged 79,866 wagons. In the first four months of 1918, the last year of the war, 149,546 wagons were exchanged. Special Welsh coal trains brought 1,290,000 tons to the naval base at Rosyth. The wartime traffic placed an unprecedented strain on the locomotive department.

The first trouble came with the loss of staff to the armed forces. The Government had agreed that railwaymen would not be recruited, but that did not prevent them from resigning their rail-

NB Class S 0–6–0 (LNER Class J37)

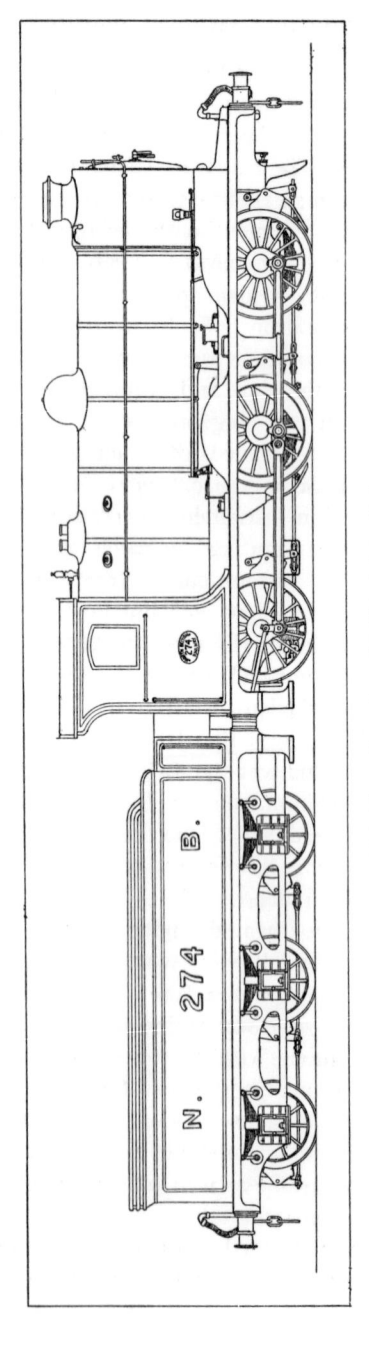

way jobs and joining up. In all such cases Jackson personally took steps to retrieve the men from the army and reinstate them on the railway. Sometimes the reinstated man ran away again and rejoined the army. On 4 February 1915 Jackson informed Scottish Command, 'I am informed that George Guild again left this company's service on 27th ultimo after working one day's notice. It is thought that he left to endeavour to join the army. Will you kindly let me hear from you on the subject when you are in a position to write me'.

Sometimes the army authorities professed to know nothing about the man inquired of, but army intransigence could not protect the 'escapee' from the long arm of W. F. Jackson. On one occasion when the army pleaded ignorance Jackson informed the Commander in Chief, Scottish Command, 'I may state that the man enlisted at Lochiel's Cameron Recruiting Office, George Square, Glasgow. The recruiting sergeant (Sgt McKay, Seaforth Highlanders) told him he did not care whether he (Donald McKay) was a railwayman or not; there was also present a captain of the same regiment'. Jackson got his man. Further he demanded that the recruiting staff be punished, and duly received the reply, 'The sergeant mentioned has been dealt with. The officer mentioned has not been traced'.

When the army seemed to be getting the better of him Jackson curtly informed the Commander in Chief, 'We are now in the position that we must either get back the men who have enlisted without permission or we will be compelled to reduce the service and probably not be in a position to give the Government the service they may require in an emergency that may arise'.

The building programme was continued, indeed was accelerated throughout the war years to meet the inordinate demands of the period. Before the Armistice was signed 54 superheated goods had been added to stock, along with 12 0-6-0 tanks, 10 Scotts and 15 of a superheated version of the 4-4-2 tank. New building barely kept pace with traffic demands. As the war dragged on passenger trains were slashed from the timetable to release engines for goods traffic. At one point the operating superintendent was allocated a meagre supply of coal and told to plan his passenger service round it. The company suffered from the lack of mineral engines powerful enough to take the heaviest coal trains—the S Class was a disappointment in this respect—and the consequent double-heading made inroads into engine power. In 1917 an NE 0-8-0 was tried on Glenfarg bank but it was 'resolved that no reason had been shown for building eight-coupled engines'.

The NB possessed many hundreds of old dumb-buffered wagons which before the war it had been getting rid of to scrap merchants for £8 each. Before the war was half way through the same wagons were fetching £40 from collieries and factory owners with private sidings and from the Ministry of Munitions. Two batches went to Greece. It was therefore with a vision of profit to come that on 31 August 1917 the general manager read a letter from the War Department from which he understood the Government intended to purchase 25 18½in goods for service in France.

Within a week the locomotive committee met to discuss this apparent windfall and decided that the proceeds of the sale plus the grant obtainable from the Government to finance the purchase of new stock needed for wartime traffic would provide enough cash for 34 new S Class locomotives. Jackson was soon closeted with Hugh Reid (of the NBL) making arrangements for construction of the engines. Reid thought he could complete the order by 31 December 1918 provided that Jackson could obtain a 'No 2 Priority'. There was an acute shortage of copper at the time but the builder undertook to provide as many copper fireboxes as possible and make the remainder of steel or Yorkshire iron.

A bonus of 34 S Class for 25 ageing 18½in goods was too good to be true. The Government was, in fact, requisitioning the engines, not offering cash for them. In the event the NB got its S Class but not through the free gift scheme which the board had envisaged.

LOCOMOTIVE FAMINE

The war left the NB devitalised; the struggle had been too much for it. Scores of old engines which in the ordinary course would have been scrapped, but had been kept going somehow, breathed their last in the first months of peace. Arrears of maintenance even on the newest stock got out of hand. Not since the bad old days of the 1850s had the locomotive department been in such dire straits. Wartime controls were still in force when on 20 December 1919 James Calder (who had succeeded Jackson as general manager) wrote to Sir Herbert Walker of the Railway Executive Committee:

I regret being under the necessity of reverting to the subject, but we are in such straits for engine power at the present time that I have no alternative but to make a representation to you in the matter. I may say that on Saturday last there was no less than 22·05 per cent of our locomotives on the non-effective list, while a large number of our engines which are in service should really be in the workshops undergoing repair.

So acute was the situation that between 12 October and 14 December the company had to run 685 Sunday specials simply because engines were not available on weekdays.

The desperation of railway managements for engine power was highlighted by a fracas that broke out between the NB and the Highland over the return of two engines which the Highland had borrowed during the war. When the NB demanded the return of the engines the Highland claimed that its service would collapse if it complied with the demand. A letter from William Park of the Highland to Calder on 9 September 1919 strikingly illuminates the contemporary scene:

I have received your letter of 6th inst. and am sorry I am unable to state precisely when we will be in a position to hand over the two North British engines which are at present serving on the Highland Railway to your locomotive superintendent at Perth.

As you are aware the position of this company in the matter of Government traffic is altogether exceptional and while we appreciate your present difficulty and are very desirous of rendering every help in our power the fact is that if we were to send your engines home the goods and mineral traffic on the line would very soon get into a state of chaos. I have been pressing Sir Herbert Walker to have a number of engines from one or more of the other railways sent to us in order to release yours, and his reply is to the effect that he will endeavour to get us an early allocation of engines from the Government pool if we desire it. The W.D. engines are altogether unfit for service on the Highland Railway and Sir Herbert's offer of engines from the Government pool is, therefore, of no use. Before we can release the NB engines it is essential that the Railway Executive Committee should furnish us with substitutes or alternatively agree to free and release the Highland Railway Company of the responsibility for traffic delays, etc.

It seems to me that engines and other rolling stock on the British railways should be allocated among the various companies according to their needs without regard to ownership.

Calder was unimpressed by Park's plea. He replied pre-emptorily, 'As we are urgently in need of the engines in question I have written to the Railway Executive Committee stating the attitude you have taken up and asking that you be instructed to hand over immediately the engines to this company.' Two days later Calder was again writing to Park, 'I am obliged by your letter of 10th inst. and note that the two NBR engines proved most useful to your company. The engines duly arrived at our Cowlairs depot.'

The company tried to cope with the situation by establishing a nightshift at Cowlairs but the tradesmen were handicapped by old run-down machinery, some of which had been in use since E & G Railway days. Engines were sent for repair to any outside contractor who would take them. Among the firms which accepted NB engines were W. G. Armstrong Whitworth, Messrs Vickers, J. F. Wake of Darlington and NBL. But the contractors were inundated with orders from railway companies and even the biggest firms could take only a few engines at a time. In January 1920 the board was grateful to receive the following letter from Vickers:

> I have pleasure in informing you that we are now in a position to receive a few more of your locomotives for repair and shall be glad if you can make arrangements to send us a further 6. It is not necessary to send all these locomotives at one time; in fact it would be preferable to send them along in twos at intervals convenient to yourselves.

Private locomotive users along the line were also in difficulties over locomotive failures and firms asked the NB to repair their locomotives or provide replacements for engines that were beyond repair. When lending an engine to Bo'ness Distillery in January 1920 Calder warned the firm, 'The engine is in disrepair and may require to be withdrawn within a week'. Wagons too were in short supply, and complaints from traders were numerous. On 18 December 1919 the Dykehead Ganister & Firebrick Company complained that its position had become intolerable with only three or four empties being supplied daily when it needed a minimum of 10 to carry on its business. Messrs Stern & Co of Bonnybridge wired, 'Works stopped for want of empties. Only 15 received during last 3 days'.

The locomotive shortage was aggravated by an acute shortage of coal. The average monthly delivery to the NB fell from 18,954 tons in 1913 to 11,207 tons in 1919, and a high proportion of the coal supplied was of a quality that would not have been accepted before the war. Complaints to the Coal Commissioner, the wartime functionary who still regulated supply, as often as not met with no reply. In December 1919 the NB presented the Commissioner with a formidable list of 33 collieries which had supplied bad coal. The locomotive department claimed that this coal had resulted in no fewer than 124 engine failures during October and November.

By mid-December stocks had dwindled well below safety level, and with the prospect of a week's closure of the Scottish pits over the New Year holidays, Hugh Inglis of the locomotive department was sent to England to search for coal. But the English railways were no better off than the NB and they were faced with a backlog of deliveries following the Christmas holidays. Calder made an urgent appeal to the Edinburgh office of the Coal Control and was given authority to requisition all loaded coal wagons lying in colliery sidings on the system and consigned to works known to be closed for the holidays.

In January 1920 the Ministry of Transport, fearing trouble in the mines, ordered all railway companies to raise their stocks of locomotive coal to the equivalent of six weeks supply. For the NB this meant 98,400 tons. Existing stocks totalled 42,105 tons, and the figure was dropping alarmingly. When Calder inquired of the Coal Controller what steps he should take to meet the requirements of the Ministry of Transport he got no reply. Two telegrams likewise produced neither reply nor acknowledgment. The company remained enmeshed in red tape until the labour situation looked really ugly, when the Government authorised the NB to seize any coal train on the system irrespective of to whom it was consigned.

Hurried experiments were made with oil fuel but these were no more successful on the NB than they were on other systems. The Scarab apparatus fitted on No 859 showed some promise, but all other oil fuel experiments had been abandoned by August 1921. Three months later the locomotive department intimated that No 859 was being refitted for coal burning adding, 'This will permit two incline engines, badly in need of general overhaul, being sent into shops.'

To deal with the complex postwar problems an aptly-named congestion committee was convened. One of its achievements was the deliberate diversion of goods traffic from railway to road. The NB hired a fleet of 20 ex-army trucks from the government with which it set up business as a road haulier.

W. P. Reid retired on 31 December 1919 and the directors took the opportunity to reorganise his department. Calder informed the secretary of the Railway Clearing House of the change:

> The directors have resolved that the work which has hitherto come under the control of the locomotive department shall, as from 1 January 1920 be carried on by two separate departments, and have made the following appointments which will operate from that day. Mr Walter Chalmers to be chief mechanical engineer and Mr J. P. Grassick to be locomotive running superintendent (indoor and outdoor).

A minute of 8 January 1920 revealed what action was taken to symbolise the change: 'Proposed to close up the door from the office in question into the drawing office and provide a new door between the office and the existing telegraph office'.

Gradually the locomotive department got the better of its problems. Long-cancelled prestige trains re-appeared in the timetable and new engines were built to haul them. Superheating of the older engines, which had been restricted during the war, was accelerated. In the three years that remained to the NB a vigorous programme of new building was pursued. In 1920 five Scotts and 12 Glens were built and in 1921 two new Atlantics, No 509 *Duke of Rothesay* and No 510 *The Lord Provost*, and six 4-4-2 tanks appeared. Goods engines added to stock in 1920 were 12 S Class and a further 10 0-6-2 tanks. In 1921 19 S Class were built bringing the total up to 104.

The S Class were versatile performers, but their failure to handle the heaviest Dunfermline–Aberdeen coal trains single-handed irked the board. Their maximum load on the run was 27. With trains exceeding that number of wagons pilot assistance was required from Townhill to Crossgates, Thornton to Lochmuir and Leuchars to Wormit, and the train had to be double-headed beyond Dundee. All in all it was a cumbersome and expensive operation. A special board meeting resolved 'that the steam pressure of the big goods engines working the Aberdeen coal traffic be increased to 180 pounds and the full load be increased by 5 wagons, no new pilot assistance being given except from Dundee to Camperdown Junction'. A month later the board, taking a more realistic view, conceded that the coal trains could be double-headed as required as far as Kinnaber Junction, but not beyond that point. Double-headed trains exceeding 30 wagons were divided at Kinnaber and run over the Caledonian as two trains.

THE QUEST FOR AN EIGHT-COUPLED ENGINE

With most of its post-war worries overcome the company sought to satisfy its long-felt need for a powerful mineral engine. There was in Cowlairs drawing office a general arrangement drawing No 2662 dated 16 May 1908 showing Reid's design for a large 0-8-0 tender engine. It used the Atlantic boiler and its outside cylinders were 19½in by 26in. The proposed engine's cab, like that of the Atlantic, had two windows on each side. Its estimated weight was 70 tons. It would have been an impressive and powerful engine, but Cowlairs showed no inclination to put the design into production.

Instead, Maj Stemp, traffic superintendent, in 1920 looked round to see what other companies had to offer in the way of eight-coupled engines, and he was particularly attracted by the performance of the GWR 'E Group' 2-8-0s on the heavy gradients in the West of England. The NB's most powerful goods engine had to be double-headed when its load reached 28 wagons. From charts supplied by his GWR opposite number, Mr Nicholls, Stemp saw that the GWR 2-8-0 regularly took 28 loaded wagons over the 9 miles 22 chains between Lostwithiel and Doublebois, where the ruling gradient was 1 in 58, in 29 minutes. The same class hauled Welsh coal trains of 38 wagons over 1 in 90 gradients with regularity and apparent ease. Stemp was convinced that this was the engine for the NB.

The company opened negotiations with the GWR on 14 December 1920. At first it seemed that there would be difficulty in obtaining a route between the engine's home territory and the Border because of gauge problems, but the difficulty was quickly overcome and on 19 December Charles Aldington, general manager of the GWR, informed Calder that he had given instructions for 2-8-0 No 2846 to be prepared for the journey to Scotland. He wrote again on 1 January 1921 to say that Churchward himself would accompany the engine.

The test was fixed for 12 January, the location being the 6 miles 53 chains between Bridge of Earn and Glenfarg where the NE

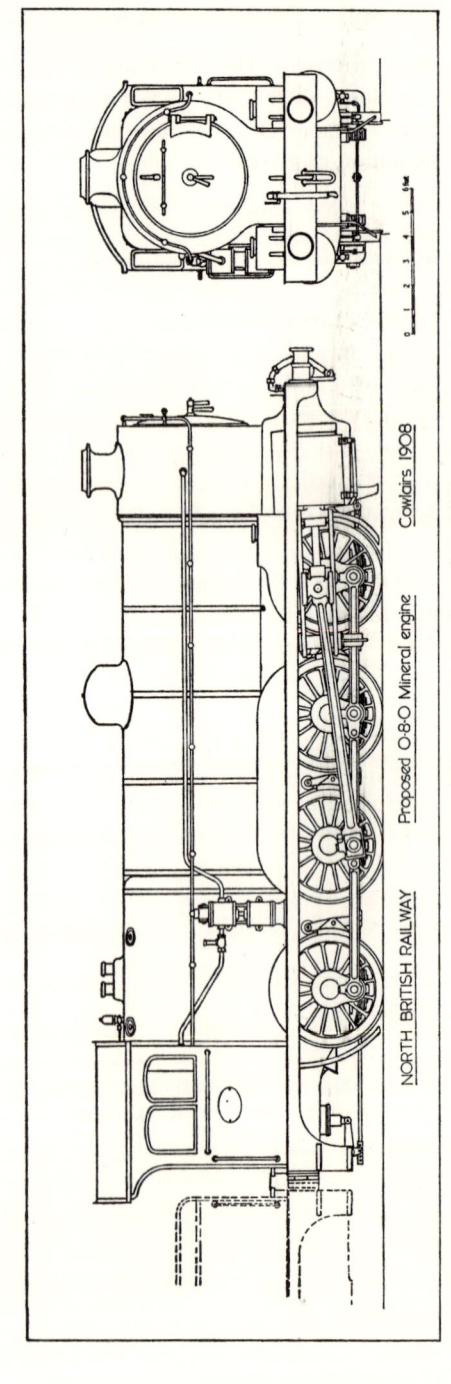

NORTH BRITISH RAILWAY   Proposed 0-8-0 Mineral engine   Cowlairs 1908

Proposed NBR 0-8-0 mineral engine

0-8-0 had been tested in 1916. The GWR engine was handed over to the NB at Berwick on 10 January and at 6.15 that evening was lodged in Haymarket shed. On the morning of the test Calder received the following letter from Aldington:

> My chairman and I are keenly interested in the tests and hope they will be satisfactory in all respects. As you know Mr Nicholls and one or two other Great Western representatives will be present, but I am sorry that it is not possible for Mr Churchward or his deputy to visit Scotland just now.

Conditions could not have been worse when the special train conveying NB and GW officers and observers from other companies reached Bridge of Earn. The test stretch was blanketed in snow and a near blizzard was blowing. The NB entrant was first at the post. With 23 loaded 16-tonners and two goods brake vans (437ton 8cwt exclusive of the brake vans) the 0-6-0 set off but stuck only a short distance up the bank. The train had to be hauled back to Bridge of Earn. The NB engine retired from the contest; it was quite unequal to the task allotted to it.

In the second test No 2846 in the charge of the GW crew and with a load of 29 wagons and two brake vans (552ton 4cwt exclusive of the vans) started away easily and, without faltering, reached Glenfarg in its scheduled time of 25min.

For the third test five wagons were added to the load bringing it up to 643ton 9cwt. Again the GW engine got away easily but about two miles from the start it encountered hard packed snow on the rails. It began to slip badly and was forced to a stand from which it failed to recover.

Three days after the tests Calder wrote to Aldington:

> Mr Nicholls will no doubt have informed you of the results of the tests. I may say that these were carried out under pretty extreme weather conditions, but they proved the superiority of your company's locomotive over ours, and will of no doubt be of great assistance to us in connection with designing engines in the future for the hauling of mineral traffic over heavy gradients. I should just like again to thank you very cordially for your kindness in giving us the loan of your locomotive.

On the following day the NB general manager called for a joint report on the tests from Stemp, Fraser (the civil engineer), Chalmers and Grassick, but it was not until 14 April that the report was forthcoming.

The NB officers generally had a high opinion of the visiting engine. They blamed its failure to complete the third test on the abnormal weather conditions and expressed their confidence in its ability to keep time with 30 loaded wagons on any NB main line under any weather conditions. They thought the GW engine could take 38 wagons of coal from Dunfermline to Aberdeen without assistance and in so doing save the company £7 6s 9d per train.

Fraser had reservations. He thought that NB track would not stand up to the regular running of such a heavy engine. He proposed a top speed limit of 25mph with severe restrictions at many selected points. It would be impossible, he pointed out, to run the engine through the platform roads at Dundee and use would have to be made of the loops.

Chalmers, too, had reservations, particularly on the question of maintenance. He wrote:

> There should be no particular difficulty in designing an engine of the power required within the limits specified but so far as repairs and renewals are concerned it is difficult to estimate such as a locomotive of the Great Western type with its enormously high boiler pressure might mean very heavy boiler repairs and consequently high maintenance cost. From the experience we have had on our own heavy engines we estimate that the increase would be not less than 30 per cent. If designing an engine however, of similar tractive power it would be feasible to considerably modify the boiler pressure without involving a greater loading effect than that produced by the engine on the test.

Stemp summed up:

> From an operating point of view the adoption of a type of engine similar in tractive power to that of the Great Western engine making the test would certainly be most advantageous if, later on, the use of such an engine could be allowed on other important main lines as well as on the Aberdeen section. It would eliminate altogether the use of the banking pilots which, taken all over would mean a very considerable saving in engine power.

One of the outside observers of the tests was Maj H. A. Watson, general superintendent of the NER. He was not entirely displeased at the failure of the GW engine on the third test, and he had no sooner returned to York when he was writing to Stemp:

> I am pleased to tell you that we have tested one of our 0-8-0 three-

cylinder freight locomotives with a load of 700 tons on a five-mile bank of 1 in 70 and it lifted the load quite satisfactorily. In fact it made up a minute compared with the standard running for the regular mineral service over the same section of line. In view of this Sir Vincent Raven will be very pleased to send the locomotive to be tested on Glenfarg bank if Mr Whitelaw so desires. I may say that on formula the tractive force of our locomotive is 36,000lb compared with the Great Western's 33,000 so it *ought* to accomplish what the Great Western engine failed to do.

The engine which Watson was offering was Raven's T3 of 1919, a three-cylinder version of the T2 which had been tested on the NB in 1916 with unimpressive results. William Whitelaw, now chairman of the NB, agreed to the tests provided that the locomotive department considered there was a possibility of the NE engine giving better results than the GW 2-8-0. The chief mechanical engineer opted for the tests, but negotiations with the NE had hardly begun when Fraser registered a strong protest. He wrote to Calder:

> I have looked into the matter carefully and find that for certain spans the effect produced by the North Eastern engine is much in excess of the effect produced by our present Atlantic type. This is to a lesser extent with the GW engine and I have come to the conclusion that it is not desirable to allow a heavier type than the latter for use between Dunfermline engine shed and Kinnaber Junction.

Three days later Fraser had an interview with Whitelaw as a result of which he modified his views. On 24 February he informed Calder:

> I am quite agreeable to this engine being brought over our system for the purpoese of a test on the Glenfarg bank, but I would not agree to the engine being adopted on the company's system for general work. I shall be very much obliged if you will give me plenty of notice of when the engine would be brought over the company's system as I would require to have a man in attendance to give instructions as to restrictions over certain bridges.

Because of the 1921 coal strike the tests were postponed and did not in fact take place until Sunday 28 August. On the previous Wednesday an NE driver had a look at Glenfarg from the footplate of an NB engine and on the following day he returned to Darlington to work the test engine, No 903, to Edinburgh. Maj Watson and Mr Stamer, assistant CME, were in the NE party.

The test engine left Haymarket for Bridge of Earn at 9 am on the Sunday and the first test run began at 12.9½. There was no question of pitting the visitor against an NB engine; it was a solo performance with No 903 hauling increasing loads on successive trips, four of which had been planned. On the first trip the engine reached Glenfarg in 33min (2min late) with a load of 617ton 5cwt. At the second attempt the climb was accomplished on schedule with 703 tons and on the third run with the load increased to 754ton 16cwt schedule was again maintained. That must have been an exhilarating day at Glenfarg. The NB officials concluded that there was no point in running a fourth test and the party returned to Edinburgh. In his report on the day's proceedings Stemp said:

> The engine proved itself to be superior to the Great Western locomotive for it accomplished all that that company's locomotive failed to do. It was, to say the least of it, really a magnificent performance, and far beyond our expectations. There is no question of the superiority of the North Eastern three-cylinder type of engine over anything that has been previously tested.

It was estimated that by using T3 locomotives on the Aberdeen coal trains the savings would be £10 9s 9d per train or £2,250 18s 9d per year. But Fraser flatly refused to accept an engine of the class for regular work and Whitelaw bowed to his decision. However, an NER T2 0-8-0 was sent to Scotland and put to work on the Aberdeen trains.

The quest for an eight-coupled engine was not yet over. For nearly 20 years there had been a Great Central influence at Cowlairs, so it came as no surprise when plans were announced for the testing of a GC 2-8-0 on the NB. But before the tests could be carried out the company had been overwhelmed by the amalgamation. No 1185 came to Scotland in July 1923. Unlike its English predecessors it was not required to run the gauntlet of Glenfarg but was put at once on revenue service with the Aberdeen coal trains alongside the T2 already working in the link.

On its first run No 1185 got away easily from Thornton with a train specially strengthened to 40 wagons and weighing 689ton 5cwt plus a 20ton brake van. It took the gradients along the route in its stride and delivered its load in Aberdeen on time. After a series of test runs in revenue service the verdict was that the GC engine was superior to both NE classes in performance and maintenance costs. Stemp reported:

This type of engine is really what is required for working our long distance mineral trains and would also be very useful in the Western district for working iron ore trains from Stobcross and Yoker to the iron works at Coatbridge and Coltness. For working long distance mineral trains we have no hesitation in stating that the Great Central type of engine is the best that has yet been tested on the North British area.

Of the 125 RODs purchased by the LNER from the War Department 10 went to Scotland and all were in service by 30 August 1924. At last eight-coupled engines were running on NB metals, although their tenders bore the legend LNER.

THE ATLANTIC TRIALS

By the summer of 1922 the writing was on the wall for the North British. But even at that late hour the old feud between the NB and the NE over the employment of NE engines on the East Coast expresses north of Berwick flared again. In the troubled 1890s the NB did not have an engine to compete with the contemporary NE engines but in the 1920s the NB Atlantics offered a formidable challenge to the most powerful NE Atlantics. The NB wanted its Atlantics to share in the East Coast through workings. A hint of the old bitterness appeared in a report by Grassick to his general manager that summer:

> You are aware that the most powerful North Eastern engines working into Edinburgh haul a load of 350 tons up the Grantshouse bank, and as you know failures to take even that load are not infrequent. In practice the load of the East Coast trains out of Edinburgh is frequently in excess of 350 tons and piloting up the bank is regularly resorted to and on occasion duplication is necessary.

As a preliminary to staking a claim for a share of the main line traffic Grassick staged an Atlantic test from Edinburgh to Berwick and back on 30 August 1922. The engine was *The Lord Provost* and the driver Samuel Bruce. The test train, 780ft long and weighing 380 tons was brought to a deliberate stand at Innerwick advance starter, but the engine had no difficulty in getting away again on the rising gradient. Its average speed up the bank was 29mph. Grassick reported, 'We are confident that it [the engine] can quite easily haul a loaded train of 380 tons over the road as scheduled and without losing time unless weather conditions are most adverse'.

The next step was to arrange with the NE for a test run with an Atlantic non-stop from Edinburgh to Newcastle and back. The test was scheduled for 23 October, again with a 380 tons train in the charge of *The Lord Provost* and *Samuel Bruce*. The NE dynamometer car was provided. Light, quick-burning coal from Fordelmains, Glencraig and Greenrigg collieries was placed in equal amounts on the tender, 8 tons in all.

The run as far as Berwick was uneventful, but south of the Border difficulties were encountered. Three permanent way checks and the consequent recovery effort put Bruce on his mettle. When water fell dangerously a 5½min stop had to be made at Alnwick. In spite of these setbacks the train arrived at Newcastle only 4min late. On the return journey Berwick was reached in 1hr 22min from Newcastle, but a water stop there occupied 8min.

The dynamometer car roll showed that on the up journey a maximum speed of 67mph was achieved at Goswick, and on the down journey the maximum was 71mph reached at Cockburnspath. The average drawbar pull on the up journey was 950 with a maximum of 1,220 recorded near the 37th milepost from Edinburgh. The corresponding figures for the down journey were 748 and 1,010, the maximum being achieved 3 miles out of Newcastle. Coal consumption per train mile was 72·25lb.

The outcome of the test was that three NB Atlantics were fitted with tender water scoops early in 1923 and thereafter took a share in the through express workings.

In October 1923 Gresley conducted tests with NB, NE and GN Atlantics between Edinburgh and Newcastle for the purpose of evaluating their relative performance. The NB engine, No 878 *Hazeldean*, came out of the contest well. It achieved the highest drawbar pull and the highest average speed on the test trains. In normal service its coal consumption was the lowest of the three engines.

The final Atlantic trials took place in November 1925. No 878 was again the engine chosen and the purpose this time was to assess the results to be obtained by using selected English coal. Engines of the D30 (Scott) and D11 (Director) classes also took part in the trials. The coal, from Maria E. Wylam and Addison collieries, was tested for calorific value on the calorimeter at Cowlairs. This instrument had been designed by Lord Kelvin, W. P. Reid's brother being a senior member of Kelvin's firm.

The trials took place with ordinary service trains between Edinburgh and Dundee and Edinburgh and Glasgow, 16 individual runs being recorded. The four Atlantics employed on the Edinburgh–Dundee route each burned an average of 73lb of coal per mile. *Hazeldean* on two tests with the regular load burned 52·7lb and 54·7lb.

Whitelaw received the figures with scepticism and he told Grassick, who had conducted the test, to see Gresley and try to reconcile his figures with those obtained in the 1922 and 1923 trials. Grassick insisted that his figures were correct and showed what an Atlantic could do when given the right kind of coal. He reported:

> From my point of view I consider the results between Edinburgh and Dundee with the Atlantic engine very satisfactory as the consumption is little higher than it is with the Director and Scott classes of engine working the same trains. Taken on the ton-mile basis the Atlantic consumption is better than that of the Scott.

THE ATLANTIC TRIALS OF 1922

The first run was from Edinburgh to Berwick and back and the second from Edinburgh to Newcastle and back. In both cases the engine was No 510 and the driver Samuel Bruce.

	30.8.22	23.10.22
Engine miles run	121	254
Train miles run	115	248
Train ton-miles	47,035	99,448
Train ton-miles (including engine)	61,065	129,704
Total coal used	8,960lb	17,920lb
Coal used per engine-mile	74·04lb	70·55lb
Coal used per train-mile	77·9lb	72·25lb
Coal used per ton-mile (including engine)	0·146lb	0·138lb
Total water used	59,530lb	97,740lb
Water per engine-mile	409·3lb	384·8lb
Water per train-mile	430·69lb	294·1lb
Water per train-mile (including engine)	0·811lb	0·753lb
Water per pound of coal	5·52lb	5·45lb

LOCOMOTIVE COAL TRIALS 1925

Engine Class	Engine No	Engine Miles	Total train ton miles	Total train ton miles plus engine	Average load per ton mile	Total (lb)	Coal lb per engine mile	Coal consumption lb per ton mile including engine	lb per train mile	Ash deposit in firebox and ashpan (lb)	Water per lb of coal (lb)
D30	9497	206	56,448	76,992	294	11,424	55·46	0·148	59·46	284	6·55
D30	9497	206	53,952	74,296	260	10,602	51·45	0·143	55·22	340	6·68
D30	9428	254	55,440	80,400	230	12,700	50·00	0·158	52·9	597	7·3
D30	9428	254	51,868	76,600	216	12,570	49·5	0·168	52·4	512	7·0
D11	6378	206	53,184	73,528	277	9,828	47·71	0·134	51·19	525	6·65
D11	6378	206	55,104	75,448	287	9,710	47·14	0·129	50·51	456	6·74
D11	6384	252	53,040	79,400	221	11,396	44·8	0·143	47·5	1,045	
D11	6384	254	54,000	80,440	226	11,829	44·6	0·141	47·2	807	
C11	9878	254	59,760	89,040	249	10,656	49·8	0·142	52·7	668	7·4
C11	9878	254	62,880	92,160	262	13,144	51·7	0·143	54·7	698	7·3

The coal used in the tests came from Addison and Maria collieries, East Wylam

CHAPTER 10

That NB Flavour

THE LAST DAYS

Time was running out for the old NB. Yet on 26 December 1922 when James Calder sat at his desk going through the morning mail there was little about the atmosphere of headquarters office to suggest that the NB had six days to live.

'The grouping' had been the subject of many discussions in recent months. On January 1 1923 the Scottish railways were to lose their identities. The NB was to join the Great North of Scotland to become the Scottish end of the London & North Eastern Railway, a vast uniform system with lines stretching from London to Lossiemouth. If there was sadness at the imminent demise of the old company there was pride in the fact that the NB's own chairman, William Whitelaw, had left for London to be head of the great new organisation. And there was comfort in the knowledge that a similar fate awaited the Caledonian. The proud, self-styled National Line was to vanish in the maw of the London Midland & Scottish Railway.

With less than a week to go Calder had not yet received official information about the organisation of the railway in Scotland after 31 December. But in the mail that morning was a letter from the chief general manager of the LNER, Ralph Wedgwood, containing the details Calder sought. He drafted out a circular to the staff.

NBR
London & North Eastern Railway
Organisation in Scotland

> It has been arranged as from 1st proximo, the date when the new amalgamated company comes into being that Scotland for organisational purposes so far as the new company is concerned shall be divided into two areas, one to be called the Southern Scottish Area with headquarters at Edinburgh and the other the Northern Scottish Area with headquarters at Aberdeen. Both areas will be under my control as General Manager, Scotland, of the London & North Eastern Railway. The Southern Scottish

Area will consist of the existing NB system but the jurisdiction of the officers of that area will terminate at Kinnaber Junction. The Northern Scottish Area will consist of the GNS system subject to the jurisdiction of the officers of that area commencing at Kinnaber Junction. The whole staff of the North British Company at Aberdeen will, under this arrangement, fall to be transferred to and be controlled by the officers of the Northern Scottish Area. The working between Aberdeen and Kinnaber Junction and at that place will be under the control of the officers of the Northern Scottish area.

Just in case the manager of the GNS got false ideas Calder wrote to him: 'I have no doubt that you will advise the GNS officers that I will take full executive responsibility in Scotland for current business as from the 1st promixo'. And to Wedgwood he replied, 'I see no reason why the new organisation, so far as Scotland is concerned, should not be brought fully into operation on the 1st proximo'.

Among the routine matters that Calder dealt with that day was a request that the NB should exhibit at its stations posters advertising the 21st Annual Motor Exhibition. The general manager wondered if it would be wise to grant the request. There was a memo from the chairman of the locomotive committee to say that it had been decided to complete all new engines and rolling stock under construction but not to start on work already authorised pending a decision by the LNER. There were notices to go out concerning the withdrawal of passenger services from the Rosyth branch on 31 December, and an estimate showing that it would cost £770 8s to replace 'NBR' with 'LNER' on staff uniforms.

Late on the afternoon of Hogmanay 1922 the doors of the office at Waterloo Place closed on 80 years of history. The North British Railway, one of the greatest businesses Scotland had known, with 1,389 miles of track covering 21 Scottish and two English counties, 61 acres of docks, 1,107 locomotives, 3,564 carriages and 57,011 wagons producing an annual revenue of £13,283,857 would, when the bells rang in the New Year from the Tron steeple, pass into alien hands. Inside the darkened boardroom on the ground floor of the old Georgian building portraits of the men who had made the NB great looked down from the walls. Left on the shelves of basement rooms and cellars to gather dust and mouse droppings over the years were the written records of the company—history recorded as it happened. There was excitement, tragedy, pathos and humour in those heaped papers. There lay the authentic NB flavour. Suppose we look at some random parting samples.

SERENDIPITY SHOP

The captains of the NB Forth steamers did an important job on the vital ferries. They were highly respected and kenspeckle figures in their own communities. When the Forth Bridge opened the steamers and their captains vanished and were forgotten. What happened to them? Four cryptic minute book entries give the answer.

13 Mar. 1890	A memorial by the captains of the goods steamers which have been withdrawn from the Burntisland–Granton ferry on the opening of the Forth Bridge for re-employment elsewhere or an allowance in respect of past services was declined, but it agreed to give the men employment if the occasion should occur.
17 Aug. 1890	Forth steamers sold for scrap to P & W McLellan, Glasgow.

Goods	Midlothian	£6,750
	Leviathan	£1,200
	Balbirnie	£1,875
	Kinloch	£1,875
Passenger	Thane of Fife	£1,000
	Auld Reekie	£1,000

Haulage machinery at Burntisland and Granton sold for £17,250.

15 Feb. 1894	Captain Elder employed as master of the Granton–Burntisland ferry until opening of Forth Bridge asks to be released of rent on company house. Rent free for one year.
12 Sept. 1895	Captain Elder asks for pecuniary assistance as well as free house. Granted £5 16s per year.

The question of staff relations cropped up again in two minute book entries made within a fortnight in 1892.

18 Feb. 1892	Referring to the payment of 7/6 per week authorised to be paid to John Robertson retired joiner of St Margarets at the last meeting it was reported that this man having been admitted to the poorhouse the payment will not now be required.

| 3 Mar. 1892 | Retirement of George Wieland. That in recognition of his long and valuable services he be presented with a sum equivalent to three years salary to be debited to the reserve fund, the same fund to be reimbursed half yearly by the addition of any saving resulting from the appointment of a secretary on a lower scale. |

The company's relationship with its operating staff appears in another light in minutes recorded following the Elliot Junction disaster of 1906. In this accident an express train hauled by an engine running tender first through a blinding blizzard crashed into the rear of a stationary train. The driver stood trial at the High Court of Justiciary and was jailed for five months. The sentence provoked a furious public outcry in which, uncharacteristically, the company joined.

| 21 Mar. 1907 | Board petitioned the Secretary of State for Scotland for the remission of the remainder of prison sentence being served by Driver Gourlay who was convicted of manslaughter following the Elliot Junction disaster of 28 December 1906. |

| 16 May 1907 | Money raised by Miss Ellaline Terris deposited in North British Savings Bank for benefit of Driver Gourlay and widows of Fireman Irvine and Guard Leslie. Payment of 15 guineas authorised to be made to four doctors who assisted at accident. |

Ellaline Terris was one of the foremost actresses of her day. All four doctors returned their bank orders to the NB. The company took the unusual step of paying Gourlay his wages while he was in prison and in arranging employment for him on release. His sentence was reduced to three months. It appears that the company was more concerned about its driver than with the passengers who were stranded after the disaster. Because of the widespread snowstorms and the blockage of the line people trying to reach their homes for the New Year holiday found themselves stranded in Dundee. They formed a Committee of Passengers, and asked the stationmaster to charter the tug *Renown* to get them out of the beleaguered city. When that gambit failed four members of the committee put their names on a telegram to Jackson: 'Indifference shown to comfort of passengers especially women and children amounts to callousness and is unworthy of NB'.

Jackson had gone home for the holiday but Calder was still in the office and he sent the telegram to the general manager's home. Jackson wired the Dundee stationmaster: 'Inform passengers everything will be done for them while snowed up'. The Elliot Junction disaster inspired a schooboy to design a snow plough. He sent his drawings to the general manager through an official of the National Bank of Scotland. Jackson gave the matter his personal attention and duly replied:

> I have examined the drawing and while the plough looks feasible it appears to me to be too elaborate and would be attended with difficulty in getting attached to engines on short notice. For all the snow experienced on this line I do not consider it necessary to go in for such an elaborate and expensive plough. The drawing is creditable to the lad.

The final acount for the Elliot Junction affair was not settled until 26 June 1910. It came to £43,637 10s 11d.

The human side of Jackson emerges from the following instruction he sent to W. P. Reid on 29 August 1907:

> Signalman Heatlie's (Gunnie North) artificial limb has given way today rendering him unfit for duty. The limb has been sent to Mr Scotland today. Press him to have it repaired speedily. Ack.

The NB agreement books yield unexpected nuggets. It happened sometimes that company gas lamps at stations lit not only the platforms but the adjoining public highways. In all such cases the NB did its best to make the local authority pay for its share of the lighting. A typical agreement allowed for the town being responsible for the cleaning of the lamps and paying a half share of the gas bill. At Markinch the difficulty was that the porter whose job it was to turn out the lamp at the station entrance went off duty at 7 pm. The town agreed to send a man to extinguish the lamp at 10 pm and to pay the company 2s 6d per annum for the extra gas consumed. When the company installed a fine clock at Leith Central station it asked Leith Town Council to pay for the electricity that lit the clock at night since all citizens benefitted from its services. The Town Council complied.

The company's most venerable clock was the turret timepiece

which was erected over the old erecting shop at St Margarets shed in 1848 and survived almost unaltered for well over a hundred years. It had a peculiarity which an NB record explains:

> Soon after the installation of the clock a hole of approximately 1½ inches in diameter was made in the boundary wall on London Road. This hole which is at normal eye level, is in direct line with the face of the south aspect of the clock, and it was made so that men could check their time on their way to work no other public timepiece being available in the vicinity.

On 1 November 1881 the NB signed an agreement with the Carron Company to provide 'merry-go-round' trains between the company's ironfield at Cadder and its furnaces at Falkirk, and in so doing anticipated a transport concept that was regarded as novel when it was reintroduced 80 years later. The agreement provided for 'the continuous output of ironstone to be conveyed by the railway'. The NB provided 90 wagons which were made up into three standard trains of 30 wagons each, the capacity of each wagon being a minimum of 7 tons. The rental for the wagons was £300 per year paid by monthly instalments with the Carron Company in addition paying 1s 5d per ton up to 40,000 tons, reducing to 1s 2d per ton for the next 20,000 tons, but increasing after that to 1s 9d per ton to cover wear and tear of the wagons. The method of operating the merry-go-round service was outlined in the agreement:

> After depositing each train at Carron Junction sidings a train of 30 empty wagons will be delivered by the Carron Company to the North British Company to be hauled by them to Cadder where the train of empties will be exchanged for a train of loaded wagons to be taken to Carron Junction sidings aforesaid and so on regularly so that a train of 30 wagons will be en route while a second train of empty wagons is in course of being loaded at Cadder, and a third train of 30 wagons in course of being unloaded at Cadder and Carron Junction respectively to the North British Company and hauled by them between these points as before described.

The company's carriages featured regularly in the correspondence, although seldom in a flattering light. On 25 March 1884 Walker complained to Inspector James McLaren:

> I have been sorry to observe for a considerable time past that our carriages have presented a rather dusty and soiled appearance and

Page 189:
Wagons: (above) *Gunpowder van*; (below) *Hopper wagon*

Page 190:
Sheds: (above) *The Burntisland roundhouse*; (below) *Eastfield after the fire of 28 June 1919. Nineteen engines were badly damaged*

I was satisfied in my mind that they were not being properly attended to. I think the annexed returns which have been made to me will prove completely that this has been the case.

Jackson in his day was constantly on the warpath over dirty and decrepit carriages. He sent this letter to Deuchars following a passenger's complaint:

It is not satisfactory that any carriage should be allowed to get into such a very bad state of disrepair as the one complained of appears to have been in, and the inspector in charge should have had the carriage put right at the proper time. Are all carriages now running on the train referred to in good condition and is it not possible to make arrangements for their being kept in a cleaner state?

In 1880 Drummond was told to design a sleeping car. He knew that the GNR was in the process of designing one and he asked Stirling if he could have a look at his drawings. Stirling sent his original drawing to Cowlairs with the comment, 'This is the only drawing in our possession of the proposed GNR sleeping car'. A few days later, when he had had time to study the drawing, Drummond reported to Walker, 'If it were at all possible to introduce the Pullman Sleeping Cars they would be a very great improvement on these carriages'.

That the NB was not above looking to other companies for inspiration in carriage design is shown by the following communications that passed between Walker and Holmes.

7 April 1884
I return the plan you left with me on the 20th ultimo and presume you are satisfied we cannot do better than make two duplicates of the L & NW saloon which we saw here the other day.

7 April 1884
If the L & NW saloon which we inspected would clear all our tunnels and bridges I have no objections to our new saloons being of the same width and design of roof as the one first mentioned.

Eyebrows must have been raised when one day in February 1897 there arrived at NB head office a letter with a Berlin postmark addressed to 'Herr General Direktor, der Nord Englischen Eisenbahn Gesellschaft'. It was from the Konigsliche Eisenbahndirektion and was in reply to a letter Conacher had addressed to that establishment some six weeks earlier.

Corridor brake third

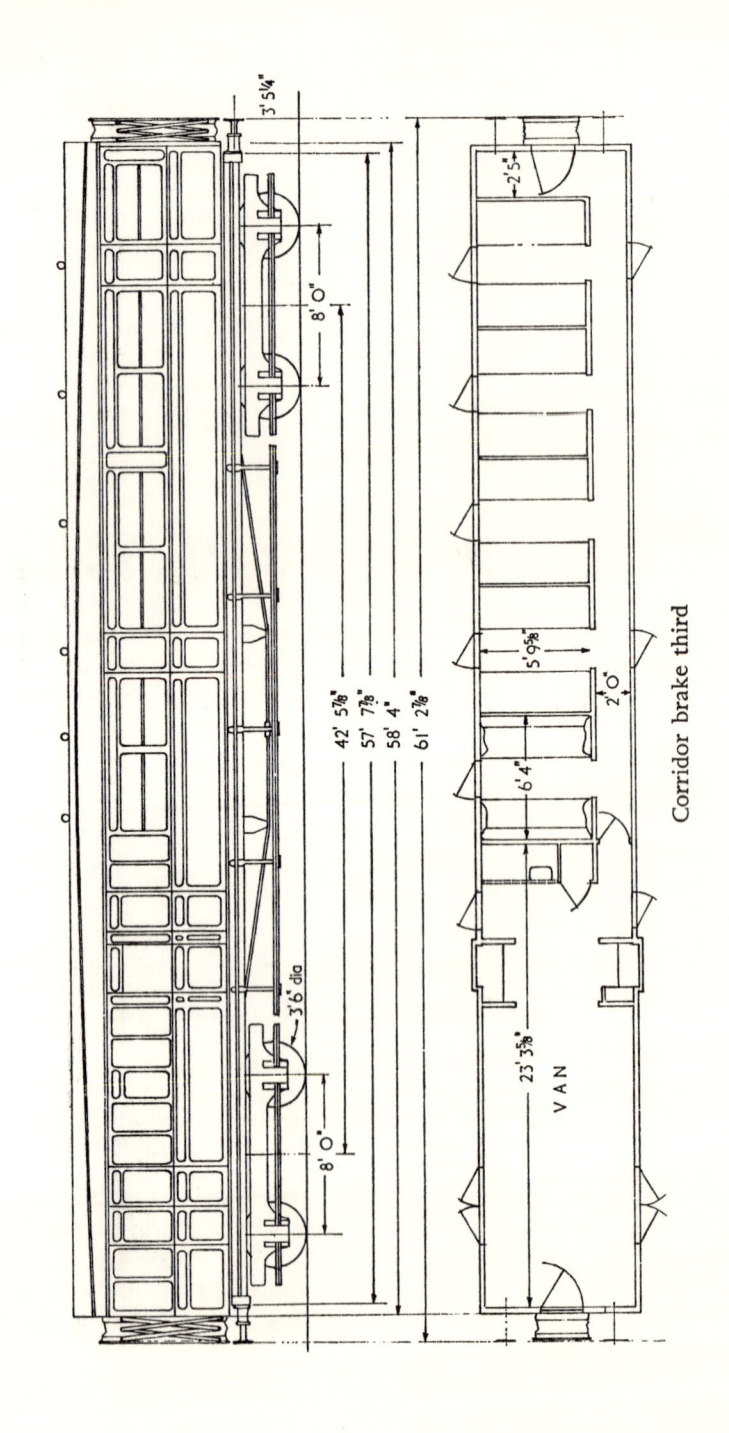

Corridor third

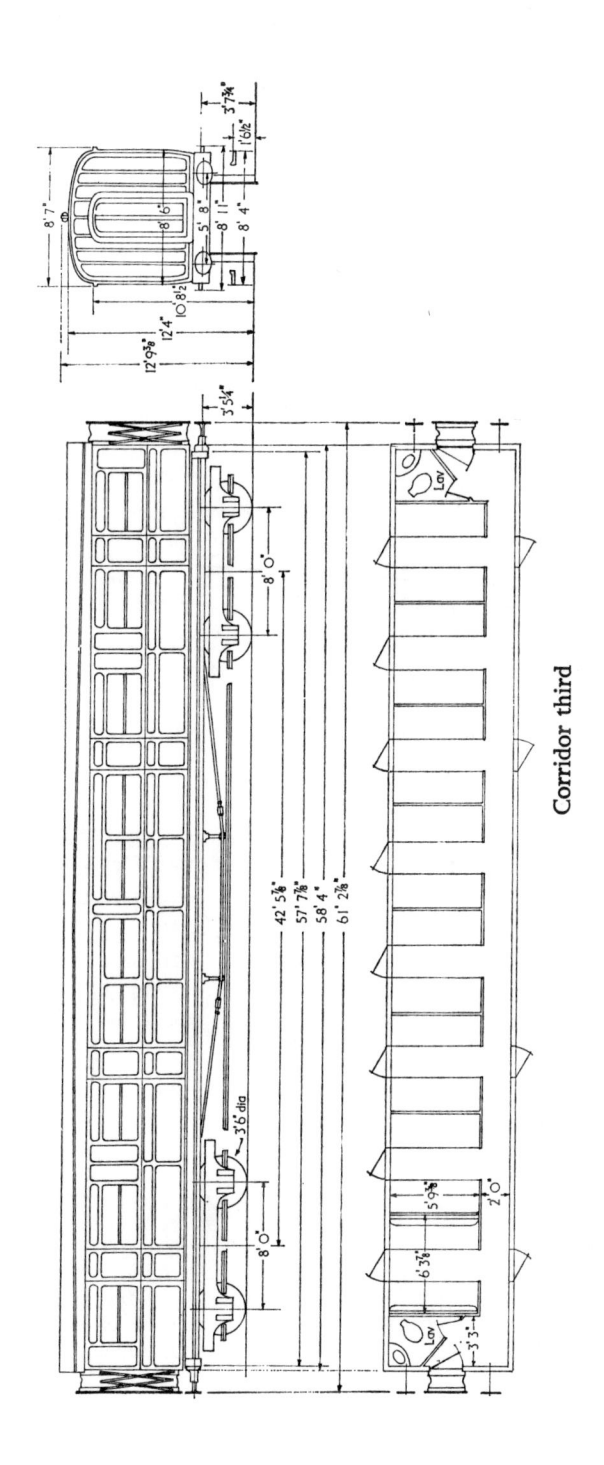

At that time the East Coast companies were designing new dining cars for the Anglo-Scottish services and Conacher, recalling an experience he had had while travelling on the Prussian State Railways in the previous summer, asked his English colleagues not to proceed with the new carriage until he had made investigations in Germany. Conacher had been served with a meal in a corridor carriage from a compact kitchen at the end of the vehicle. 'I also observed', Conacher informed the German authorities, 'that the passengers sitting on the corridor side of each compartment had their meals served on folding tables of a very ingenious and compact nature, and it would be an advantage to us if you could kindly tell me where I could obtain one of the tables in question'.

When no reply had been received by mid-January Conacher outlined the construction of the German vehicle to Holmes and told him to work out a similar idea. At the same time he dispatched a somewhat sharp reminder to the 'Royal Railway Management'. The eventual reply gave particulars of the carriage and the name of the manufacturer of the folding table that had so intrigued Conacher. The general manager passed the German drawings to Holmes, but the English managers opted for conventional dining cars.

NB track frequently was host to private locomotives. Sometimes they were brand new engines in transit from builder's works to their owners, but more often they were colliery engines being transferred from one pit to another. The usual procedure was for the engines to be certified mechanically fit by an NB locomotive inspector before being allowed on to the main line. Some private owners were allowed to move their traffic over NB metals on a regular basis. The inspection of such engines after the initial test seemed to be perfunctory. An NB inspector submitted to W. P. Reid the following report on a Barclay pug which had been working regularly over the NB main line:

> 74 water space stays broken in firebox, 35 right side 28 left side and 14 top of back plate. All firebox stays are defective, firebox sideplate are badly bulged between the stays along the bottom. All the tubes are very short and driven in past the face of tubeplate fully one-eighth of an inch. The tube plate is badly bulged out and leaking badly. I may state that this engine has been working in a very dangerous condition.

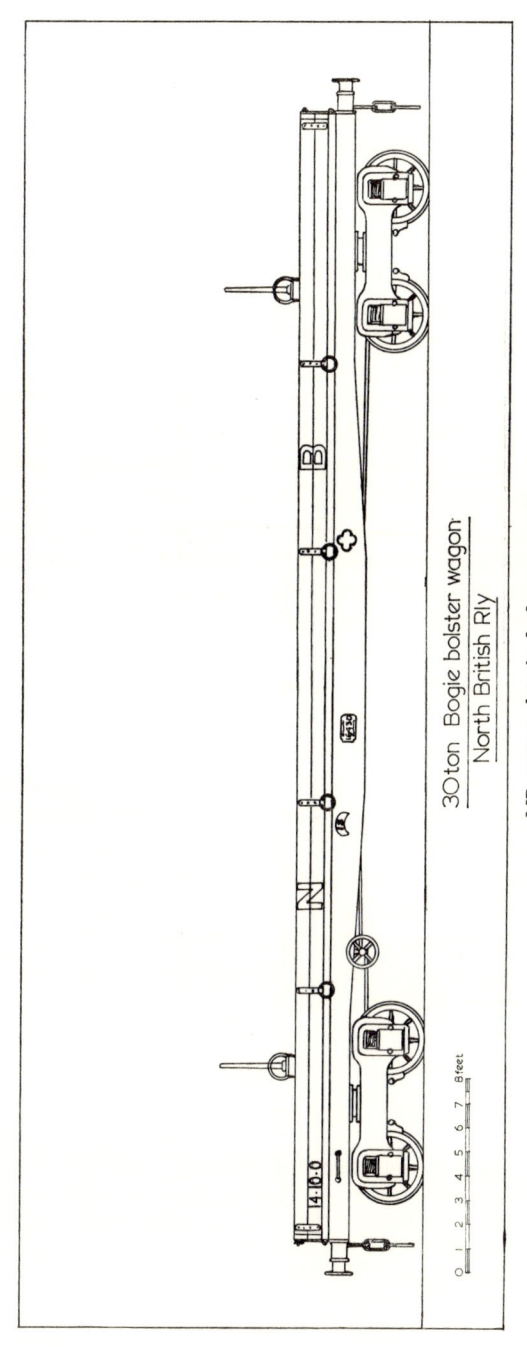

NB 30ton bogie bolster wagon

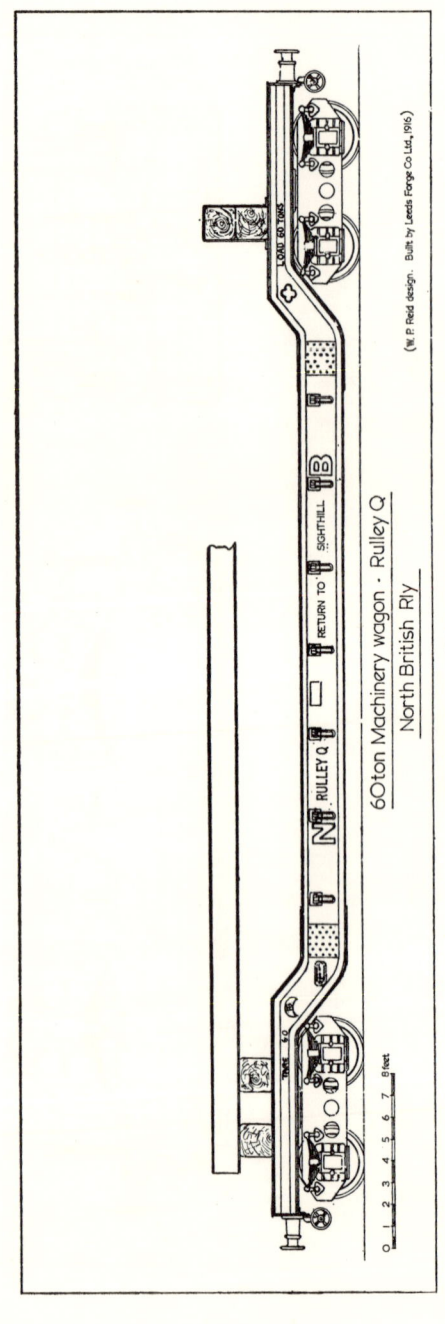

NB 6oton machinery wagon

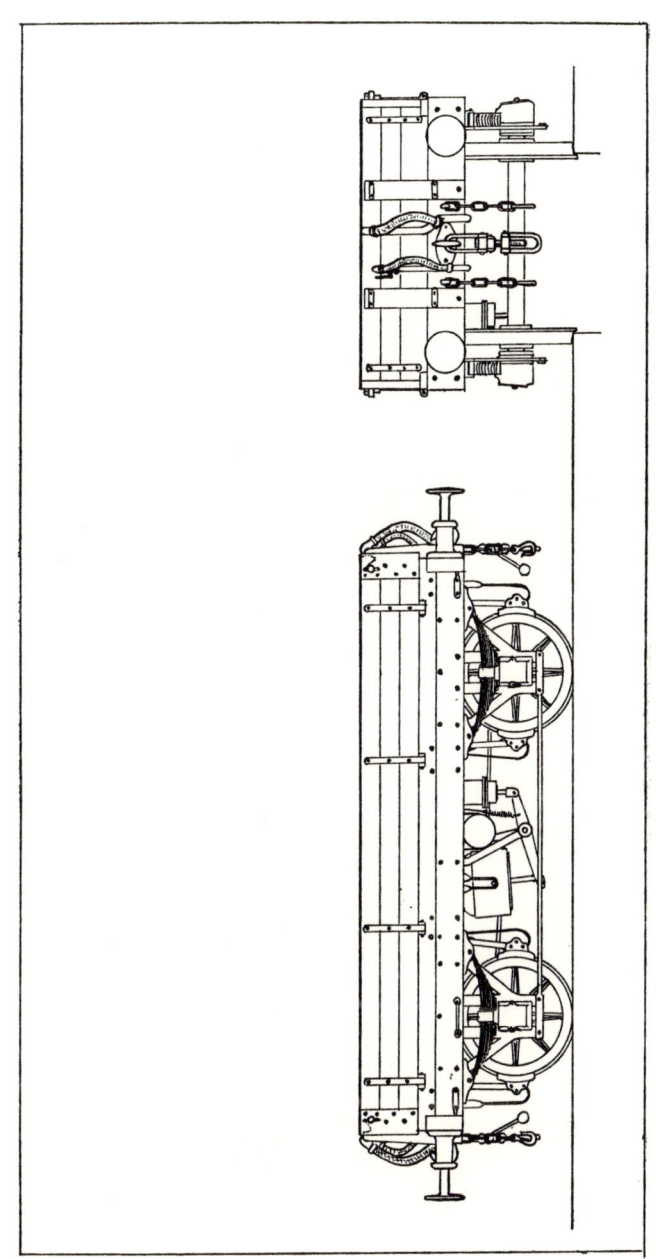

NB 3ton fish wagon

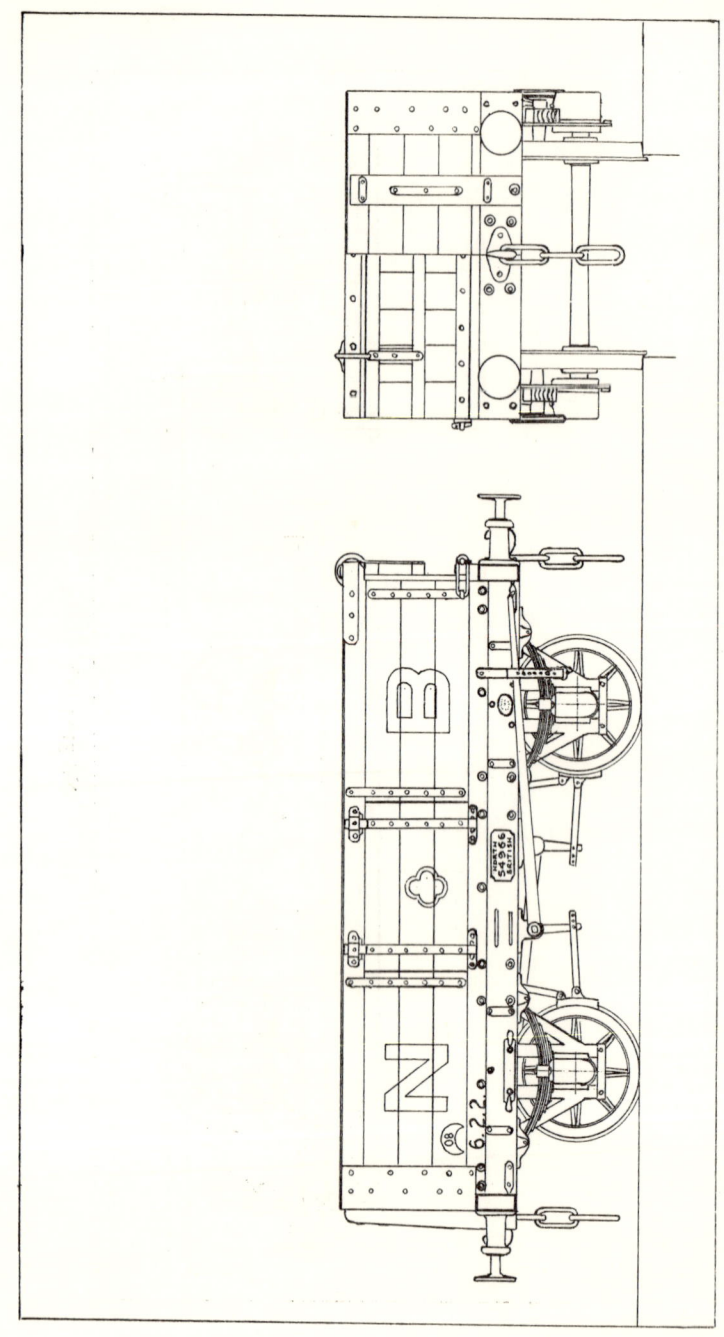

NB 8ton mineral wagon

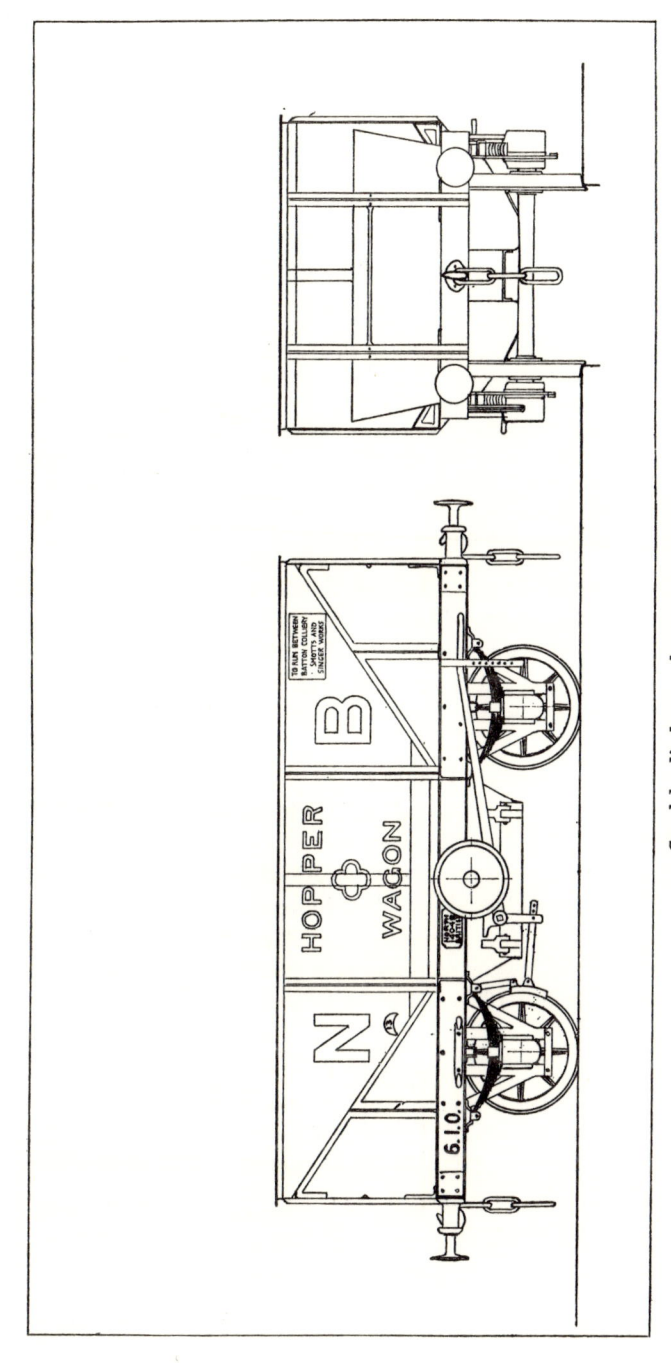

Steel bodied 9ton hopper wagon

Sometimes the crews of private engines were no better equipped for their job than were their charges. In the course of an accident investigation Drummond was infuriated to find that a driver who had been using the NB main line was illiterate and had only a rudimentary knowledge of signalling.

The 'complaints' file contains many gems. For instance in October 1881 the manager of the Lumphinans Iron Company saw fit to write to Walker as follows:

> We some time ago informed you that we had been the victim of a robbery of empty wagons after they had been placed in our sidings. Since then similar outrages have been perpetrated on us and this morning the fourth one occurred. The result of the latter is that while from the wagons in our siding last night we judged it safe to arrange for extra workmen today we have been compelled to send all our men home and close our works because the wagons have been secretly moved during the night.

Walker admitted having removed the wagons 'because of a pressure in another quarter'. But he added, 'I learn that you have been in the habit of detaining our wagons in your sidings for long periods and using them privately for conveying dross between your pits, and I now ask you to be good enough to let me have an explanation of this'.

Thomas Story was a farmer at Walby in Cumberland and his complaint was that the company's bridges over the Silloth line, which intersected his fields, were not strong enough. The company had warned Story on numerous occasions not to run his traction engine over the bridge without first informing the district engineer, but the farmer neither answered the letters nor heeded the warnings. The outcome was revealed in a letter which Story wrote to Walker in January 1881:

> Yours of the 9th to hand. Excuse me for not answering yours of December 22nd but I had mislaid it. I am sorry that I broke through Easton Bridge, but it was no fault of mine. I give you my distinct assurance that it will not be repeated as I will not cross another of the bridges in the state they are in at present. Trusting to oblige.

That the NB found itself in trouble when it established a manure depot next to a distillery is apparent from this letter which passed between Walker and the distiller's solicitor:

> I understand that this complaint originated from Mr Mackie

manager to the Distillers Company at Queensferry. He says the smell from the Glasgow manure prevents him from experimenting with his blending. In fact he has consulted his doctor on the point.

Letters about the NB–Caledonian relationship are legion. It was the custom for railway companies to station men on overbridges when the royal train was due to pass. On one occasion the Caledonian put a man on the NB bridge carrying the Waverley route across the Caledonian main line north of Carlisle and an 'incident' resulted. Writing to Deuchars on the matter Jackson had this to say:

> I shall be glad if you will arrange for a man being stationed on our bridge in all cases in future when the royal train may pass underneath when running on the Caledonian Railway with a view to give warning in the event of any such incident occurring. You will not of course inform the Caledonian of our intention to do so.

A notable fracas took place in 1888 at Whifflet in Lanarkshire where the Caledonian exercised running powers over a length of NB main line. At 11.5 am a Caledonian goods train was offered which the NB saw fit to accept at 11.40. The Caledonian driver required access to the sidings at R. B. Tennent's works, but this was refused by the NB inspector present for reasons best known to himself. The Caledonian driver was ordered to clear the section immediately. He refused to move.

At this point a Caledonian train arrived on the down line with a load for Dundyvan Basin on the Monkland Canal. Access to the site, however, was blocked by the rear of the first Caledonian train which was fouling the points. The recalcitrant driver was appealed to again but still he refused to move. When the driver of the second Caledonian train was asked to set back he refused and deadlock followed. The NB main line was totally blocked.

This state of affairs persisted until 2.30 in the afternoon when the first Caledonian driver was persuaded to move. But the down driver, denied permission to enter Dundyvan basin, refused to budge, whereupon the NB instituted single line working round the obstruction. The NB inspector's official report explained what happened next: 'At 2.50 pm two of our engines pushed the second Caledonian train back over the catch points so as to clear our own main line'. The laconic wording of the report does less than justice to the grand spectacle of the joust between the rival locomotives.

The NB drove the enemy over the catch points but the Caley man had plenty of fight left in him as is shown by the concluding sentences of the report:

> The driver of CR engine No 616 came forward again and fouled our main line notwithstanding that the signals were at danger. I personally remonstrated with this driver, but it was not until 4 pm that the Caledonian Company agreed to discontinue their obstruction and at 4.20 the ordinary working was resumed.

THE GREAT SILENCE

If there was one poignant moment above all in the history of the North British it occurred at eleven o'clock on the morning of 11 November 1919. On the eve of the first anniversary of the armistice that had ended World War I His Majesty King George V had issued a proclamation in which he asked that 'at the eleventh hour of the eleventh day there may be for the brief space of two minutes a complete suspension of all normal activities. During that time except in the rare cases where this may be impracticable all work all sound and all locomotion should cease so that in perfect stillness the thoughts of everyone may be concentrated on reverent remembrance of the glorious dead'.

The NB ordered 'complete suspension of normal business and locomotion together with a cessation of sound from engines'.

And so on that winter morning a great silence fell over the the North British—a silence symbolic of the stillness that had fallen over the battlefields when the guns had stopped firing a year ago to the very minute. All over the system from Northumberland to Inverness-shire, on main lines and branches, in yards and sheds, passenger trains, goods trains and shunting engines stopped wherever they happened to be. Engine crews stood bareheaded on their footplates, passengers sat silent in the compartments. Great stations fell suddenly silent, travellers froze into immobility. People had much to remember; few in those trains and stations had not lost a relative or friend in the recent war. Of the 4,836 NB men who had joined the armed forces, 775 had not returned.

At two minutes past eleven the platform trolleys rumbled again and the hiss of steam rose from the engines. Trains everywhere started up simultaneously.

TAILPIECE

1 January 1923 was a national holiday in Scotland. King's Cross and Euston had to accept the fact that on the first day of the new railway empires they would have to carry on without the active participation of their Scottish outposts. On New Year's Day James Calder, LNER general manager in Scotland, was disconcerted to read in his newspaper under the heading 'Our New Name' an advertisement in which the Caledonian extolled the virtues of the London Midland & Scottish Railway. Next morning he wrote to his chief general manager in London:

> I send herewith copies of advertisement which appeared in the leading Scottish newspapers of yesterday and today. It seems to me that we must have sooner or later a counterblast.

New name or not the auld enemy was the auld enemy.

Appendix

A NORTH BRITISH CHRONOLOGY 1880–1923

1 February 1880	Dundee & Arbroath Railway becomes joint line (NB and CR)
1 October 1880	NB Arbroath & Montrose Railway opened to Inverkeillor and Letham Grange for goods
8 October 1880	NB Arbroath & Montrose Railway opened to Lunan Bay for goods
1 March 1881	NB Arbroath & Montrose Railway opened throughout
2 June 1881	One mile of track laid experimentally with coiled iron keys by Anderston Foundry Co
18 July 1881	Montrose & Bervie Railway vested in NB
1 August 1881	Wemyss & Buckhaven Railway opened to Buckhaven
15 May 1882	Craigendoran pier opened
27 July 1882	Resignation of Dugald Drummond as locomotive superintendent. Appointment of Matthew Holmes
1 October 1882	Strathendrick & Aberfoyle Railway opened
1 December 1882	Glasgow, Yoker & Clydebank Railway opened.
1 May 1883	NB Arbroath & Montrose Railway. First through NB trains to Aberdeen
1 September 1883	Anstruther & St Andrews Railway opened to Boarhills
5 April 1884	Standard 84lb rail adopted in place of former 75lb rail. The rail was reversible and ⅜in thicker on one side than the other
31 October 1884	Edinburgh Suburban & Southside Jct Railway opened for goods
1 December 1884	Edinburgh Suburban & Southside Jct Railway opened for passengers
2 February 1885	Partick–Yorkhill opened

APPENDIX 205

1 August 1885	Kelvin Valley Railway absorbed by NB
15 March 1886	Glasgow City & District Railway opened
13 December 1886	City of Glasgow Union Railway: Barnhill opened for passengers
1 January 1887	City of Glasgow Union Railway: Springburn opened for passengers
1 February 1887	Glasgow City & District Railway: Circular route opened
20 April 1887	New Tay Bridge opened
5 May 1887	Wemyss & Buckhaven Railway opened to Methil
1 June 1887	Craiglochart station opened
2 July 1888	Kilsyth & Bonnybridge Railway opened
31 July 1888	North Monkland Railway incorporated in NB
1 February 1889	NB trains stop at Stonehaven (CR)
1 February 1889	Loch Lomond Steamboat Co purchased by NB
13 July 1889	NB and G & SW tickets to Clyde coast made interavailable
26 July 1889	Wemyss & Buckhaven Railway purchased from R. E. Wemyss
4 March 1890	Forth Bridge opened
13 March 1890	Disused shed at Forth Bridge works sent to Kipps as replacement for engine shed which had been destroyed by fire
28 April 1890	Forth Bridge station renamed 'Dalmeny for Forth Bridge'
2 June 1890	Dalmeny–Saughton Jct and Dalmeny–Winchburgh Jct opened (Forth Bridge connecting lines)
16 April 1891	100 sets of wheels and axles ordered from D. Drummond & Son, Govan 'at their reduced price of £21 per ton'
13 April 1891	Eyemouth Railway opened
23 April 1891	Death of John Walker
9 July 1891	Robert Chalmers, chief draughtsman, appointed assistant locomotive superintendent
1 August 1891	Blane Valley and Strathendrick & Aberfoyle railways absorbed in NB

11 August 1891	John Conacher appointed general manager
10 December 1891	Prizes for best kept stations instituted
17 March 1892	George Wieland appointed director
1 May 1892	2nd class abolished in express trains
1 May 1892	Express fares abolished on Edinburgh–Glasgow service
12 May 1892	New paint shop at Cowlairs insured for £20,000 with the Hong Kong Fire Insurance Co
24 November 1892	Passenger and goods station at Dumbuck authorised but not built (the site was between Bowling and Dumbarton)
1 March 1893	2nd class abolished on Anglo-Scottish trains
16 March 1893	Green substituted for white as 'all clear' signal
20 July 1893	Rebuilding of Waverley station authorised
23 November 1893	David Deuchars (assistant general manager, outdoors) appointed superintendent of line
23 November 1893	Ticketless travel: names of passengers found to be travelling without tickets ordered to be inscribed on 'caution bills' and exhibited at stations
7 August 1894	West Highland Railway opened
1 September 1894	Charlestown branch opened for passengers
17 September 1894	Kilbagie (between Clackmannan & Kennet and Kincardine) opened for passengers and goods
1 January 1895	WHR: Inverlair renamed 'Tulloch for Loch Laggan and Kingussie'
22 April 1895	Powderhall (between Leith Walk and Bonnington South Jct) opened for passengers only
31 May 1895	WHR: Banavie branch opened for general traffic. No fixed signals. Train staff had key for Lucas and Aird (WHR contractor) siding and siding at Banavie station
1 June 1895	Banavie branch opened for passengers
4 August 1895	Buchlyvie Junction (Forth & Clyde Junction Railway) moved from original site to Buchlyvie station

Page 207:
(above) *The North British Hotel, Edinburgh;* (below) *Train departure indicator at Waverley station East End in November 1922*

Page 208:
NB engines in BR livery: (above) *No 62060 at Eastfield;* (below) *A line-up of newly-overhauled J37s at Inverurie Works in the late 1950s*

APPENDIX 209

4 December 1895	Waterside Jct–Bridgend Jct (Garngaber Junction Railway) opened
1 April 1896	Killearn Old renamed Dumgoyn Hill; Killearn New renamed Killearn
1 May 1896	Whistlefield station opened
28 July 1896	City of Glasgow Union Railway partitioned. Springburn–College East Jct taken over by NB
13 December 1896	Whiteinch East Jct–Clydebank doubled
14 December 1896	Whiteinch Victoria Park opened for passengers
8 May 1897	Clydebank Jct–Dalmuir Jct opened for goods. Sighthill–Fort William goods used line from 10 May
20 June 1897	Inverkeillor–St Vigeans doubled
4 August 1897	CR exercise running powers for all traffic over Bervie branch (Broomfield Jct–Bervie)
20 December 1897	Crianlarich station–Crianlarich East Jct (Callander & Oban) opened
10 March 1898	Station authorised at Ardoch (between Dalreoch and Cardross) provided that 23 feus for substantial houses are taken up. Sidings for materials to be provided during building. The station was never built
17 April 1898	Waverley suburban platforms opened
18 August 1898	East Fife Central Railway opened for goods only, East Fife Central Jct (between Cameron Bridge and Leven) to Lochty
1 January 1899	Kinniel opened for passengers
	Port Carlisle branch closed to goods minerals and livestock
1 May 1899	Port Carlisle branch reopened for goods, minerals and livestock using horse traction
30 June 1899	CR cease to exercise running powers to Bervie
1 July 1899	William Fulton Jackson appointed general manager
30 September 1899	Through carriages discontinued between Edinburgh and Ayr (NB and G & SW)
24 April 1900	Milngavie branch doubled

1 May 1900	Hillfoot station opened
1 April 1901	WHR: Mallaig Extension opened
2 July 1901	Lauder Light Railway opened
14 October 1901	Gifford & Garvald Light Railway opened
8 May 1902	Proposal to construct a monorail between Edinburgh and Glasgow considered by board but rejected
1 December 1902	John Conacher reports on proposal to build railway to summit of Ben Lomond
12 January 1903	Glasgow City & District Railway; Circle service discontinued
7 May 1903	Matthew Holmes resigned for health reasons and W. P. Reid was appointed for a probationary period of six months
22 July 1903	Invergarry & Fort Augustus Railway opened Worked by Highland Railway
27 August 1903	Board agrees to contribute £2 2s to St Margarets staff library. General manager to supervise choice of books
7 November 1903	Consideration of W. P. Reid's permanent appointment delayed for a further six months
2 June 1904	W. P. Reid appointed locomotive superintendent
8 September 1904	Two motor cars purchased for the North Berwick–Gullane service at £560 each from the Mo-car Company, Paisley
17 November 1904	Lauder Light Railway: proposed extension to join Berwickshire Railway opposed by NB
1 December 1904	Possilpark Goods–Saracen opened
23 March 1905	'Motor car house' at North Berwick approved
25 June 1905	Severe flood damage to line at Whitrope, Galashiels and Tulloch
3 December 1905	Robert Chalmers, assistant locomotive superintendent, resigns
11 January 1906	Walter Chalmers appointed chief draughtsman
8 March 1906	Board considers building 15 'covered carriage trucks for the conveyance of motor cars'

APPENDIX

3 April 1906	'Ladies Only' compartments abolished
2 July 1906	Kincardine & Dunfermline Railway opened
13 July 1906	1,500 footwarmers at 8s 6d each and 500 at 8s 9d each purchased
15 January 1907	NB buy Galloway Saloon Steam Packet Co
7 March 1907	Reported that the Trossachs Road account was £1,074 6s 5d in credit
18 April 1907	Two Arrol Johnston motor cars for North Berwick–Gullane service purchase for £700 each less £250 trade-in price on old motor cars
1 May 1907	NB take over working of Invergarry & Fort Augustus Railway
3 November 1907	Kilbowie diversion and Singer station opened
29 November 1907	Decision taken to work Cowlairs incline by adhesion
15 December 1907	Tests take place with locomotive hauled trains on Cowlairs incline
1 February 1908	Maryville closed
4 June 1908	Mr Rintoul, stationmaster at Waverley fatally injured by drunken passenger. Widow awarded one year's salary plus £6, this being an unclaimed amount in the books of the Edinburgh hotel
23 June 1908	Decision taken to abandon electric lighting of carriages (first introduced in 1906) as soon as electrical fittings in stock are used up. 'Incandescent light to be used in all new carriages and gradually in existing modern vehicles as they come into the shops for repair'
31 July 1908	Dalhousie closed
1 August 1908	Newtongrange opened
31 October 1908	Rope haulage discontinued on Cowlairs incline (since 11 February 1908 empty stock trains not attached to the rope had been locomotive assisted)
19 November 1908	Questions asked in the House of Commons on NB's refusal to allow member of staff at Ladybank to take town council seat to which he had been elected

12 December 1908	William Whitelaw appointed director
22 January 1909	Newburgh & North Fife Railway opened for general traffic
25 January 1909	Newburgh & North Fife Railway opened for passengers
4 July 1909	New up and down slow passenger lines Piershill Jct–Craigentinny opened
8 August 1909	New up and down main lines Craigentinny–Portobello West opened
26 August 1909	Cowlairs incline haulage rope removed
23 September 1909	Cowlairs incline stationary engine broken up for scrap and used at Cowlairs. Engine house became electrical switch room
2 December 1909	Electric light rejected in favour of gas for new directors' saloon
3 February 1910	NB exhibit sent to international exhibition in Japan
3 March 1910	William Whitelaw appointed deputy chairman
9 February 1911	Track circuit between Partick and Yorkhill removed having proved unsatisfactory 'in consequence of the proximity of the electric tramways'
30 September 1911	David Deuchars, superintendent of the line, retires
19 October 1911	All four-wheeled carriages to be fitted with three-ply wooden seats except Ashbury carriages and vehicles used on the Edinburgh suburban and Glasgow–Hamilton services
7 March 1912	William Whitelaw appointed chairman
5 September 1912	Agreement with Glasgow Garden Suburb Tenants Ltd where the society agrees to guarantee receipts at a proposed Westerton Garden Suburb station near Milngavie Jct
22 February 1913	Collision at Dalmuir attributed to the obscuring of signalman's view by mullioned windows of box. Mullions ordered to be removed from all boxes

APPENDIX

1 June 1913	Extra train added to Glasgow–Fort William service every other day. Dep Fort William Monday, Wednesday, Friday, dep Glasgow Tuesday, Thursday, Saturday
19 June 1913	Four-wheeled vehicles of wheelbase less than 9ft 6in barred from express trains
10 July 1913	Christopher Cumming appointed district locomotive superintendent, Burntisland (Cumming later became locomotive superintendent of the Highland Railway)
July 1913	Through carriages instituted between St Andrews and North Berwick and London. Two services a day from North Berwick. The St Andrews carriage was conveyed on *The Flying Scotsman*
1 August 1913	Invergarry & Fort Augustus Railway re-opened
30 October 1913	Electric lighting in carriages re-introduced. '20 new carriages to be lighted with the Leeds Forge Company system of electricity'
4 January 1914	Finnieston station to be closed daily at 6.30
6 April 1914	Horse haulage with train staff and ticket discontinued and replaced by one engine in steam working on the Port Carlisle branch
16 December 1914	Public highway from Falkirk High station to the town, formerly partly owned and maintained by NB, taken over wholly by the burgh
30 December 1914	Decided to lift Fort Augustus pier extension and take materials into stock
1 July 1915	Rosyth Dockyard station opened
8 August 1915	Gretna–Longtown closed
24 February 1916	William Whitelaw and W. F. Jackson in their capacities as NB representatives on the Burntisland Harbour Commission tried in the High Court of Justiciary, Edinburgh, for an alleged offence against the Defence of the Realm Act. Found not guilty
13 March 1916	Meadows Jct (NB) to Seafield Rd (CR) opened

12 April 1916	Inverkeithing South Jct–Rosyth Naval Base Jct doubled
5 July 1916	Telegraph wires alongside the railway where it crossed the end of the runway at Raploch Aerodrome, Stirling, lowered to within two feet of the ground at the expense of the War Office
19 July 1916	Passenger service on the Newburgh & North Fife Railway resumed after temporary withdrawal owing to staff shortage
7 February 1917	Board decided to offer apprenticeships in Engineers' Drawing Office, Edinburgh. 'When an apprentice enters the company's service with a BSc degree the period of unpaid apprenticeship shall be restricted to three years'
21 March 1917	Pittenweem and Boarhills stations (closed as a wartime emergency) reopened on alternate days as unstaffed goods sidings for full wagon loads. Loading and unloading and covering and uncovering of wagons to be done by consignors and consignees
14 March 1918	Jessie Davidson makes history by becoming the first lady member of the locomotive department staff. She was employed as a comptometer operator at £90 per year
1 August 1918	Hugh Inglis appointed chief assistant in the running department at Cowlairs at £500 per year
22 November 1918	Free issue of lemonade to hotel staff discontinued and one shilling added to weekly wage
1 February 1919	Dining car services resumed after wartime cancellation
6 February 1919	William Whitelaw orders the following letter to be 'engrossed in the minutes of the meeting and that it be preserved in the archives of the company'

APPENDIX 215

> HMS Queen Elizabeth
> 22 January 1919
>
> Sir
>
> On the conclusion of the Christmas leave to ships of the Grand Fleet I desire to express my appreciation of the excellent arrangements made by your company for the rapid and comfortable conveyance of the officers and men to and from their destinations especially as it is fully realised that the transport of such a large number of men must have created an exceptional strain.
>
> I am, Sir,
> Yours faithfully,
> DAVID BEATTIE
> Admiral

(The NB carried 14,000 men in 32 trains)

4 May 1919	Representatives from NB attend national memorial service for railwaymen killed in the war; St Paul's Cathedral, London
23 November 1919	South Queensferry halt opened for passengers
23 December 1919	Glasgow City & District line through Queen Street Low Level opened at night for goods traffic for short period to relieve congestion
31 December 1919	W. P. Reid retires. Title of locomotive superintendent abolished
1 January 1920	Walter Chalmers appointed chief mechanical engineer
1 January 1921	Blackdyke renamed Blackdyke halt
12 January 1921	GWR 2-8-0 No 2846 tested on Glenfarg bank
1 March 1921	Saughton closed
1 April 1921	Yorkhill closed
30 July 1921	Bangour Railway closed
15 August 1921	Government wartime control of railways ended at midnight
3 October 1921	Leuchars Old closed

1 November 1921	Loch Leven closed
1 December 1921	Clackmannan Rd closed
2 March 1923	Last Annual General Meeting of the North British Railway Company
12 March 1923	NBR war memorial in Waverley station main hall unveiled by Duke of Buccleugh
1 July 1923	Alexandra Park renamed Alexandra Parade, Junction Road renamed Junction Bridge, Thornton renamed Thornton Junction, and Crossgates renamed Crossgates (Fife). These changes were made because of the similarity of NB station names to station names elsewhere on the LNER

Bibliography

NBR Board and committee minute books, 1880–1923
NBR General manager's letter books. Selected 1880–1923
NBR Service and public timetables
NBR Sundries books
NBR Traffic note books
NBR Agreement books
NBR Original letters of David Deuchars, superintendent of the line
NBR Batches of miscellaneous letters and documents in West Register House, Edinburgh
NBR LNER Official reports and correspondence concerning locomotive trials
Forth Bridge Railway Company. Minute books
Forth Bridge Railway Company. Letter books
West Highland Railway. Minute books
Invergarry & Fort Augustus Railway. Minute books
Blane Valley Railway. Minute books
Strathendrick & Aberfoyle Railway. Minute books
The Conacher papers
The Breadalbane papers
Corporation of Glasgow records
Acts of Parliament relating to the NBR
Transactions of the Institution of Engineers and Shipbuilders in Scotland
Sir William Arrol: A Memoir. Sir R. Purvis
The Golden Years of the Clyde Steamers. A. J. S. Paterson
The Victorian Summer of the Clyde Steamers. A. J. S. Paterson
Newspapers and periodicals:
Glasgow Herald, The Scotsman, North British Daily Mail, St Rollox and Springburn Express, The Railway Magazine, Railway Gazette, The Locomotive, The Engineer, Engineering

Acknowledgements

This book is based largely on source material located in the Scottish Record Office, Edinburgh. I am indebted to the Keeper of the Records of Scotland and his staff, and particularly to Mr George Barbour for their assistance and especially for their approval to reproduce railway documents. The locomotive drawings are from originals by James Watson. I am also indebted to William Caldwell of British Rail, Alex McLean and friends who have contributed photographs to the volume.

Index

Aber Bay, 122
Aberdeen, 44-5, 48, 49, 56
Aberfoyle, 128, 130
Aldington, Charles, 173
Alloa, Dunfermline & Kirkcaldy Rly, 134
Alloa Railway Co., 133
Amalgamation, 183
Anstruther, 133
Anstruther & St Andrews Rly., 204
Ardoch, 209
Arrol Wm., 19 et seq
Armistice, 202

Baker, Benjamin, 19
Banavie, 112, 206
Bangour Rly., 215
Bank of Scotland, 147
Barlow, W. H., 18
Barnhill, 143
Beattie, Admiral, 215
Beattie, Hamilton, 149
Bell, James, 74, 158
Ben Lomond Railway (proposed), 210
Blackford Hill, 146
Blane Valley Rly., 64, 127
Borrowdale Burn, 113
Botanic Gardens, 142
Bouch, Sir Thomas, 16, 69, 145
Bridge of Orchy, 112
Buchlyvie Jct., 206

Calder, James, 183-4, 203
Caledonian Rly., 12, 45, 46, 47, 98, 122, 124, 134, 201
Calton Hill, 25
Cathles, John, 41

Cambrian Rlys., 35
Carntyne, 145
Carriages, 64-70, 66, 156, 192, 193
Carron Co., 188
Carlisle, proposed NB line from Glasgow, 105 et. seq.
Castlecary Viaduct, 105
Chalmers, Robert, 70, 157, 205
Chalmers, Walter, 172, 176
Charing Cross, 142, 143, 144
Charlestown branch, 206
City of Glasgow Union Rly., 143, 205
Clackmannan Rd, 216
Cleminson's Patent Elastic Wheelbase, 67
Clocks, 187-8
Clyde, Ardrishaig & Crinan Rly., 117
Clydebank, 144
Coal shortage, 170-1
Cockburnspath, 82
College, 140
Communication cord, 65
Conacher, John, 11, 12, 32, 38, 40, 135 et. seq.
Cowlairs incline, 101, 140, 141, 161, 163, 211
Cowlairs Works, 63, 64, 68, 75, 158-9, 163
Craigendoran, 110, 117, 119, 204
Crianlarich, 209

Dalmeny, 21
Dalkeith, 147
Deuchars, David, 35, 39-43, 58, 103
Devon Valley, 133

Dolphinton, 147
Drem, 81
Drumburgh, 72
Drummond, D., 63-72
Dubton, 46
Duddingston, 146
Duke of Montrose, 127, 129
Dumbuck, 206
Dumgoyn Hill, 130, 209
Dundee & Arbroath Rly., 39, 64, 204

Earl of Dalkeith, 140
East Fife Central Rly., 209
Edinburgh International Exhibition, 74
Edinburgh, Perth & Dundee Rly., 78, 133
Edinburgh, Southside & Suburban Rly., 145, 204
Electric coach lighting, 143, 211, 212, 213
Ellaline Terris, 186
Elliot Jct., 186
Eyemouth Rly., 205

Falshaw, Sir James, 69
Fife, 133 et. seq.
Finnieston, 213
Flanders Moss, 129, 130
Forth Bridge, 19-22, 85; excessive speed of trains, 29-30, 53; paint, 26
Forth Bridge Railway Co., 18, 25-31
Forth ferries, 185
Fort Augustus, 114-115, 111
Fort William, 49, 108-10, 138
Forth & Clyde Junction Rly., 127

Galbraith, W. R., 107
Garngaber, Jct. Rly., 209
Garngad, 143
Glasgow, City & District Rly., 141, 205, 210
Glasgow & Inveraray Steamboat Co., 118
Glasgow-Kings Cross traffic, 58-9

Glasgow & South Western Rly., 108, 143
Glenfarg, 107, 173, 175
Glenfinnan Viaduct, 113
Gorgie, 146
Gorton, 112
Gourlay, Driver, 186
Grantshouse. 81
Grassick, J. P., 172, 181
Gullane, 147

Haymarket West Jct., 147
Highland Rly., 115, 169
Hillfoot, 210
Hilton Jct., 133
Holmes, Matthew, 54, 72-7, 81
Horses, 70-2
Hotels, 147-51
Holy Loch, 120

Inglis, Dr. J., 119-21
Inglis, Hugh, 214
Invergarry & Fort Augustus Rly., 114-16, 210, 211, 213
Inverlair, 206
Inverness, 100, 108, 114
Inverurie, 208

Jackson, W. F., 12, 28, 29, 144

Kelso, 71
Kelvin Valley Rly., 64, 205
Kent Rd., 141
Keyden, James, 127
Kilbagie, 206
Kilbowie, 211
Kincardine & Dunfermline Rly., 211
Kinnaber Jct., 46, 53, 58, 184
Kirkcaldy, 134
Krupp of Essen, 68

Ladybank, 133
Lauder Light Rly., 210
Leadburn, 147
Leith Central, 147, 187
Lenzie, 77
Letter books, 11, 70

INDEX 223

Leuchars (Old), 215
Leven, 133
Light engine mileage, 160-1
Lingard, John, 70
Lochend Jct., 147
Loch Fyne, 118
Lochgilphead, 117
Loch Leven, 216
Loch Lomond, 108-9, 120-6
Loch Lomond Steamboat Co., 205
Locomotives:
  Drummond 0-4-4T 63; Holmes 17in goods 72; Holmes 592 Class, 73, 86; Holmes 0-4-4 passenger tank, 74; Holmes 0-4-0 saddle tank, 74; Holmes 795 Class tank, 75; Holmes 18in 0-6-0, 75; Holmes West Highland bogie, 75-6; Holmes 729 Class, 76; Holmes 317 Class, 76; petrol shunter, 71; Reid 0-6-0 dock tank, 152; the Atlantics 154-9, 179-182, 137; *Sir Walter Scott*, 162; the Reid Intermediates, 162; Reid 0-4-4 passenger tanks, 163; Reid 4-4-2 passenger tanks, 163, 164; *The Dugal Cratur*, 163; *Hal o' the Wynd*, 165; *Redgauntlet*, 165; Reid S Class 0-6-0, 165, 166; Reid 0-8-0 mineral engine (proposed), 174
Locomotive trials:
  Atlantics, 179-182; GWR 2-8-0 No 2846, 173; NER 0-8-0 No 903, 177; NER 0-8-0 T2, 178; GCR 2-8-0 No 1185, 178; NBR No 510, 181; NBR No 878, 180
London Chatham & Dover Rly., 67
London Brighton & South Coast Rly., 36
London & South Western Rly., 67
London & North Eastern Rly., 184 et. seq.
Lossiemouth, 183

McAlpine, Robert, 113
MacBrayne, 117
McLaren, Inspector, 82
McLelland, Inspector, 53, 55, 59
Macmerry, 147
Mallaig, 113
Marindid, Major, 42, 144
Map of system, 14
Mason, Charles, 35
Mason, S. L., 35
Mawcarse, 133
Merry-go-round trains, 188
Milngavie, 209
Minute books, 11
Mo-car Company, 210
Monorail (proposed), 210
Moor of Rannoch, 110
Musselburgh. 147

Neele, G. P., 35
Neilson, Reid & Co., 75
Newburgh & North Fife Rly., 212, 214
Newington, 146
Newport Rly., 64
Niddrie North Jct., 146
North Berwick, 72, 147
NB Arbroath & Montrose Rly., 204
North Leith, 72
North Monkland Rly., 205

Oakley, Sir Henry, 35, 36, 47, 48
Obstruction of traffic by Caledonian, 45-7
Oil firing, 171

Park, Wm., 169
Peebles, 147
Penicuik, 147
Perth, 46-7
Petrol shunter, 71
Polton, 147
Port Carlisle, 72, 209
Portbello, 146
Powderhall, 206

Princess Street Gardens, 25
Prussian State Railways, 194

Quadrupling (proposed) of E&G main line, 102
Queen Victoria, 35

Race to the North, 11, 49–52, 53, 55–6, 60–2
Railway Clearing House, 80
Reid, W. P., 152–72
Rothesay Dock, 120
Rosyth Dockyard, 213
Running powers, 79

Saughton, 215
Scottish Central Rly., 35, 37, 39
Sharp Stewart & Co Ltd., 75
Singer, 144, 211
Sleeping cars, 191
Snowstorms, 112
South Queensferry, 215
Spitting in carriages, 145
Springburn, 143
Steamboats, 117–126
St Margarets, 65, 75
Strathendrick & Aberfoyle Rly., 127, 204
Strathendrick & Loch Lomond Rly., 127
Stroudley, Wm., 70
Superheating, 163–5

Taff Vale Rly., 36

Tay Bridge, 16, 20, 22, 53, 63, 69
Tayport, 41, 133
Tender tyres, 68
Ticketless travel, 206
Timetables, 47
Trossachs, 126 et. seq.
Trossachs tour, 132
Trossachs road, 131, 211
Tulloch, 206
Tweeddale, Lord, 36, 37, 42, 135
Tweedmouth, 80

Underground workings, 102

Wagons, dumb buffered, 168
Walker, John, 17, 29, 44–5, 146
War memorial, 216
Warming pans, 65
Water tube boiler, 153
Waverley route, 84, 106–8, 137
Waverley station, 23–5, 33, 48, 50, 104
Wedgwood, Ralph, 184
Wemyss & Buckhaven Rly., 64, 204
Wemyss, Randolph, 42–3, 84, 134
West Highland Rly., 65, 75–6, 108–14, 138
Westinghouse brake, 64, 73
Whifflet, 201
Whitelaw, Wm., 183
Wieland, George, 35, 135, 136, 148, 186
Workers services, 144–5, 146